Understanding Animal Abuse and How to Intervene with Children and Young People

Understanding Animal Abuse and How to Intervene with Children and Young People offers a positive, compassion-based and trauma-informed approach to understanding and intervening in animal abuse. It provides an accessible cross-disciplinary synthesis of the current international evidence on animal abuse and a toolkit for professionals working with people and/or animals to help them understand, prevent and intervene in cases of animal abuse.

With contributions from experts in the field, this essential text offers ten user-friendly chapters with questions for reflection and key summary points. It offers a definition of animal abuse, synthesises the latest research on children, young people and animal abuse, explores the link between animal abuse and other forms of abuse and outlines legal perspectives on animal abuse. The second half of the book presents a practical toolkit for professionals, offering guidance and strategies for the prevention of and intervention in cases of animal abuse. It provides multidisciplinary perspectives on interventions; from teachers' and social workers' roles in the detection and intervention of childhood animal abuse, to the roles of enforcement agencies and veterinarians in legal cases of adult animal abuse.

Together with a final chapter proposing new directions for research, policy and practice, this guide is for all who work with children, young people and/or animals, including psychologists, social workers, veterinarians, educational professionals and animal welfare educators. It is also a key reading for those involved in legal and policy issues relating to animal welfare.

Gilly Mendes Ferreira joined the Scottish SPCA in 2005 and, together with amazing colleagues, creates innovative solutions to address key animal welfare concerns, conducts research in the fields of animal welfare and human-animal interactions and engages at a political level to ensure current animal welfare legislation meets modern-day issues.

Joanne M. Williams is Professor of Applied Developmental Psychology and an expert in children's interactions with animals. Her research spans the positive effects of pets on children's development to psychological risk factors for animal cruelty. She works extensively with the Scottish SPCA and other welfare charities to promote children's compassion to animals.

Praise for *Understanding Animal Abuse and How to Intervene*

'I would encourage all people working with animals and people to read this book.

Based on evidence, this book highlights the link between animal and human welfare and identifies the power professional agencies working together, can have in intervening in animal abuse cases.

The authors inspire the integration of animal abuse prevention into the school curriculum from the early years and also provide a structure to follow when dealing with possible childhood animal abuse cases.

This was a valuable read.'

Karen Bowman, *Primary School Teacher*

'I'm sure this book will be of great interest to animal professionals and those working in the social sector. It brings together experts who show an evidence-based understanding of the facets of animal abuse and how it can be tackled. An well-referenced book that would be easy to dip into or read cover to cover. It skilfully explains the aspects of each topic and the case studies from around the world give the reader a better understanding of how these have been tackled.

Whilst reading I kept thinking how different colleagues needed to read each chapter and can imagine that this book being essential reading for anyone in the sector.'

Tracy Genever, *Head of Welfare Standards and Education, Blue Cross*

'This book is a fantastic explanation of the different facets of animal abuse, child abuse and domestic violence and how they intersect and relate to one another from the perspective of all the different professionals who need to be involved in these cases. It clearly demonstrates both the need and the mechanisms for greater interagency understanding, co-operation and joint working.'

David Martin BVSc MRCVS, *Group Animal Welfare Advisor IVC Evidensia*

'This is an important book. It has profound implications for social work practice and training. It will help social workers to understand how crucial assessing the role of animals in children's lives is, the early warning signs to look out for and the impact this can have on their development and behaviour, and provides clear advice on how to prevent and intervene in cases of animal abuse. Justice social workers will want to consider the implications in cases of domestic abuse and how we deliver interventions to achieve successful outcomes, including diversionary measures such as Diversion from Prosecution, restorative justice and as part of a community payback order. I cannot recommend this book highly enough.'

James Maybee, *Justice Policy & Practice Lead, Social Work Scotland*

'This book could save lives, animal and human. The link between human abuse and animal abuse could not be clearer, the evidence is laid bare, and for many professionals working in social care or animal welfare the effects of this link will be sadly familiar. This seminal book shows how we can intervene, whether we are a teacher, social worker, a vet, or animal welfare professional, we have a role to play and if we work together to spot signs early and act in alliance, we can prevent the worst from happening.

Importantly Gilly and Jo, both experts with a long history in this field, take us further still to explore ways in which we can prevent animal abuse happening through evidence based education programmes for children at risk of abusing or more generally as part of their education.

Whether you are in animal welfare, a teacher, a vet or a social worker I would recommend this as a must read book, it is highly informative, practical and for me, an inspiration.'

Kelly Grellier, *Chief Operating Officer, Blue Cross*

Understanding Animal Abuse and How to Intervene with Children and Young People

A Practical Guide for Professionals Working with People and Animals

Edited by Gilly Mendes Ferreira and Joanne M. Williams

Routledge
Taylor & Francis Group

LONDON AND NEW YORK

Cover image: Getty

First published 2023
by Routledge
4 Park Square, Milton Park, Abingdon, Oxon OX14 4RN

and by Routledge
605 Third Avenue, New York, NY 10158

Routledge is an imprint of the Taylor & Francis Group, an informa business

© 2023 selection and editorial matter Gilly Mendes Ferreira,
Joanne M. Williams; individual chapters, the contributors

British Library Cataloguing-in-Publication Data
A catalogue record for this book is available from the British Library

ISBN: 978-0-367-76111-0 (hbk)
ISBN: 978-0-367-76113-4 (pbk)
ISBN: 978-1-003-16555-2 (ebk)

DOI: 10.4324/9781003165552

Typeset in Bembo
by MPS Limited, Dehradun

Contents

Contributing Authors

Phil Arkow is the coordinator of the National LINK Coalition – the National Resource Center on The LINK between Animal Abuse and Human Violence in the U.S.A. – and edits its monthly LINK-Letter. He teaches college courses and lectures internationally on The Link between animal abuse and human violence, humane education, animal care and control, the human–animal bond and animal-assisted therapies.

Angus Nurse is the head of the Department of Criminology and Criminal Justice at Nottingham Trent University. His main research is in wildlife law and its enforcement, and the causes of crimes and harms against animals. His books include *Animal Harm* (Ashgate, 2013) and *Wildlife Criminology* (with Tanya Wyatt, Bristol University Press, 2020).

Janine C. Muldoon is an experienced interdisciplinary researcher with interests in developmental transitions, relationships (with people and pets) and emotional wellbeing. Her work has focused on understanding children's and young people's perspectives, as well as practitioners' perspectives, to identify how best to support them.

Mike Flynn has been with the Scottish SPCA since 1987 and is currently the Society's Chief Superintendent. He wrote the first inspectors manual that was approved by the Crown Office, created the First Strike campaign in Scotland and has assisted in implementing legislation in Jersey, Northern and Southern Ireland, Canada and Catalonia. He was awarded an MBE for his services to animal welfare in the Queen's 80th Birthday honours list.

Laura Wauthier is completing her PhD in clinical psychology at the University of Edinburgh, which investigated the psychological risk factors for animal cruelty and evaluated the Scottish SPCA's Animal Guardians programme. She completed her undergraduate degree in zoology at the University of Cambridge and a master's in philosophy of mind at the University of Edinburgh, before converting to psychology.

Freda Scott-Park is a veterinary surgeon and was Chairman of the Links Group UK (a multi-agency group promoting the welfare and safety of vulnerable children, animals and adults). As the president of the British Small Animal Veterinary Association and of the British Veterinary Association, she sought to ensure that veterinary surgeons understood their role in recognising animal abuse.

1 Animal abuse: A concern for all

Gilly Mendes Ferreira[1] and Joanne M. Williams[2]
[1] Scottish SPCA
[2] Clinical and Health Psychology, University of Edinburgh

Aims of the book and this chapter

The aim of this book is to be a key resource for professionals who may encounter animal abuse as part of their professional lives. Some professionals will encounter animal abuse regularly as part of their usual practice (e.g., police, animal welfare practitioners, social workers and veterinarians). However, other professionals may encounter animal abuse less frequently or may not recognise it as a core professional concern for their own practice and feel less well equipped to intervene (e.g., teachers and health professionals).

This book is divided into two broad sections: the first section examines background theory and research on psychological approaches to understanding animal abuse, social approaches to understanding of the link between animal abuse and human abuse and legal perspectives on animal abuse; the second section focuses on the work of the international societies for the prevention of animal cruelty and includes chapters for professional groups, approaches to prevention and evaluation of interventions, conclusions and future directions. Throughout, the aim of the book is to provide you with an evidence-based practical guide to identifying, preventing and intervening in animal abuse.

This chapter provides a 'roadmap' of how to use this book, defines animal abuse and outlines who has a role in preventing and intervening in animal abuse.

Introduction

This book is a result of a long-standing collaboration between the editors and chapter authors on trying to understand, prevent and intervene in animal abuse. Over time it has become increasingly clear that a wide range of professionals are potentially involved in tackling this societal issue, but that many

DOI: 10.4324/9781003165552-1

professions do not see it as within the scope of their role or professional training. For example, despite links between animal abuse, domestic abuse and child abuse, domestic violence advocates and child protection workers rarely ask questions about pets in the family (Randour and colleagues, 2021). Within the veterinary profession although experience of animal abuse is common, and vets feel a strong moral duty to act, they can lack confidence in intervening (Williams, Wauthier, Scottish SPCA & Knoll, 2022). This book provides a resource for a wide range of professionals to understand when and why animal abuse can occur and to provide some simple guidance on what can be done in practice to prevent it and intervene when it is identified.

How to use this book

This book provides a key resource for professionals who might come across instances of animal abuse in their professional practice, including those working with children, adults and animals. This book has been created in two sections: theoretical and research evidence; and practical guides for professional practice.

Each chapter has been written by an expert in their field and has been written for professional audiences who are not necessarily experts in animal abuse, or for non-professionals who are concerned about animal abuse (e.g., parents). This book can be treated as a guide from theory to practice and can be read in it's entirety, or chapters can be read as stand-alone pieces, some of specific interest to particular professional groups. Each chapter has clear aims and key messages to support you as the reader in consolidating your knowledge and to ease your journey through the book.

The remainder of this chapter considers animal abuse as part of broader human-animal interactions, defines animal abuse and illustrates the range of professionals potentially involved in preventing and intervening in cases of animal abuse.

The following three chapters provide a synthesis of theory and research on animal abuse. Chapter 2 focuses on psychological research on children and adolescents to examine when they might engage in animal abuse and how this behaviour can be interpreted. Chapter 3 focuses research on the 'Link' between animal abuse and other forms of abuse (e.g., partner abuse, child abuse and elder abuse). It includes research and theory that explains the connections between different forms of abuse, features of perpetrators of abuse and actions professionals can take to intervene to support victims and survivors. This research has derived from social work and criminology research and illustrates how animal abuse should be viewed as part of a wider societal issue. Chapter 4 considers international legal perspectives on animal abuse to set the context for how this behaviour is viewed and treated within different national and legal frameworks.

Chapter 5 presents an overview of the workings of the Societies for Prevention of Cruelty towards Animals (SPCA's) across the world and presents a series of case studies of animal abuse, mainly from the UK. These examples are used to examine the range of psychological, social, environmental and legal contexts involved in animal abuse and highlight the need for inter-agency working. We invite readers to track the example cases of animal abuse through the legal process and consider how evidence of animal abuse is gathered and used in legal cases. We also present cases of animal abuse by children and young people and consider age-appropriate non-legal approaches to intervening in animal abuse.

The next four chapters focus on what we can do to prevent and intervene in animal abuse through a range of professional lenses. Chapter 6 considers veterinary perspectives and what vets can do to identify cases of animal abuse, including non-accidental injuries, and how they can intervene to support the animal involved, including collecting evidence for legal cases. Chapter 7 considers what parents and professionals working with children (e.g., teachers, social and health professionals) can do to prevent childhood animal abuse and how they can intervene if they suspect a case of animal abuse. Chapter 8 focuses on animal abuse prevention programmes that have been developed for children and young people and evidence for their efficacy. Chapter 9 presents an evidence-based evaluation toolkit for evaluating animal abuse prevention and intervention programmes. This toolkit is designed to support professional practice in animal abuse intervention development and evaluation.

The book draws to a conclusion with Chapter 10, which synthesises what we know and what we do not yet know about animal abuse. We will consider what has been shown to work to prevent and intervene in cases of animal abuse, and what professionals can do to promote positive interactions between people and animals to prevent animal abuse. We will also highlight areas of new concern such as the role of digital technology in both preventing but also perpetrating animal abuse.

In some chapters the Scottish SPCA's (Scottish Society for the Prevention of Cruelty to Animals) **ANIMAL** approach to intervening in animal abuse has been applied to a particular case (Figure 1.1) and it is worth keeping this approach in mind as you review the various case studies that have been included throughout this book.

Human–animal interactions and animal abuse in context

It is important to see harmful and abusive behaviours towards animals within the broader context of the many different ways we interact with animals. Animals play a significant role in people's everyday lives: Offering comfort and security (companion animals), providing food for human consumption (farm animals) and forming part of our natural environment (wild animals). The important interconnections between humans, animals and the environment are increasingly acknowledged. For example, pet ownership is common, especially in Western countries, and has been growing (PDSA, 2022).

ASSESS

What is the situation?
Is the person
vulnerable? Are they
in immediate danger?
Where is the animal
concerned?

LISTEN

Listen and learn. What
is the impact of your
decision? What have
you learnt from the
experience? What
would you do
differently next time?

NEED

What does the person
need? What does the
animal need?

Take the ANIMAL approach

ACTION

Put the safeguarding
four R's into action—
Recognise, Respond,
Refer, Record.
(NSPCC, 2021)

INSIGHT

What information do
you have that will help
you make a decision?
Is the person a minor?
Are other agencies
involved?

MAKE A DECISION

What are you going to
do? Do you take
action? Do you wait
and monitor? Do you
seek advice? If so
from who?

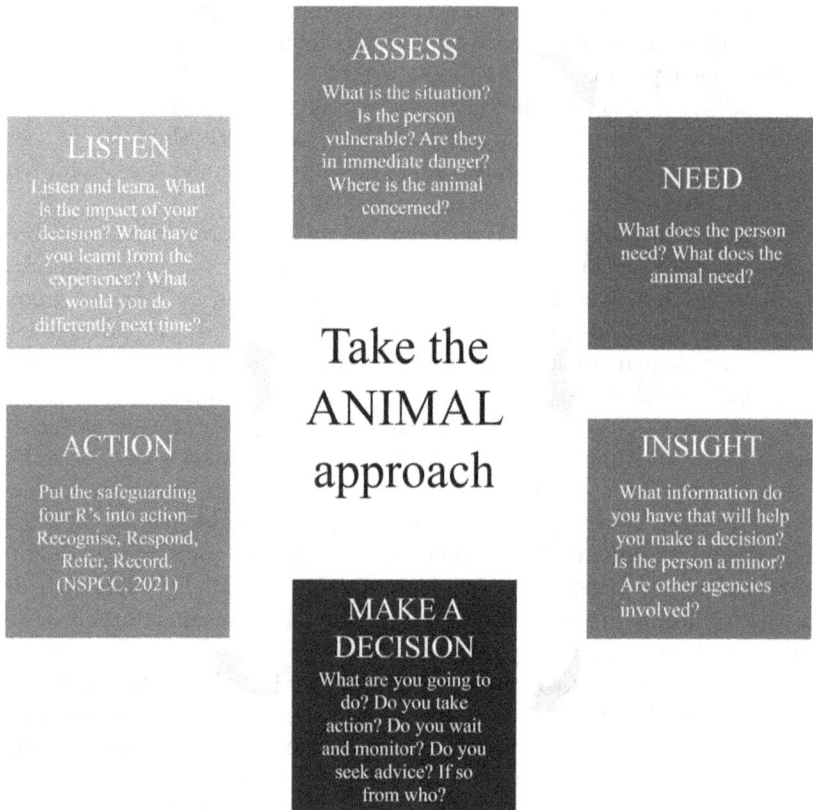

The ANIMAL approach a decision making process when faced with an animal abuse incident

Figure 1.1 Scottish SPCA's applying the ANIMAL approach to an abuse incident.

In the United States it's estimated that 70% of households own a pet (American Pet Products Association, 2022). In France, 65% of households have a pet (Statista, 2022) and in the UK it's estimated that 62% of households have pets (PFMA, 2022). Environmental concerns about the climate impact of meat production have led to increases in veganism (Sanchez-Sabate & Sabaté, 2019) and there is a greater acknowledgement of the positive impact nature can have for our mental health (e.g., Tillmann and colleagues, 2018).

The One Welfare framework has been developed to recognise links between animal welfare, human well-being and environmental well-being (Pinillos, 2018). Jegatheesan and colleagues (2020) uses Bronfenbrenner's bioecological systems model (Bronfenbrenner & Morris, 2006; see also Chapter 2) to show that animal abuse can be seen as a result of a combination of biological, psychological and social factors that influence human behaviour towards animals.

Building upon One Welfare and biopsychosocial theoretical frameworks the Scottish SPCA's Animal WISE® Footprint Framework (Figure 1.2) illustrates how negative factors can counteract the positive influences on a person's or animal's life. By actively forming partnerships between those who support a person's or animals' health and development (education, medical, animal welfare and veterinary sectors) with those who are tackling the more negative societal/environmental issues such as animal abuse, drug addiction, alcoholism, poverty and other Adverse Childhood Experiences (ACEs) (enforcement agencies, charities, justice system, social care sector and medical profession), the footprint that a person and/or animal leaves behind has the potential to be a positive one, providing the right support is given. Sitting at the heart of this framework is promoting positive human-animal relationships and protecting the human-animal bond. The Human Animal Bond Research Institute (HABRI) defines the human-animal bond as *a mutually beneficial and dynamic relationship between people and animals that is influenced by behaviors that are essential to the health and well-being of both. This*

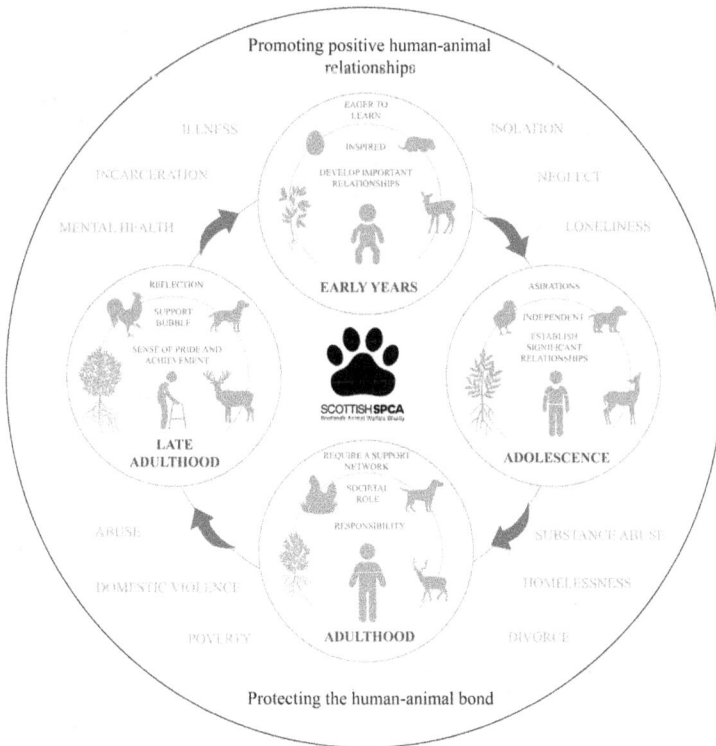

The developmental life cycle of both humans and animals showing positive and negative effects on their lives

Figure 1.2 Scottish SPCA's Animal WISE® Footprint Framework.

includes, but is not limited to, emotional, psychological and physical interactions of people, animals and the environment. Thus, the positive interactions between people and animals can outweigh the negative societal/environmental influences that can affect people's lives and this needs to be recognised.

Interactions between humans, animals and the environment are also influenced by historical and economic factors. So, what are the current challenges humans and animals face?

Current challenges humans and animals face

In 2022, the Royal Society for the Prevention of Cruelty to Animals (RSPCA) together with the Scottish SPCA launched the Animal Kindness Index. This UK survey examines people's attitudes towards animals. Over 4,000 people were surveyed and it was found that animal welfare is one of the top most important issues for people: (1) Mental Health, (2) Conservation and Environment and (3) Animal Welfare. Importantly, 69% of people stated they were animal lovers, four in five (81%) believe animal welfare should be protected by law, 75% took action to help animals in the last 12 months and 84% think that animal welfare should be taught in schools. So, in the UK there is a high level of public support for animal welfare. However, the cost of living affects our treatment of pets and ability to care for them. The Kindness Index (RSPCA, 2022) found that 69% of pet owners said that looking after their pet was more expensive than last year (2021). In addition, 72% of UK pet owners reported that increases in the cost of living would impact their animals, 28% of pet owners are worried about being able to care for their pets and 19% are worried about feeding their pets. There was a 153% rise in people searching online for 'can i give my dog paracetamol' between 2019 and 2022, suggesting many people are trying to treat their pets at home without veterinary care. A Scottish study found that those with lower resources (indicated through employment status, receiving means tested benefits and use of food banks) were most likely to experience challenges related to pet ownership including pet relinquishment (Williams, Muldoon, Scottish SPCA & Blue Cross, 2022). Scottish SPCA research has revealed that over 75% of Scottish tenants who responded to a survey stated they had a pet for emotional (77%) and mental health (83%) support. It was also found that 37% of tenants have had to choose between a pet and a roof over their head, 28% of tenants stated it took them 12 months to find pet friendly accommodation and 69% of tenants said they would risk becoming homeless if it meant they could stay with their pets (Scottish SPCA, 2022). These findings indicate the challenges pet owners are currently facing due to the economic factors and the lack of availability of pet-friendly housing.

The PDSA PAW Report (PDSA, 2022) for the UK highlighted worrying emerging trends in our treatment of animals including increased number of pets acquired from abroad. The report also highlighted increases in concerns over pet behaviour issues in the UK. There has also been an increase in both the estimated dog population (now 10.2 million was 9.6 million in 2021) and the proportion of adults owning a dog (27% of UK adults now own a dog was 26% in 2021). Many dogs acquired during the Covid-19 pandemic seem to be experiencing separation-related behaviour problems, and there are increasing rates of pets being relinquished. The expectation is that the economic challenges coupled with impact of Covid-19 (Miyah and colleagues, 2022) and impact of climate change on human health (Valentová & Bostik, 2021) will have long-term effects.

These economic and social contexts can put pressure on our interactions with animals, including our ability to care for pets. Families may have to make difficult choices about housing, feeding themselves, children or pets and seeking veterinary support when pets are ill, or relinquishing their pet. Thus, pets may come to harm because of the complex situations their owners find themselves in. So how do we define animal harm, and what is animal abuse?

What is animal abuse?

The terms 'animal cruelty' and 'animal abuse' are often used interchangeably to denote situations where a human harms an animal. However, there are a range of perspectives on how to define 'animal abuse', often emerging from different disciplines and professional groups.

From a veterinary perspective, Dr Helen Munro (veterinary pathologist) together with Professor Michael Thrusfield (veterinary epidemiologist) published ground-breaking papers that highlighted the types of non-accidental injuries (NAIs) sustained by companion animal victims and drew parallels to the non-accidental injuries sustained in cases of child abuse (e.g., Munro & Thrusfield, 2001). They highlighted four categories of animal abuse: physical abuse (may also be referred to as non-accidental injury (NAI); neglect; emotional abuse; and sexual abuse (see also Williams, Wauthier, Scottish SPCA & Knoll, 2022).

Social scientists and psychologists have moved away from using the term 'animal cruelty' to using the term 'animal abuse', in line with terminology used in relation to human violence and aggression. Furthermore, social scientists and psychologists define animal abuse more around the intentions and actions of the perpetrator, rather than the animal's injury patterns, or other forms of abuse they cause to the animal.

Ascione (1993, p. 83) initially defined animal abuse as:

> "all socially unacceptable behavior that intentionally causes unnecessary pain, suffering or distress and/or death of an animal".

Later Ascione and Shapiro (2009, p. 570) revised this, removing reference to intentionality, to define animal abuse as:

"non-accidental, socially unacceptable behavior that causes pain, suffering or distress to and/or the death of an animal".

More recently Vincent and colleagues (2019) stated that descriptions of abuse generally include intentional physical injury or death of an animal, and the lack of appropriate food, water, shelter or medical care, along with definitions of what is considered 'appropriate' standards for animal care.

However, within the legal framework for animal welfare (see Chapter 4), intention to harm is not a defining characteristic of animal abuse because acts of omission or commission that lead to an animals' welfare being compromised are also acts of 'animal abuse'.

In UK law (Animal Welfare Act 2006 and Animal Health and Welfare (Scotland) Act 2006) and indeed in many countries around the world, it is recognised that animals have five welfare needs where there is a duty of the person responsible for an animal (i.e., the owner) to ensure the animal's welfare. An animal's needs include:

1   It's need for a suitable environment
2   It's need for a suitable diet
3   It's need to be able to exhibit normal behaviour patterns
4   It's need to be housed with, or apart from, other animals
5   It's need to be protected from pain, suffering, injury and disease

These welfare needs vary with species (e.g., dog, cats and rabbits), so our behaviours towards animals, including pet care, need to be adjusted to meet animals' needs. A suitable environment and diet will be different for cats, rabbits and goldfish. Thus, meeting an animal's welfare needs is complex and unintentional neglect or injury would fall within 'animal abuse' because of the harm caused to the animal. Most cases of animal abuse reported by vets are cases of neglect rather than non-accidental injuries (Williams, Wauthier, Scottish SPCA & Knoll, 2022).

Recognition of animal sentience (Animal Welfare Sentience Act 2022) and the acknowledgement that vertebrate animals (those that have a backbone) can experience feelings such as pain or joy has resulted in many organisations advocating for those responsible for animals to take these five freedoms to the next level and consequently adopt what is known as the five domains model when caring for or interacting with animals (Mellor and colleagues, 2020). The five domains model places more emphasis on an animal's mental state, so it is seen as equal to the other needs that are required to be met, and in order for an animal to have a life worth living they must have the opportunity to not just be kept free from negative experiences but also have positive experiences. Animal abuse is certainly a negative experience and people's beliefs in animal sentience (i.e., that animals have feelings) can impact their behaviour towards that animal.

Consequently, throughout this book we use the term 'animal abuse' to include intentional and unintentional acts of omission (failing to act) and commission (allowing an act to happen) that leads to welfare compromise, injury and death of an animal. The issues of defining animal abuse and re-cognising it are revisited in various chapters throughout this book (e.g., Chapters 4 and 5).

Who needs to know about animal abuse?

Different professionals view animal abuse in different ways and how they respond to an animal abuse incident will vary both between professions and within professions (Figure 1.3).

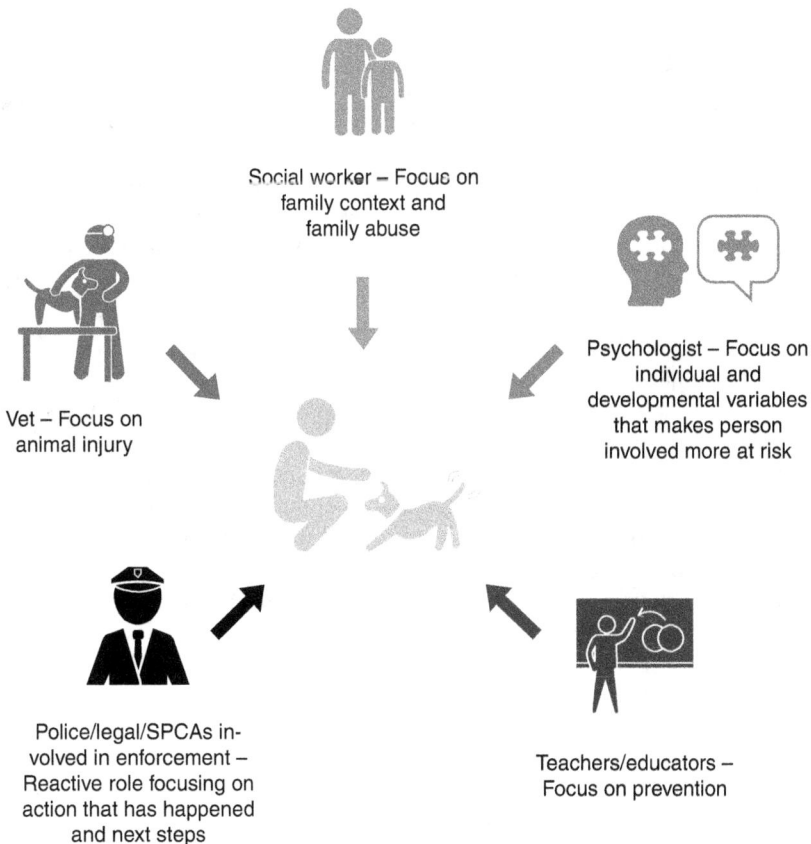

Social worker – Focus on family context and family abuse

Psychologist – Focus on individual and developmental variables that makes person involved more at risk

Vet – Focus on animal injury

Police/legal/SPCAs in-volved in enforcement – Reactive role focusing on action that has happened and next steps

Teachers/educators – Focus on prevention

Types of professionals that are linked with animal abuse cases

Figure 1.3 Professionals engagement with animal abuse.

Here is a case example where a number of professionals could or should be involved and their predicted role.

Case: A complaint has been made to an animal welfare organisation that a dog is not being cared for properly and is being attacked by a child on a regular basis. Video footage has been shared as part of the complaint showing the child attacking the dog in the garden. When an animal welfare inspector arrives at the address an unkempt child opens the door. It is estimated that the child is around six years old. The child's parent does come to the door eventually and the inspector informs the parent why they are there and asks to see the dog. The dog is quite fearful, is underweight and has scratch marks across it's nose. Only the mum and child live in the house, there is not much furniture and the mum states that she struggles with her mental health.

Looking at Figure 1.3 who should be involved?

1   **Veterinarians** – The vet's role would be to conduct a full health check on the animal. If the animal was just brought into a vet practice with no history the vet would certainly focus on the treatment of that animal. Would they look to find out more information and refer? Some vets would, some vets might not.

2   **Police/Legal/Animal Welfare Organisations (i.e., SPCAs)** – The enforcement roles would be to conduct a full investigation and identify if a deliberate act of animal abuse has taken place and whether legislation such as failure to meet the needs of the animal (i.e., the duty of care to provide the five needs to that animal) has been breached. Focus would be on both the animal and the people involved. Dependent on who is leading the investigation sometimes one profession will focus on only the animal or only the person and they will not make the connection between the two.

3   **Social Workers** – The social worker's role will be to identify what family support is required and to address any safeguarding concerns with regards to the child involved and also mum. Some social workers will look to ensure the welfare of the animal involved by calling the relevant agencies, whereas others will just focus on the human side.

4   **Clinical and Educational Psychologists** – The psychologist's role will be to support both mum's mental health and the child's mental health and development. Social work and/or the enforcement agencies may ask for support as part of the investigation and indeed courts may ask for background reports to be provided if a case is being brought forward. Psychologists will focus on the individuals involved. A minority will look at the link between animal abuse and the person's relationships with others, whilst others will focus solely on the individual and psychological and developmental influences.

5   **Teachers/Educators** – The teacher/educators' roles will be to support the child involved. They may be asked to provide background information when it comes to the child's engagement with education. They may not be told fully about the animal abuse incident that has happened or make that connection between animal abuse and everything else that may be going on in that child's life.

In most cases like this each professional role operates in isolation and a case discussion involving all professionals does not take place. As seen earlier in this chapter, the definition of animal abuse often varies between these professions making it even harder to find a common ground and to recognise the benefits of partnership working. This book therefore aims to encourage partnership work between different professionals, and recognition of what role each profession can play when faced with a situation that involves both a human and an animal. The book also highlights best professional practice in relation to animal abuse, so that both human and animal welfare is protected.

Conclusions

Animal abuse occurs in context and is part of our broader interactions with animals. Defining animal abuse can be complex because of the different professional and disciplinary perspectives on the issue. While vets may focus on an animal's injury patterns and case history, psychologists may focus on the intentions to harm the animal and psychosocial characteristics of the perpetrator, and legal professionals focus on laws including those relating to property, domestic violence and animal welfare. The issue of defining and identifying animal abuse will be a recurring theme throughout the following chapters. A range of professional groups and the public, including parents, all have roles to play preventing and intervening in animal abuse and their roles may be more or less central to this endeavour. Importantly, working together is likely to be most effective in preventing and reducing animal abuse. This book provides some guidance on how we can all help to create a society that is more compassionate towards animals resulting in more positive human-animal interactions.

Questions to consider

1   What insights are you hoping to gain from reading this book?
2   Do you have a good understanding of what animal abuse actually is from this chapter?
3   Are the professions highlighted in this chapter as involved in a case of animal abuse the professions that you would expect?

Key Points

- Animal abuse has been defined in different ways and definitions have changed over time.
- A range of professionals have a role in preventing and intervening in animal abuse.
- This book can be used as a complete guide or you can focus on specific chapters that are of most interest to your professional practice.

References

American Pet Products Association (2022, August 22). *2021–2022 National Pet Owners Survey*. https://www.americanpetproducts.org/pubs_survey.asp

Ascione, F. R. (1993). Children who are cruel to animals: A review of research and implications for developmental psychopathology. *Anthrozoos*, 6, 226–247.10.2752/089279393787002105.

Ascione, F. R., & Shapiro, K. (2009). People and animals, kindness and cruelty: Research directions and policy implications. *Journal of Social Issues*, *65*, 569–587. 10.1111/j.1540-4560.2009.01614.x

Bronfenbrenner, U., & Morris, P. A. (2006). The bioecological model of human development. In W. Damon & R. M. Lerner (Eds.), *Handbook of child psychology; Theoretical models of human development* (Vol. 1, pp. 793–828). New York, NY, USA: Wiley.

Jegatheesan, B., Enders-Slegers, M. J., Ormerod, E., & Boyden, P. (2020). Understanding the link between animal cruelty and family violence: The bioecological systems model. *International Journal of Environmental Research and Public Health*, *17*(9), 3116.

Mellor, D. J., Beausoleil, N. J., Littlewood, K. E., McLean, A. N., McGreevy, P. D., Jones, B., & Wilkins, C. (2020). The 2020 five domains model: Including human–animal interactions in assessments of animal welfare. *Animals*, *10*(10), 1870.

Miyah, Y., Benjelloun, M., Lairini, S., & Lahrichi, A. (2022). COVID-19 impact on public health, environment, human psychology, global socioeconomy, and education. *The Scientific World Journal*, *2022*. 10.1155/2022/5578284.

Munro, H. M. C., & Thrusfield, M. V. (2001). 'Battered pets': Features that raise suspicion of non-accidental injury. *Journal of Small Animal Practice*, *42*(5), 218–226.

Pet Food Manufacturers Association (2022, August 22nd). *Pet Population*. https://www.pfma.org.uk/news/new-pfma-pet-population-data-highlights-pet-peak-but-the-number-of-owners-giving-up-their-pet-is-huge-concern-

PDSA. (2022). Animal Wellbeing Report. https://www.pdsa.org.uk/what-we-do/pdsa-animal-wellbeing-report/paw-report-2022.

Pinillos, R.G. (Ed.). (2018). One welfare: A framework to improve animal welfare and human well-being. Cabi.

Randour, M. L., Smith-Blackmore, M., Blaney, N., DeSousa, D., & Guyony, A. A. (2021). Animal abuse as a type of trauma: Lessons for human and animal service professionals. *Trauma, Violence, & Abuse*, *22*(2), 277–288.

RSPCA Kindness Index Report (2022, August 22nd). *RSPCA Kindness Index Report*. https://www.rspca.org.uk/whatwedo/latest/kindnessindex/report

Sanchez-Sabate, R., & Sabaté, J. (2019). Consumer attitudes towards environmental concerns of meat consumption: A systematic review. *International Journal of Environmental Research and Public Health*, *16*(7), 1220.

Scottish SPCA. (2022). Pets and Tenants Together Action Plan. SCAS Conference September 2022.

Statista. (2022, August 22). *People ownership rate in France 2021, by type*. https://www.statista.com/statistics/764729/possession-desire-animal-company-french/#:~:text=In%202021%2C%20more%20than%2065,a%20cat%20within%20their%20household

Tillmann, S., Tobin, D., Avison, W., & Gilliland, J. (2018). Mental health benefits of interactions with nature in children and teenagers: A systematic review. *Journal of Epidemiology and Community Health*, *72*(10), 958–966.

Valentová, A., & Bostik, V. (2021). Climate change and human health. *MMSL*, *90*(2), 93–99.

Vincent, A., McDonald, S., Poe, B., & Deisner, V. (2019). The link between interpersonal violence and animal abuse. *Society Register*, *3*(3), 83–101.

Williams, J. M., Muldoon, J., Scottish SPCA, & Blue Cross. (2022). Pet ownership challenges: Socioeconomic and pet type variations. ISAZ 2022 conference presentation.

Williams, J. M., Wauthier, L., Scottish SPCA & Knoll, M. (2022). Veterinarians' experiences of treating cases of animal abuse: An online questionnaire study. *Veterinary Record*, 191/5.

2 Psychological risk factors for animal harm and abuse among children and young people

Joanne M. Williams and Laura M. Wauthier
Clinical and Health Psychology, University of Edinburgh

Aims of chapter

This chapter starts by focusing on the role of pets in children's lives and presenting the 'spectrum' of interactions children can have with animals. The focus is on children and adolescents because early development influences later behaviour towards animals, and intervening early can prevent later animal abuse. We present four case studies to illustrate different types of harm towards animals and a range of factors at play.

We then move on to considering developmental psychological risk factors for animal abuse. We focus on: age and gender as risk factors; attachment strategy and attachment to pets; self-regulation and behaviour; individual differences in empathy and personality variables such as callous-unemotional traits; cognitive development and understanding of welfare needs; attitudes to animals; and the social environment the child grows up in and the impact that has on their behaviour to animals.

The chapter closes with a focus on the need to support children's positive relations with animals, and a call to treat children who abuse animals with compassion and understanding.

Introduction

Around 70% of children in the UK, and many other Western societies own pets (Marsa-Sambola, Williams, Muldoon and colleagues, 2016). Through growing up with pets, and forming emotional attachments to their pets, children learn about their own pets' needs, likes and dislikes. Human–animal interaction (HAI) is especially complex for children and adolescents who are themselves developing socially and cognitively. Furthermore, children's interactions with animals are guided by family expectations, norms and responsibilities (Muldoon and colleagues, 2015). For example, cleaning out pets is usually seen as a mothers' job, and parents can sometimes discourage some

DOI: 10.4324/9781003165552-2

pet care activities by children for child safety reasons. Children may view pets as playmates and enjoy positive interactions with their pets (Muldoon and colleagues, 2016), which may contribute to positive welfare in species where play is a part of their natural behavioural repertoire (e.g., dogs and rats). However, sometimes play can be inadvertently rough, and rough handling, as we will see, may lead to harming an animal unintentionally. So, children's developing behaviour, knowledge and attitudes, influence their behaviour towards animals.

The other side of the equation is the animals, and here we have complexity too. Most children in Western societies direct interaction with animals involves companion animals and there are concerns about children's lack of understanding and contact with farm animals and wildlife (Burich & Williams, 2020). Many different species are kept as companion animals and in the UK the three main species are dogs, cats and rabbits (PDSA, 2022). Species have different welfare needs, and welfare needs can differ within species depending on factors such as breed, age and history. Pets also have different personalities so, for example, not all dogs of the same breed behave in the same way (Menchetti and colleagues, 2018). A child may have grown up with 'Lucky' the black Labrador, but another black Labrador may not like the same type of handling or react in the same way as the pet they know well and love. Thus, human-animal interactions are complex interactions between two complex organisms and children's experiences of interacting with animals, positive and negative, will shape their future attitudes to animals and their compassionate behaviour.

Childhood animal abuse as part of a spectrum of interactions

In view of this complexity, it is important to view animal harm as part of a spectrum of possible interactions between children and animals, with a variety of outcomes for the child and the animal involved. Figure 2.1 highlights the potential interactions between animal welfare and harm and child wellbeing and harm. These child-animal interactions are nested within the social contexts the child and animal are living in (e.g., family, culture, material resources, age and development). Thus, child-animal interactions can lead to four potential outcomes: reciprocal benefits for child and animal; reciprocal harm to child and animal; benefits to child but harm to animal; or harm to child and benefits to animal. The majority of research on children and animals has focused on the positive side of the model, exploring the benefits of pets for child and adolescent development (Purewal and colleagues, 2017), or the positive impact of animal-assisted interventions on children's mental health, well-being and learning (Brelsford and colleagues, 2017; O'Haire, 2013). However, two outcomes involve animal harm: harm to the animal but not to the child (e.g., a child hitting a dog) and reciprocal harm to the child and the animal (e.g., a child hits a dog who then bites the child). Especially in cases of reciprocal harm, we can see that prevention is not only an animal welfare issue

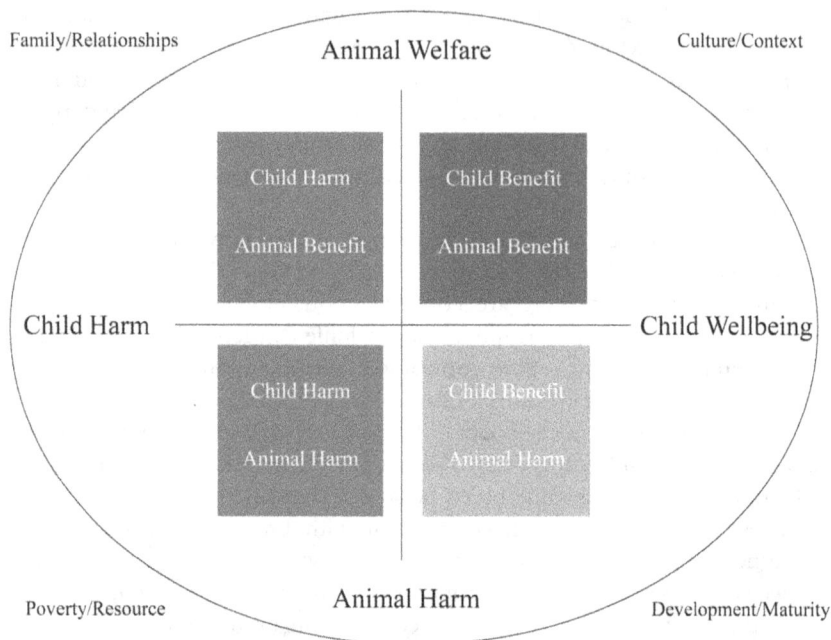

Interactions and influences between child harm/wellbeing and animal harm/welfare

Figure 2.1 Interactions between child and animal harm and welfare.

but can also be a child safety issue and can prevent a cycle of phobias or negative attitudes (see for example the literature on dog bite prevention).

It is important to note that a single negative interaction is not necessarily representative of the child's overall relationship to animals; a child may harm an animal in a moment of frustration, but still be very attached to their pet and have a positive view of animals. We explore childhood animal harm in detail below, giving case study examples of childhood and adolescent animal harm and drawing on research evidence to explore the psychological factors involved.

Defining childhood animal harm

As outlined in Chapter 1 there are different ways of defining animal abuse. A commonly used definition of animal abuse is "non-accidental, socially unacceptable behavior that causes pain, suffering or distress to and/or the death of an animal" (Ascione & Shapiro, 2009, p. 570).

Many children's and adolescents' harmful behaviours towards animals are accidental or at least not carried out with the intention of harming the animal. Furthermore, if a child's level of cognitive maturity means that their understanding of animal welfare needs is low and that they are not able to recognise pain, distress or discomfort from the animal's behaviour, or they have a low level of understanding that animals are sentient with thoughts and feelings, then they may not be aware that their behaviour is actually harmful. There is also an issue of framing cruelty around "social acceptability" because this varies between and within national contexts and cultures, and may be different from legal frameworks (as reviewed in Chapter 4). For these reasons we recently defined children's harm to animals as:

> "Any act, of commission or omission, where a child negatively impacts an animal's welfare, intentionally or unintentionally."
>
> (Wauthier & Williams, 2022, p. 193)

Ascione (2001, see also Ascione, 1993; Lee-Kelland & Finlay, 2018) outlines a theoretical set of motivations for childhood and adolescent animal harm. These are divided into non-pathological and pathological abuse (adapted from the originals below):

Non-pathological motivations for animal abuse include:

1   Curiosity or exploration (animal is harmed while being examined or played with)
2   Peer pressure (peer pressure to abuse an animal)
3   Mood enhancement (animal abuse to relieve boredom or mental state)
4   Animal phobias (pre-emptive attacks on the feared animals)

Pathological motivations for animal abuse include:

1   Sexual abuse (sexual activity with an animal)
2   Forced abuse (coercion into abuse by more powerful other)
3   Identification with the child's abuser (victimising a less powerful other in the context of child abuse)
4   Post-traumatic play (re-enacting violence with an animal victim)
5   Imitation (copying other's behaviours)
6   Self-injury (provoking animal to inflict injury)
7   Rehearsal for interpersonal violence (practicing violent behaviours)
8   Vehicle for emotional abuse (injuring animal to harm the person who cares about it)

While this early work was immensely helpful in beginning to explore the motivations behind child and adolescent animal abuse, it has not been fully borne out by subsequent research evidence, and is very much focused on animal abuse within the context of other forms of violence and abuse (see Chapter 3 for more information). Furthermore, it does not capture the full range of unintentional animal abuse or harm to animals that is a consequence of broader behavioural and emotion regulation issues experienced by some children. So, while these motivations are a good starting point, they do not fully encompass the behaviours or psychological mechanisms involved in childhood animal abuse.

Let us consider some cases to explore the complex factors surrounding childhood animal harm. In the boxes below four cases are presented, preserving the anonymity of the children and adolescents involved, and some discussion of the cases is also presented.   .

Example 1   A case of unintentional harm due to low welfare knowledge

A 7-year-old girl is playing with dolls and toy prams at her friend's house. She picks up her friend's cat, Ellie, and forces her into the pram, holding her down to prevent the cat from escaping from the pram. Ellie struggles to free herself and is distressed and injures her leg when escaping the pram. Ellie was a rescue cat and easily stressed and the girl has pets and loves animals but has no experience with cats, only dogs.

In this situation the child's intention is not to harm Ellie, they lack knowledge of cats and cat care, and the specific history of this cat. She did not read the cat's behaviour accurately, and the harm to the animal was distress and minor physical injury not requiring veterinary intervention.

Increased knowledge of appropriate handling of cats, and the specific cat's likelihood of distress may have prevented this from occurring. Adult supervision of playing around pets and intervening to explain when an animal is in danger of becoming distressed or injured may have been enough to prevent this case of animal harm.

Example 2   A case of animal harm linked to issues with emotional regulation

A young person has recently been rough handling and hitting a dog called Rocco in their new foster carers' home. When they get frustrated, they take their emotions out on Rocco by grabbing him, kicking him and punching him. Their harmful behaviour towards Rocco causes emotional distress to the foster family. The young person had to leave their family dog behind when entering their foster home. They speak positively about the dog they used to have and how much they are missing it. They have a history of being great with animals and always showing kindness towards them.

In this case, a range of psychological factors is involved in the abusive behaviour. The young person has a history of positive behaviour towards dogs, and therefore seems capable of understanding canine welfare needs and recognising canine emotions. This behaviour may be a reaction to the circumstances, including difficulties in communicating their distress with the foster family. They may miss their previous family and their dog which might lead to feelings of resentment towards the current foster family and Rocco, or the behaviour may simply be a way to lash out when overwhelmed. On top of this, the young person may be coping with a range of psychological issues such as attachment disruptions and trauma, and consequently may have difficulties managing their emotions and controlling their behaviour.

As animal abuse in foster care settings can be a cause of placement breakdowns, intervention is required. Any intervention should be careful to take a non-stigmatising approach and coordinate with other health professionals working with the young person to ensure they are supported. The intervention would need to remind the young person that Rocco has emotions and welfare needs the same as the previous dog he loved, while providing support in emotion regulation and behavioural control, and taking a trauma-informed approach may also be important to understand the broader context of the animal abuse.

Example 3   A case of intentional animal harm linked to low empathy and psychopathic traits

A young teenage boy goes out alone and seeks out wildlife to harm when he is distressed or angry. He targets wildlife such as birds, birds' nests and insects and on one occasion intentionally killed a hedgehog. The boy has had a challenging life growing up, with multiple homes, and multiple schools and has always been disengaged from learning. Although he has no known diagnosis (such as ADHD or Autism), he scores high on the Adverse Childhood Experiences chart and struggles to control his emotions.

A key feature of this case study is that the animal abuse occurs when the young person is angry, is premeditated and has occurred several times. In common with Example 2 the young person has experienced trauma and Adverse Childhood Experiences and struggles with emotion regulation and behavioural control. However, while in the previous case the harm occurred in the 'heat of the moment' in a child who otherwise had positive relationships with animals, in this case the harm is fully intentional and done in secret. This pattern of abuse which is intentional, frequent and severe, suggests factors such as low empathy to animals and callous-unemotional traits may be involved.

Intervention for this young person would need to go beyond enhancing knowledge of welfare needs and changing attitudes about cruelty to animals. It would need to provide support for emotion regulation and behaviour control and address callous–unemotional traits. Shifting psychopathic traits may require longer-term psychotherapeutic intervention. As before, a child–centred approach which is non-stigmatising will be important for positive engagement. As the young person is struggling with education a multi-agency approach might also be beneficial.

Example 4   A case of animal abuse linked to negative attitudes and peer pressure

A group of three older teenagers has started teasing neighbourhood cats in a pattern of escalating harm. They started by pulling cats' tails and using one of their dogs to chase the cats, but this has escalated to trying to tie them down and lighting them on fire. The teenagers have also turned to social media to document and brag about their 'tough' behaviour against the 'weak and stupid cats' and use the videos to intimidate their peers.

One of the main features of this case is that the animal abuse has occurred as part of a group and the cats seem to act as 'props' within a larger social dynamic. The teenagers clearly have negative attitudes towards cats and the group setting encourages an escalation of behaviour. There is intent to harm as in Case 3, but in this case peer pressure may be a large factor in motivating this behaviour, and animal harm may be occurring within a larger pattern of emerging delinquency.

Intervening in cases of animal cruelty that are part of a group dynamic adds a layer of complication since practitioners need to understand the group dynamic on top of the complex histories of each individual. Working to shift attitudes towards cats and acceptance of harm will be important, as well as discussing ethical and moral issues. Adolescents can work well in group interventions in which practitioners co-construct goals with them, and there may be scope to bring in elements from interventions for adults. Working with the school and the broader community may help to shift overall attitudes in the larger peer group as well.

From the cases above, it is clear that a wide range of factors is involved in children's harmful behaviour towards animals. If you heard about these cases, or witnessed one of these cases, what would you do? Who would you seek advice from? Do you think it is always easy to identify whether the animal harm being committed is intentional or unintentional?

In the section below, key risks and protective factors for animal abuse are discussed. It is important to understand the risk and protective factors involved in animal abuse because they help guide how we should intervene to prevent or reduce child and adolescent harm to animals. As a first step, however, we need to know whether a child or adolescent is harming animals.

How can we tell if a child has harmed an animal?

Most of the research on child and adolescent animal abuse highlights the difficulty in identifying childhood animal abuse (Lee-Kelland & Findlay, 2018) and thus estimates of animal abuse rates vary from 1.8% to 50% between studies (Ladny & Meyer, 2020). Firstly, if a child understands that it is not appropriate to harm animals, this behaviour may be hidden. Furthermore, if the harm caused to an animal is accidental and the animal does not require veterinary treatment then the child may not tell anyone about it. Equally some harmful behaviours toward animals may be observed by parents/carers but not deemed to be 'animal abuse', and therefore opportunities to intervene may be missed. Examples that might fit into this category include a child: trimming a cat's whiskers; locking pets in cupboards; hitting pets if they disrupt a game or toys; shouting at pets if they do not do as the child wishes them to do. In these cases, if the behaviour is viewed as exceptional within the context of usually positive child-animal interactions, then parents/carers/professionals may not consider it to be animal abuse. When correctly identified, these situations provide valuable opportunities to improve children's interactions with animals while increasing skills such as perspective-taking and caregiving.

There are some occasions when a child or adolescent may not hide abusive behaviour towards animals. For example, if a child has psychological risk factors such as low empathy or high callous-unemotional traits (see further on in this chapter as to what this means) they may not see the need to hide the behaviour. Another example might be a child who acts impulsively or reactively to the animal, and who does not have a chance to conceal it. In the context of adolescence and cultural contexts where animal abuse is more common, it may be made actively visible through social media (Whyke & López-Múgica, 2020). Finally, if a child is growing up in a context typified by violence, then abusive behaviour towards animals might be the norm and highly visible (Wauthier, Scottish SPCA & Williams, 2022).

Researchers have tried to measure child and adolescent animal abuse, and acknowledge the challenges of achieving this. Childhood animal abuse measures include: The Child Behaviour Checklist (Achenbach, 1991) which includes a single item on animal abuse; the Children and Animals (Cruelty to Animals) Assessment Instrument Ascione and colleagues, 1997); The Cruelty to Animals Inventory (Dadds and colleagues, 2004; Guymer and colleagues, 2001); and the Childhood Trust Survey on Animal Related Experiences (Boat and colleagues, 2008). Other approaches to enable children to talk about their experiences of animal abuse include using vignettes of animal abuse incidents (Wauthier, Scottish SPCA & Williams, 2022), and asking children about their attitudes towards animal abuse (Connor and colleagues, 2021; Hawkins and colleagues, 2020). While there is no gold standard measure or standardised assessment tool, a list of measures used in research on childhood animal abuse is provided in a recent literature review (Wauthier & Williams, 2022). Given the difficulties in reliably identifying children who have harmed animals, it is important to have preventative interventions in place before harm occurs and to reduce stigma around receiving interventions when animal abuse has already happened.

Despite the variability in measures, three dimensions of animal harm are consistently associated with greater psychological risks and worse outcomes: clear intentionality, higher frequency and greater severity. For example, using samples of prison inmates, Hensley and colleagues (2009) found that only repeated acts of animal abuse in childhood were predictive of repeated acts of interpersonal violence in adulthood, while Kellert and Felthouse (1985) found that more severe acts of animal abuse were much higher in a group of aggressive criminals compared to non-aggressive criminals and non-criminals. Although intentionality has received less attention, studies with adolescents suggest that intentional harm is associated with higher rates of delinquency compared to accidental harm (Connor and colleagues, 2021). Using these three dimensions (frequency, intentionality and severity), Table 2.1 proposes a theoretically informed scale that can help quickly assess the level of risk

Table 2.1 Assessing animal harm in children and adolescents

Please answer the following questions about any harm or distress the child or young person has caused animals. Answer only for vertebrates (e.g., fish, reptiles, birds, mammals) do not include behaviour towards invertebrates (e.g., insects, worms, molluscs).	
1. What type(s) of harm or distress has the child/young person caused animal(s)? (Circle all that apply)	
a) Child/young person has never caused an animal distress *(skip remaining questions)*	*[0 points]*
b) Child/young person has caused an animal physical distress (e.g., rough handling, hitting)	*[1 point]*
c) Child/young person has caused an animal emotional distress (e.g., teasing, yelling at)	*[1 point]*
d) Child/young person has neglected an animal (e.g., forgetting food or water, tying up for very long periods)	*[1 point]*
2. How many times has the child/young person caused an animal harm or distress in the last six months?	
a) Not in the last six months	*[0 points]*
b) 1–2 times	*[1 point]*
c) 3–5 times	*[2 points]*
d) More than 5 times	*[3 points]*

(Continued)

Table 2.1 (Continued)

If there is more than one instance you can think of, answer the remaining questions for what you consider to be the most serious case

3. Do you think the child/young person caused the animal's harm or distress on purpose?

a) No, it was an accident	[0 points]
b) Not really, the young person didn't realise what they were doing in the moment (e.g., they reacted impulsively)	[1 point]
c) Yes, but the young person's primary goal was not to cause the animal distress (e.g., they wanted to 'correct' bad behaviour)	[2 points]
d) Yes, the young person did it specifically because they wanted to cause the animal harm or distress	[3 points]

4. How much harm or distress did the child/young person cause the animal?

a) Mild: e.g., animal was uncomfortable, but it did not last beyond the incident	[1 point]
b) Moderate: e.g., animal had lasting pain and/or fear	[2 points]
c) Severe: the animal needed to go to the vet and/or died	[3 points]

Score	Associated Risk	Primary Intervention	Example
0	Very low risk	Prevention	Scottish SPCA 'Animal Wise'
2–4	Low risk	Animal welfare education	Animal Guardians
5–6	Moderate risk	Welfare education and assess for further intervention	Animal Guardians [+ AniCare] *or* BARK
7–12	High risk	Psychotherapy	AniCare Child/Adult

associated with animal abuse incident(s). Using simple, non-stigmatising language, it can be completed by parents, social workers or health care workers to determine what level of intervention might be required.

Psychological risk and protective factors for animal abuse

In this part of the chapter, we will draw heavily on two published systematic reviews of the evidence of risk and protective factors for childhood animal abuse (Hawkins, Hawkins & Williams, 2017; Wauthier & Williams, 2022). The research on childhood and adolescent animal abuse is very limited compared to other aspects of children's behaviour and development. Furthermore, research has focused on the more extreme end of the animal abuse scale, with animal abuse seen as an indicator or 'red flag' for developmental psychopathology (Boat and colleagues, 2011; Wauthier & Williams, 2022). Unfortunately, this research tendency has led to childhood animal harm being treated as 'abnormal', 'pathological' and often highly stigmatised. Furthermore, research has been heavily influenced by researchers in social work and criminology, often working with highly vulnerable children and families (e.g., those involved in domestic violence) and rarely carried out directly with children themselves, often relying on parent, teacher or practitioner reports of animal abuse.

The section below covers both protective and risk factors since a single variable (e.g., empathy) can act as both; for example, high empathy might be protective against animal harm, while low empathy might increase risk. If a child or adolescent exhibits risk factors for animal harm this does not mean that they will harm an animal, they are just more likely to harm an animal than someone with low risk. A risk factor is not a determinant of behaviour, there is always scope for intervention and prevention, especially with children, as we will see in Chapters 7 and 8.

In the review of psychological factors below, we draw on two theoretical frameworks commonly used in developmental and health psychology. The *biopsychosocial* model can be used to describe the interaction of biological and environmental factors in creating psychological outcomes and the interaction of these domains through development. Bronfenbrenner's *bioecological systems model* places the individual and their psychological risks within a wider social context, starting with intra-personal factors (the microsystem) and moving outward to consider increasing broad institutions, from families to schools and neighbourhoods (the mesosystem) to overall cultural influences (the macro-system; see e.g., Bronfenbrenner & Ceci, 1994) (Figure 2.2).

Biological risk factors

Across a range of studies, boys are more likely to engage in animal abuse than girls (for a review see Lee-Kelland & Finlay, 2018). Boys more commonly engage in rough and tumble play as children (Hart & Tannock, 2019), which may be a risk for accidental harm to animals, and are more likely to engage in physical aggression in childhood and adolescence, which can include violent behaviour to people and animals (Galán and colleagues, 2022). Boys report less attachment to pets in adolescence, but there may be reporting biases here as boys may be less likely to discuss their emotional bonds with animals (Muldoon, Williams & Currie, 2019). Furthermore, the precise mechanisms underlying this sex difference in animal abuse are not well understood.

Age is also a predictor of animal abuse. In a UK longitudinal study (McEwen and colleagues, 2014) it was found that animal abuse was more common among younger children, however, other studies have highlighted an increase in animal abuse among adolescents coinciding with increases in anti-social behaviour and delinquency (Ascione, 2005). It is important to note that the types of animal abuse might change with age from unintentional to more intentional abuse, and that psychological risk factors might vary across ages.

Finally, genetics can also play a role in determining a child's susceptibility to impulsive or aggressive behaviour. Several genes involved in neurotransmission have been identified as increasing a child's risk of externalising disorders such as Conduct Disorder and ADHD (Fairchild and colleagues, 2019). For example, one study reports that low-activity variants of the monoamine oxidase A (MAOA) enzyme increase risk of aggressive behaviour when male children are also exposed to abuse (Fergusson and colleagues, 2011), illustrating the importance of considering gene-environment interactions.

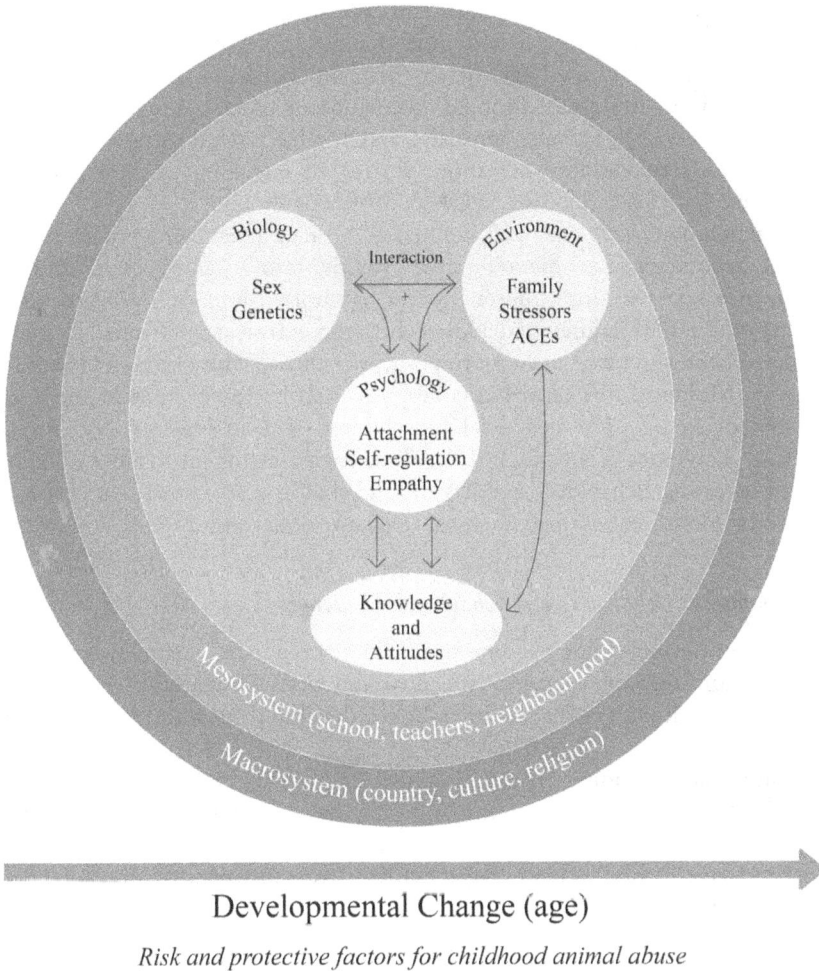

Developmental Change (age)

Risk and protective factors for childhood animal abuse

Figure 2.2 Risk and protective factors for childhood animal abuse.

Attachment style and relationships with animals

Children's relationships with pets have been a key focus of research; how we define these relationships remains unclear. Veterinary perspectives on relationships with companion animals refer to the 'bond' but psychologists focus on human attachment theory (e.g., Bowlby, 1969) and extend this body of knowledge to pets. Attachment theory as it relates to humans sees the attachment between a child and primary caregiver as an essential part of development. Reciprocal attuned behaviour between the child and caregiver, where the child's needs are met is seen as a foundation of emotional development, with consequences for later mental health. Children who are insecurely attached (e.g., Ainsworth and colleagues, 1978) to caregivers are most at risk of psychological difficulties including behaviour problems and mental health difficulties (Van Ijzendoorn and colleagues, 1999). In fact, attachment is an important foundational building block for arousal regulation, interpersonal skills and empathy, and we have demonstrated that insecurely attached children are more at risk of engaging in animal harm (Wauthier, Farnfield, Scottish SPCA & Williams 2022).

Pet attachment is not as well defined as human attachment but pets can become secondary attachment figures, provide comfort in times of distress and form a safe base for children (Marsa-Sambola, Muldoon, Williams and colleagues, 2016). Children and adolescents who are strongly attached to their pets have been shown to have more positive mental health outcomes (Marsa-Sambola, Muldoon, Williams and colleagues, 2016). However, attachment to dogs seems to be most beneficial for children and adolescents (Muldoon, Williams, Lawrence & Currie, 2019). While high attachment to a pet is likely to lead to caring behaviours, we have found that low attachment to pets is a risk factor for animal harm (Hawkins, Williams & Scottish SPCA, 2017b).

Self-regulation, impulsivity and behavioural challenges

As children develop, they become more able to regulate their own emotions and behaviour through a range of executive functions (Diamond, 2013). Three core executive functions that are inter-linked develop through early childhood:

- Inhibition (including resisting impulses and self-control)
- Working memory (to retain and manipulate information over short periods of time)
- Cognitive flexibility (allowing them to sustain or shift attention to apply different rules to different settings)

As children's executive functions develop they become more able to regulate their behaviour and emotions and behave appropriately in different contexts. As much of the animal abuse we see among young children is accidental and unintentional it is clear that the child's ability to regulate their behaviour and avoid impulsivity plays a role in their interactions with animals (see Case Studies above). For example, imagine a situation where a pre-school child is playing a game with building bricks or a doll's house and the family dog knocks all their toys and destroys their game. They may feel angry and upset, they may want to lash out at the dog. They have to regulate their emotions and behaviour and control their impulses. Importantly, we can support children in developing self-regulation and avoid risks of animal abuse in cases where a child may be having difficulties regulating their own behaviour. Interacting with animals can be an approach to supporting children to build skills in self-regulation and emotion regulation (Boyer, 2014).

As with all areas of psychological development, there are individual differences and high impulsivity and aggression are associated with animal abuse among adults (e.g. Newberry, 2018) and children and adolescents (e.g. Walters, 2019). Similarly, some children's behaviour leads them to be diagnosed with a Conduct Disorder defined as "repetitive and persistent pattern of behaviour in which the basic rights of others or major age-appropriate societal norms or rules are violated" (DSM V). Animal abuse was added to the diagnosis of conduct disorder in the 1980s, and has been found to be one of the earliest indicators of childhood-onset Conduct Disorder (Miller, 2001). Thus, age-related difficulties in regulating emotions and behaviour and individual differences in levels of impulsiveness and challenging behaviour are associated with a range of developmental outcomes, including increased risk of animal abuse, and may require specialist support and intervention.

Empathy and callous–unemotional traits

Personality traits were the focus of early research on animal abuse that was often based on adult forensic samples. The *Macdonald Triad* proposed that the co-occurrence of enuresis (bed wetting), fire-setting and animal cruelty in childhood was predictive of later violence, especially serial-killing (Felthous & Bernard, 1979; Macdonald, 1963; Parfitt & Alleyne, 2020). The Graduation Hypothesis that animal abuse in childhood is predictive of later human–directed violence has been influential in our thinking about childhood animal abuse, but has not stood research scrutiny (Hensley and colleagues, 2018). Similarly, the Dark Triad of the personality variables Narcissism, Machiavellianism and Psychopathy has been found to be predictive of attitudes to animals and animal abuse among adults (Kavanagh and colleagues, 2013). However, personality traits are still developing in childhood and childhood psychological risk factors can lead to a range of developmental outcomes (Cicchetti & Rogosch, 1996).

Focusing on children, empathy was found to be associated with concern for animals and (Ruckert, & Arnold, 2018) behaviour towards them (Hartman and colleagues, 2019). Empathy develops over childhood and is multifaceted including: the ability to understand another's perspective (cognitive empathy); experiencing an emotional reaction to another's emotions (affective empathy); and behavioural responses to support an animal in need (sometimes referred to as: behavioural empathy, compassionate concern or intention to comfort) (Overgaauw and colleagues, 2017). Most measures of empathy relate only to humans and research has shown that empathy to humans may not directly link to empathy towards animals (Paul, 2000). So, although we know that empathy towards people typically develops over childhood, less is known about the factors that affect empathy to animals. It is likely to include a range of cognitive skills such as: recognising animal emotions and understanding that animals are sentient (cognitive empathy), feeling distress when an animal is harmed (affective empathy) and engaging in a behavioural reaction to comfort an animal (behavioural empathy).

Some children show atypical development of empathy, developing callous-unemotional (CU) traits where they demonstrate a lack of empathy, shallow affect and uncaring attitude. CU traits are a risk factor for childhood animal abuse (Hartman and colleagues, 2019), and are associated with psychopathy (Craig and colleagues, 2021). Psychopathy consists of three elements: affective dysfunction (analogous to CU Traits), interpersonal style (e.g., arrogant and deceitful, narcissistic view of self and manipulative behaviour) and impulsive and irresponsible behaviour (Forth & Kosson, 2003). High psychopathic traits in children and young people are associated with animal abuse (Dadds and colleagues, 2006).

So, while empathy development is part of typical child development, among some children there is an atypical development of empathy, and development of CU traits and psychopathic traits that can be risk factors for animal abuse. This area of risk factors is complex, and assessing a child for CU traits and psychopathy requires psychological/psychiatric training. Children experiencing low empathy and high CU and psychopathic traits may require specialist support and intervention.

Knowledge and attitudes

As children grow their intellectual ability increases (for review see Barrouillet, 2015) and their ability to understand complex science concepts such as illness and animal welfare needs increases too (Muldoon and colleagues, 2016). However, understanding an animal's welfare needs is cognitively complex. As outlined in Chapter 1 from an animal welfare perspective each animal has five freedoms of welfare needs:

1   Need for a suitable environment
2   Need for a suitable diet
3   Need to exhibit normal behaviour
4   Need to be housed with or apart from other animals
5   Need to be protected from pain, suffering, injury and disease

These welfare needs vary with species (e.g., dog, cats and rabbits), so our behaviours towards animals, including pet care, need to be adjusted to meet an animals' needs. A suitable environment and diet will be different for cats, rabbits and goldfish. It is even more complex than that because children also have to learn about within species differences. So, for example, different breeds of dogs may have specific behavioural needs and health care requirements (e.g., Great Dane *(Canis lupus familiaris)* versus Mexican Hairless Dog (*Xoloitzcuintli*)). Some fish are tropical, some marine and some cold water, and so have different environmental needs. Young and ageing pets may have different welfare needs, with puppies requiring socialisation opportunities to meet their behavioural needs, whereas elderly dogs may require more rest and enhanced healthcare.

We have found that low levels of knowledge of animal welfare needs and low understanding of animal minds are risk factors for unintentional animal harm (Hawkins & Williams, 2016). Optimistically we can enhance knowledge and understanding through age-appropriate educational interventions (Hawkins, Williams & Scottish SPCA, 2017a; Williams and colleagues, 2022; see Chapter 8). Knowledge of welfare needs does not always translate into positive behaviour, so supporting children in developing behavioural skills in handling and interacting with animals may help to bridge the gap between knowledge and behaviour.

Attitudes to animals and attitudes about animal abuse are also important in influencing children's behaviour to animals. While most children generally have positive attitudes to animals, attitudes that animal abuse is acceptable is a predictor of abusive behaviour (Hawkins and colleagues, 2020). Therefore, in addition to increasing knowledge about animal welfare needs it is important to increase positive attitudes to the treatment of animals in order to reduce the risk of animal abuse. Children's knowledge and attitudes are affected by the families, communities and education systems they grow up in, so it is important to consider the impact of the broader social environment on children's behaviour to animals.

Social environment and adverse childhood experiences

Children grow up in families, communities and cultural norms that affect their behaviour towards animals. Children will model behaviour they witness in their homes or communities, a phenomenon called social learning (Bandura & Walters, 1977), this will include caring and abusive behaviour. Cultural and friendship norms also influence adolescents' behaviour towards animals (Arluke, 2012). So, promoting positive behaviour towards animals in the home and community will impact children's behaviour towards animals.

The kind of neighbourhood a child lives in and levels of community adversity also impact a child or adolescents' behaviour towards animals. Reese and colleagues (2020) studied animal abuse cases recorded by police in Detroit and found that neighbourhood conditions of economic stress, vacancy and high crime rates were most predictive of cases of animal abuse. Thus, the neighbourhood context in which a child or young person lives will have an impact on their exposure to animal abuse. Adverse Childhood Experiences and exposure to violence are risk factors for animal harm (Wauthier, Scottish SPCA, & Williams., 2022) and childhood animal abuse may be an indicator of family trauma (Bright and colleagues, 2018). There is growing evidence of the link between child abuse and animal abuse (Becker & French, 2004) and other forms of abuse (see Chapter 3 for more information). Thus, children who abuse animals are themselves likely to be vulnerable and in need of support.

Interactions between risk and protective factors

Risk and protective factors for animal abuse co-occur and interact with each other, and change over development. For example, Adverse Childhood

Experiences may be associated with exposure to violence and attachment difficulties that are all associated with childhood animal abuse (Wauthier, Scottish SPCA & Williams, 2022). Empathy, emotion and behaviour regulation, aggression and attitudes to animals are linked (Schipper & Petermann, 2013; Taylor & Signal, 2005). Furthermore, attachment difficulties and trauma may be risk factors for childhood animal abuse, but strong attachment to a pet (Carr & Rockett, 2017), or animal-assisted interventions, might counterbalance these risks (Balluerka and colleagues, 2014).

Understanding the range of psychological risk factors for animal harm in childhood and adolescence is an important step in developing effective prevention and intervention programmes. Cases of animal harm are inherently complex and multifaceted, and a 'one-size-fits-all' approach is unlikely to be effective. From a prevention perspective, understanding psychological risk factors can help identify children who are most likely to benefit from educational intervention before harm occurs. Where harm has already occurred, having an awareness of the range of issues can improve referral procedures and help practitioners identify children's areas of concern and tailor interventions accordingly. It also highlights the importance of having interdisciplinary teams and referral routes when complex cases of animal abuse are identified.

Returning to the case studies, we can see that the four cases require different levels of intervention, targeting different risk factors. Child 1's behaviour can be attributed primarily to lack of knowledge and may benefit from a simple educational intervention covering animal sentience and welfare needs. Child 2's behaviour should be recognised as a 'cry for help', and they may need a psycho-educational intervention which also covers emotional-behavioural regulation and coordination with a mental health team to ensure a positive transition into a fostered environment. Child 3's behaviour does not stem from a lack of knowledge or lack of behavioural control but from redirected frustration and anger. They may need more specialist and long-term psychological intervention which can help guide them through their tendency to harm others in an attempt to deal with their frustration. Finally, for the teenagers in case 4, behaviour stems from negative attitudes to cats amplified by group dynamics promoting aggressive behaviour. We might consider a mixed approach providing both individual intervention and group-based work, with further prevention through the school to reach a wider section of peers.

Conclusions

Childhood animal abuse occurs on a spectrum of possible interactions with animals from positive to negative. Harm to animals by children is often accidental and unintentional, but where intentional abuse occurs it is associated with psychological difficulties. A wide range of risk and protective factors affect children's likelihood of abusing an animal and these often co-occur. They range from factors within the child, to factors within the child's family, to those in the broader community. Although childhood animal abuse is complex there is a range of intervention points to prevent harm and intervene when it has happened to support the child (see Chapters 7 and 8). Taking a non-judgemental and compassionate approach to both the children and animals is essential to support those involved in animal abuse and to prevent recurrence.

Questions to consider

1   Have you come across any similar case examples as those outlined in this Chapter?
2   Thinking back to your childhood, was there a particular animal that was important to you?
3   From reading this chapter would you now observe interactions between children and animals differently?

Key Points

1   Child-animal interactions are complex and multi-faceted and animal abuse is just one possible outcome.
2   Childhood animal abuse is not always visible and can be difficult to detect and interpret.
3   Childhood animal abuse may not be intentional it may be due to a lack of knowledge of welfare needs.
4   Sex, age and emotion and behavioural regulation are implicated in childhood animal abuse.
5   Empathy, callous-unemotional traits and psychopathy are linked to childhood animal abuse.
6   High knowledge of welfare needs and attitudes that animal abuse is not acceptable are protective of animals.
7   Family environments, the experience of trauma and exposure to violence are risks for childhood animal abuse.
8   Children and young people who harm animals may be in need of support, it is important to treat them with compassion to protect them and the animals they interact with.

References

Achenbach, T. M. (1991). *Manual for the* Child Behaviour Checklist/4-18 *and 1991 Profile.* Burlington: University of Vermont Department of Psychiatry.

Ainsworth, M. D. S., Blehar, M. C., Waters, E., & Wall, S. (1978). *Patterns of attachment.* Hillsdale, New Jersey: Lawrence Erlbaum Associates.

Arluke, A. (2012). Interpersonal barriers to stopping animal abuse: Exploring the role of adolescent friendship norms and breeches. *Journal of Interpersonal Violence*, *27*(15), 2939–2958.

Ascione, F. R. (1993). Children who are cruel to animals: A review of research and implications for developmental psychopathology. *Anthrozoös*, *6*(4), 226–247.

Ascione, F. R. (2001). *Animal abuse and youth violence*. Washington: United States Department of Justice, Office of Justice Programs.

Ascione, F. R. (2005). *Children and animals: Exploring the roots of kindness and cruelty*. West Lafayette, USA: Purdue University Press.

Ascione, F. R., Thompson, T. M., & Black, T. (1997). Childhood cruelty to animals: Assessing cruelty dimensions and motivations. *Anthrozoös*, *10*(4), 170–177.

Ascione, F. R., & Shapiro, K. (2009). People and animals, kindness and cruelty: Research directions and policy implications. *Journal of Social Issues*, *65*(3), 569–587.

Balluerka, N., Muela, A., Amiano, N., & Caldentey, M. A. (2014). Influence of animal-assisted therapy (AAT) on the attachment representations of youth in residential care. *Children and Youth Services Review*, *42*, 103–109.

Bandura, A., & Walters, R. H. (1977). *Social learning theory* (Vol. 1). Englewood Cliffs: Prentice Hall.

Barrouillet, P. (2015). Theories of cognitive development: From Piaget to today. *Developmental Review*, *38*, 1–12.

Becker, F., & French, L. (2004). Making the links: Child abuse, animal cruelty and domestic violence. *Child Abuse Review: Journal of the British Association for the Study and Prevention of Child Abuse and Neglect*, *13*(6), 399–414.

Boat, B. W., Loar, L., & Phillips, A. (2008). Collaborating to assess, intervene, and prosecute animal abuse: Acontinuum of protection for children and animals. In F. R. Ascione (Ed.), *International handbook of animal abuse and cruelty: Theory, research, and application* (pp. 393–422). West Lafayette, IN: Purdue University Press.

Boat, B. W., Pearl, E., Barnes, J. E., Richey, L., Crouch, D., Barzman, D., & Putnam, F. W. (2011). Childhood cruelty to animals: Psychiatric and demographic correlates. *Journal of Aggression, Maltreatment & Trauma*, *20*(7), 812–819.

Bowlby, J. (1969). *Attachment and loss, Vol. 1: Attachment*. New York: Basic Books.

Boyer, W. (2014). Using interactions between children and companion animals to build skills in self-regulation and emotion regulation. In M.R. Jalongo , *Teaching compassion: Humane education in early childhood* (pp. 33–47). Dordrecht: Springer.

Bright, M. A., Huq, M. S., Spencer, T., Applebaum, J. W., & Hardt, N. (2018). Animal cruelty as an indicator of family trauma: Using adverse childhood experiences to look beyond child abuse and domestic violence. *Child Abuse & Neglect*, *76*, 287–296.

Bronfenbrenner, U., & Ceci, S. J. (1994). Nature-nuture reconceptualized in developmental perspective: A bioecological model. *Psychological Review*, *101*(4), 568.

Brelsford, V. L., Meints, K., Gee, N. R., & Pfeffer, K. (2017). Animal-assisted interventions in the classroom—A systematic review. *International Journal of Environmental Research and Public Health*, *14*(7), 669.

Burich, L., & Williams, J. M. (2020). Children's welfare knowledge of and empathy with farm animals: A qualitative study. *Anthrozoös*, *33*(2), 301–315.

Carr, S., & Rockett, B. (2017). Fostering secure attachment: Experiences of animal companions in the foster home. *Attachment & Human Development*, *19*(3), 259–277.

Cicchetti, D., & Rogosch, F. A. (1996). Equifinality and multifinality in developmental psychopathology. *Development and Psychopathology*, *8*(4), 597–600.

Connor, M., Currie, C., & Lawrence, A. B. (2021). Factors influencing the prevalence of animal cruelty during adolescence. *Journal of Interpersonal Violence, 36*(7–8), 3017–3040.

Craig, S. G., Goulter, N., & Moretti, M. M. (2021). A systematic review of primary and secondary callous–unemotional traits and psychopathy variants in youth. *Clinical Child and Family Psychology Review, 24*(1), 65–91.

Dadds, M. R., Whiting, C., Bunn, P., Fraser, J. A., Charlson, J. H., & Pirola-Merlo, A. (2004). Measurement of cruelty in children: The cruelty to animals inventory. *Journal of Abnormal Child Psychology, 32*(3), 321–334.

Dadds, M. R., Whiting, C., & Hawes, D. J. (2006). Associations among cruelty to animals, family conflict, and psychopathic traits in childhood. *Journal of Interpersonal Violence, 21*(3), 411–429.

Diamond, A. (2013). Executive functions. *Annual Review of Psychology, 64*, 135.

Fairchild, G., Hawes, D. J., Frick, P. J., Copeland, W. E., Odgers, C. L., Franke, B., Freitag, C. M., & De Brito, S. A. (2019). Conduct disorder. *Nature Reviews Disease Primers, 5*(1), 1–25.

Felthous, A. R., & Bernard, H. (1979). Enuresis, firesetting, and cruelty to animals: The significance of two thirds of this triad. *Journal of Forensic Science, 24*(1), 240–246.

Fergusson, D. M., Boden, J. M., Horwood, L. J., Miller, A. L., & Kennedy, M. A. (2011). MAOA, abuse exposure and antisocial behaviour: 30-year longitudinal study. *The British Journal of Psychiatry, 198*(6), 457–463.

Forth, A. E., & Kosson, D. (2003). *The hare PCL: Youth version.* Toronto, ON: Multi-Health Systems.

Galán, C. A., Feldman, J. S., & McClaine, R. N. (2022). Using the social information processing model to understand gender differences in the manifestation and frequency of aggression. *Aggression and Violent Behavior*, 101766.

Guymer, E. C., Mellor, D., Luk, E. S., & Pearse, V. (2001). The development of a screening questionnaire for childhood cruelty to animals. *The Journal of Child Psychology and Psychiatry and Allied Disciplines, 42*(8), 1057–1063.

Hart, J. L., & Tannock, M. T. (2019). Rough play: Past, present and potential. In P. K. Smith & J. L. Roopnarine (Eds.), *The Cambridge handbook of play: Developmental and disciplinary perspectives* (pp. 200–221). Cambridge University Press.

Hartman, C., Hageman, T., Williams, J. H., Mary, J. S., & Ascione, F. R. (2019). Exploring empathy and callous–unemotional traits as predictors of animal abuse perpetrated by children exposed to intimate partner violence. *Journal of Interpersonal Violence, 34*(12), 2419–2437.

Hawkins, R. D., & Williams, J. M. (2016). Children's beliefs about animal minds (Child-BAM): Associations with positive and negative child–animal interactions. *Anthrozoös, 29*(3), 503–519.

Hawkins, R. D., Hawkins, E. L., & Williams, J. M. (2017). Psychological risk factors for childhood nonhuman animal cruelty: A systematic review. *Society & Animals, 25*(3), 280–312.

Hawkins, R. D., Williams, J. M., & Scottish SPCA. (2017a). Childhood attachment to pets: Associations between pet attachment, attitudes to animals, compassion, and humane behaviour. *International Journal of Environmental Research and Public Health, 14*(5), 490.

Hawkins, R. D., Williams, J. M., & Scottish SPCA. (2017b). Assessing effectiveness of a nonhuman animal welfare education program for primary school children. *Journal of Applied Animal Welfare Science, 20*(3), 240–256.

Hawkins, R. D., Scottish SPCA, & Williams, J. M. (2020). Children's attitudes towards animal cruelty: Exploration of predictors and socio-demographic variations. *Psychology, Crime & Law, 26*(3), 226–247.

Hensley, C., Browne, J. A., & Trentham, C. E. (2018). Exploring the social and emotional context of childhood animal cruelty and it's potential link to adult human violence. *Psychology, Crime & Law, 24*(5), 489–499.

Hensley, C., Tallichet, S. E., & Dutkiewicz, E. L. (2009). Recurrent childhood animal cruelty: Is there a relationship to adult recurrent interpersonal violence? *Criminal Justice Review, 34*(2), 248–257.

Kavanagh, P. S., Signal, T. D., & Taylor, N. (2013). The Dark Triad and animal cruelty: Dark personalities, dark attitudes, and dark behaviors. *Personality and Individual Differences, 55*(6), 666–670.

Kellert, S. R., & Felthous, A. R. (1985). Childhood cruelty toward animals among criminals and noncriminals. *Human Relations, 38*, 1113–1129.

Ladny, R. T., & Meyer, L. (2020). Traumatized witnesses: Review of childhood exposure to animal cruelty. *Journal of Child & Adolescent Trauma, 13*(4), 527–537.

Lee-Kelland, R., & Findlay, F. (2018). Children who abuse animals: When should you be concerned about child abuse? A review of the literature. *Archives of Disease in Childhood, 103*(8), 801–805.

McEwen, F. S., Moffitt, T. E., & Arseneault, L. (2014). Is childhood cruelty to animals a marker for physical maltreatment in a prospective cohort study of children? *Child Abuse & Neglect, 38*(3), 533–543.

Macdonald, J. M. (1963). The threat to kill. *American Journal of Psychiatry, 120*(2), 125–130.

Marsa-Sambola, F., Muldoon, J., Williams, J., Lawrence, A., Connor, M., & Currie, C. (2016). The short attachment to pets scale (SAPS) for children and young people: Development, psychometric qualities and demographic and health associations. *Child Indicators Research, 9*(1), 111–131.

Marsa-Sambola, F., Williams, J., Muldoon, J., Lawrence, A., Connor, M., Roberts, C., & Currie, C. (2016). Sociodemographics of pet ownership among adolescents in Great Britain: findings from the HBSC study in England, Scotland, and Wales. *Anthrozo's, 29*, 559–580.

Menchetti, L., Calipari, S., Guelfi, G., Catanzaro, A., & Diverio, S. (2018). My dog is not my cat: Owner perception of the personalities of dogs and cats living in the same household. *Animals, 8*(6), 80.

Miller, C. (2001). Childhood animal cruelty and interpersonal violence. *Clinical Psychology Review, 21*, 735–749. 10.1016/S0272-7358(00)00066-0

Muldoon, J. C., Williams, J. M., & Lawrence, A. (2015). 'Mum cleaned it and I just played with it': Children's perceptions of their roles and responsibilities in the care of family pets. *Childhood, 22*(2), 201–216.

Muldoon, J. C., Williams, J. M., & Lawrence, A. (2016). Exploring children's perspectives on the welfare needs of pet animals. *Anthrozoös, 29*(3), 357–375.

Muldoon, J. C., Williams, J. M., Lawrence, A., & Currie, C. (2019). The nature and psychological impact of child/adolescent attachment to dogs compared with other companion animals. *Society & Animals, 27*(1), 55–74.

Muldoon, J. C., Williams, J. M., & Currie, C. (2019). Differences in boys' and girls' attachment to pets in early-mid adolescence. *Journal of Applied Developmental Psychology, 62*, 50–58.

Newberry, M. (2018). Associations between different motivations for animal cruelty, methods of animal cruelty and facets of impulsivity. *Psychology, Crime & Law, 24*(5), 500–526.

O'Haire, M. E. (2013). Animal-assisted intervention for autism spectrum disorder: A systematic literature review. *Journal of Autism and Developmental Disorders, 43*(7), 1606–1622.

Overgaauw, S., Rieffe, C., Broekhof, E., Crone, E. A., & Guroglu, B. (2017). Assessing empathy across childhood and adolescence: Validation of the empathy questionnaire for children and adolescents (EmQue-CA). *Frontiers in Psychology*, 8, 870.

Parfitt, C. H., & Alleyne, E. (2020). Not the sum of it's parts: A critical review of the MacDonald triad. *Trauma, Violence, & Abuse, 21*(2), 300–310.

PDSA (2022). PDSA Animal Wellbeing Report. *PDSA*.

Paul, E. S. (2000). Empathy with animals and with humans: Are they linked? *Anthrozoös, 13*(4), 194–202.

Purewal, R., Christley, R., Kordas, K., Joinson, C., Meints, K., Gee, N., & Westgarth, C. (2017). Companion animals and child/adolescent development: A systematic review of the evidence. *International Journal of Environmental Research and Public Health, 14*(3), 234.

Reese, L. A., Vertalka, J. J., & Richard, C. (2020). Animal cruelty and neighborhood conditions. *Animals, 10*(11), 2095.

Ruckert, J. H., & Arnold, R. (2018). Empathy-related reasoning is associated with children's moral concerns for the welfare and rights of animals. *Ecopsychology, 10*(4), 259–269.

Schipper, M., & Petermann, F. (2013). Relating empathy and emotion regulation: Do deficits in empathy trigger emotion dysregulation? *Social Neuroscience, 8*(1), 101–107.

Taylor, N., & Signal, T. D. (2005). Empathy and attitudes to animals. *Anthrozoös, 18*(1), 18–27.

Van Ijzendoorn, M. H., Schuengel, C., & Bakermans–Kranenburg, M. J. (1999). Disorganized attachment in early childhood: Meta-analysis of precursors, concomitants, and sequelae. *Development and Psychopathology, 11*(2), 225–250.

Walters, G. D. (2019). Animal cruelty and bullying: Behavioral markers of delinquency risk or causal antecedents of delinquent behavior? *International Journal of Law and Psychiatry, 62*, 77–84.

Wauthier, L. M., & Williams, J. M. (2022). Understanding and conceptualizing childhood animal harm: A meta-narrative systematic review. *Anthrozoös, 35*(2), 165–202.

Wauthier, L., Scottish SPCA, & Williams, J. M. (2022). A qualitative study of children's accounts of cruelty to animals: Uncovering the roles of trauma, exposure to violence, and attachment. *Journal of Interpersonal Violence, 37*(9–10), NP6405–NP6438.

Wauthier, L., Farnfield, S., Scottish SPCA, & Williams, J. M. (2022). A preliminary exploration study of the psychological risk factors for childhood animal cruelty: The roles of attachment, self-regulation and empathy. *Anthrozoos*, 1–23.

Whyke, T. W., & López-Múgica, J. (2020). Content and discourse analysis of cruelty towards stray dogs as presented in Chinese social media. *Society & Animals, 1*(aop), 1–20.

Williams, J. M., Cardoso, M. P., Zumaglini, S., Finney, A. L., Scottish SPCA, & Knoll, M. A. (2022). "Rabbit Rescuers": A school-based animal welfare education intervention for young children. *Anthrozoös, 35*(1), 55–73.

3 The links between animal abuse and domestic violence/abuse

Phil Arkow

Coordinator, *The National Link Coalition – The National Resource Center on The Link between Animal Abuse and Human Violence* Etowah, N.C., U.S.A.

Aims of this chapter

Survivors of domestic violence (or domestic abuse, as it's called in the U.K.) worldwide routinely report that threats of harm or death to their pets are tactics of emotional extortion employed by abusers to coerce and control human family members and hold them hostage in toxic relationships. This chapter reviews how survivors and their children's emotional attachments to their pets make companion animals "soft targets" for manipulation and exploitation and create barriers to family members seeking safety. It reviews the scope and manifestations of domestic violence, how household pets are affected by these dynamics, representative statistics of animal abuse within domestic violence scenarios, the pernicious impact that this polyvictimisation has on children, legislative initiatives to protect animal victims of domestic violence and the development of shelters and refuges that accommodate the needs of survivors who have pets. We explore a new dimension of healthcare engagement, namely the role of veterinarians when clients are victimised by domestic abuse. Implications for practice among domestic violence service providers, animal welfare organisations, veterinary professionals, social workers, legislators, corporate and philanthropic funders and individuals are presented.

Introduction

Decades of research confirm that the dangers faced by survivors of domestic violence are magnified when the welfare of pets must also be taken into consideration. While there are numerous legal, financial, familial and emotional reasons why abused partners fail to leave adverse relationships, or continue to return to them, fear for their pets' welfare is a relatively unexplored barrier that forces thousands of survivors to remain in dangerous

DOI: 10.4324/9781003165552-3

homes rather than seek a journey to safety. The threat or actual harm of pets is a form of emotional extortion that often holds human survivors of domestic violence hostage and keeps them from leaving their abusers. The emotional attachment that survivors and their children have for their pets makes the animals "soft targets" for exploitive abusers who will use any tool at their disposal to find a point of vulnerability that can coerce and control family members and exert power over them.

Meanwhile, for those adult and child survivors who do escape abuse without their pets, the shortage of domestic violence safehouses (called "shelters" in the U.S., "refuges" in the U.K.) that accept pets not only puts the animals' well-being and lives in jeopardy but also deprives the human family members of important emotional support which can be vital to the psychological health and recovery of people in crisis.

Scope of the problem: Domestic violence in the U.S.

Domestic violence is an extremely pervasive issue embodying a highly complex constellation of confounding factors that affect not only individuals and families but also communities and workplaces. Each community's responses to best support survivors must consider their comprehensive and unique needs.

It must first be pointed out that domestic violence is not just physical abuse. It is a spectrum of coercive, controlling behaviours that can include multiple forms of intimidation, physical and sexual assault, emotional and psychological abuse, economic abuse, stalking and threats as part of a systematic pattern of power and control by one partner over another (Pennsylvania Coalition Against Domestic Violence, 2021).

It must also be noted that while the overwhelming majority of incidents involve a man exerting power and control over a woman, there are instances of women abusing men and intimate partner violence in same-sex relationships (National Domestic Violence Hotline, 2021). However, for the purposes of this chapter, we will simplify matters and assume that the topics under discussion involve a male abuser and a female victim (and potentially her children, pets and livestock).

More than 10 million people in the U.S. are subjected to domestic violence each year, with an estimated 1 in 4 women and 1 in 7 men experiencing serious physical or sexual violence or stalking from an intimate partner during their lifetime. State and local hotlines receive more than 19,000 calls every day, or more than 13 calls every minute (National Coalition Against Domestic Violence, 2020). Despite these numbers, many people still do not understand the prevalence and impact of domestic violence, and fewer still fail to include the companion animal members of families within the prevention and services available in response to the domestic violence dynamic.

People often ask, "Why doesn't she just leave?" The answer is: it's not that easy. Abusers go to great lengths to prevent their victims from escaping, and the risk of getting killed greatly increases when they are in the process of leaving or have just left. Barriers to seeking safety include:

- Being isolated from friends and family.
- Lack of financial and transportation resources.
- Restricted access to bank accounts.
- Fear of death, more abuse or losing custody of the children.
- "Gaslighting" tactics whereby the abuser causes her to feel like she is responsible for the abuse.
- Escalating health issues emanating from the long-term emotional and physical toll of abuse.
- A state of denial in believing the abuser's promises to change (National Network to End Domestic Violence, 2021).

Animal abuse within the context of domestic violence/abuse

These obstacles become exacerbated when survivors must also fear for the safety of their pets. Domestic violence and animal protection agencies increasingly recognise that fear of leaving animals behind with abusers is a significant barrier to human victims seeking safety. The dangers faced by survivors are magnified when pets become "soft targets" and collateral damage and their welfare must also be taken into consideration when deciding whether to escape.

One unfortunate and extremely effective technique by which abusers reinforce power and control (Figure 3.1) is to threaten, hurt or kill family pets as a warning of what would happen if anyone tries to leave (Urban Resource Institute and National Domestic Violence Hotline, 2021). Women are the primary caregivers of pets in 80% of homes (American Veterinary Medical Association, 2012) and pets are predominantly found in homes with children (American Veterinary Medical Association, 2007). For many who have found themselves isolated as a result of prolonged and systematic abuse, companion animals often provide vital emotional and social support, as many victims rely on them to manage stress (Newberry, 2017). Abusers are cognisant that the strong attachment victims of domestic violence often have to their companion animals becomes an exploitable point of vulnerability. As a result, threats of animal abuse and the killing of pets are powerful tools by which abusers can perpetuate the context of terror for victims and their children (Ponder & Lockwood, 2000).

While domestic violence frequently involves physical and sexual violence, these tactics often surround and reinforce a constellation of subtle, continual behaviours of power and control: coercion and threats, intimidation, emotional abuse, isolation, using children, male privilege, economic abuse and minimising, denying or blaming (Domestic Abuse Intervention Project, 2021). The National Link Coalition has described how these dynamics affect household animals in domestic violence contexts (Arkow, 2019 and Figure 3.1):

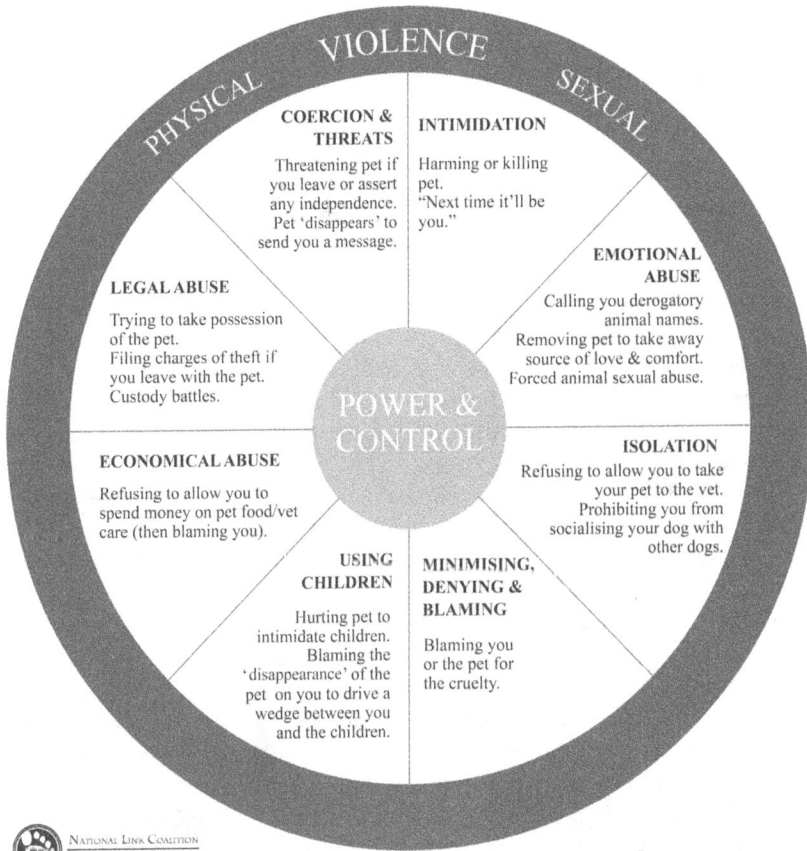

Animal abuse and the power and control wheel

Figure 3.1 Animal abuse and the power and control wheel.

- **Coercion:** Threats to kill or harm the animals if she leaves or asserts any independence.
- **Intimidation:** Targeting pets of family or friends who help her escape. Warning her that "I did it to your pet, I can do it to you."
- **Emotional abuse:** Giving pets away to deprive her of a source of emotional support and comfort. Forcing her to have sex with animals or watch animal pornography.
- **Isolation:** Refusing to allow her to take the pet to the veterinarian or socialise with others in dog parks.
- **Using the children:** Hurting children's pets to intimidate them. Blaming the pets' disappearance on her.

- **Legal abuse:** Engaging in custody battles over ownership of the animals. Filing theft charges if she leaves with the pet.
- **Economic abuse:** Refusing to allow her to spend money on pet food or veterinary care (and then blaming her for the animal's condition).
- **Minimising, denying and blaming:** Blaming her for the abuse.

Among the more significant and representative findings from surveys of survivors contacting domestic violence crisis lines and women in domestic violence shelters in the U.S., Canada, U.K. and New Zealand are:

- As many as 89% of victims with pets reported their abusers threatened, hurt or killed their pets as leverage to prevent them from leaving or to force them to return in order to care for the animals (Barrett and colleagues, 2018).
- Ninety-four percent of domestic violence shelter staff reported their clients indicated a history of animal abuse in their homes (Krienert and colleagues, 2012).
- The pets of family and friends who help victims leave were also targeted as revenge. Abusers admitted they specifically harm animals because they believe that police do not care about animal abuse (Roguski, 2012).
- Actual or threatened harm to animals ranks with low education level, history of mental illness and substance abuse as one of the four greatest risk factors for becoming a domestic violence abuser (Walton–Moss and colleagues, 2005).
- Domestic violence abusers who also abuse pets are more dangerous and use more forms of controlling behaviors and violence than those who do not also harm animals. This results in victims being more fearful to report domestic violence incidents (Simmons & Lehmann, 2007).
- Eighty-seven percent of intimidating attacks against animals occur in the presence of the spouse or partner; 75% occur in the presence of a child (Quinlisk, 1999).
- Abusers who victimise both animals and people have more than double the rate of access to guns. Seventy-eight percent of victims whose abusers also have histories of pet abuse fear they will be killed, and 76% have been strangled. The risk of death to first responders in cases where domestic violence and animal abuse co-occur doubles (Campbell, 2021).
- Forty-nine percent of domestic violence professionals were aware of cases where pets had been killed; 89% knew of cases where pets had been used as a tool for emotional abuse; 59% knew of cases where an owner's ability to care for pets had been impacted by financial abuse (Dogs Trust Freedom Project, 2021).
- A Canadian study of women in shelters described coercive-control animal abusers as "intimate terrorists" and said that reporting one's intimate partner for threatening or actual animal abuse increased the probability of her experiencing emotional or financial abuse by 38.6% (Fitzgerald and colleagues, 2022).

- In a survey of 2,480 individuals calling the National Domestic Violence Hotline in the U.S., 97% of respondents said that keeping their pets with them was an important factor in deciding whether to seek shelter; 50% would not consider shelter if they could not take their pets with them. 48% feared their abuser would kill or harm their pets, while 37% said the abuser had already threatened the animals and 29% had actually killed or hurt pets. Ninety-one percent said their pets' emotional support and physical protection were significant in their ability to survive and heal. But 72% of survivors were not aware that some domestic violence shelters either accept pets or have foster care arrangements for pets with community agencies, creating additional risk to both human and animal victims of domestic violence (Urban Resource Institute and National Domestic Violence Hotline, 2021).

Between April 2012 and April 2022, the National Link Coalition recorded 821 mainstream news media accounts of individuals arrested on charges of animal cruelty in conjunction with other alleged crimes, including domestic violence, child abuse, child sexual abuse, elder abuse, homicide, burglary, narcotics and weapons offenses and many others. Of this total, 231 (28.1%) included domestic violence – by far the most over-represented ancillary crime co-occurring with polyvictimising animal abuse. Recent representative cases include:

- A Utah man was charged with criminal trespass, arson, theft and animal torture for allegedly stealing and setting a woman's dog on fire in retaliation for a failed relationship (Reavy, 2021).
- A New Hampshire man was charged with animal cruelty and criminal threats for allegedly putting two severed rabbit heads on the car of a woman he had been text-threatening (Feely, 2021).
- A Nevada man was charged with allegedly killing his girlfriend's dog in anger after winning, and then losing, $500 in a Las Vegas casino (Garcia, 2021).
- A Nebraska man was charged with murder, child abuse and animal cruelty for allegedly killing his fiancée and her dog and leaving their bodies for her two children to find (Nelson, 2020).
- An Idaho man who believed his separated wife was having an affair was charged with burglary, arson, assault and animal cruelty for allegedly breaking into her home and throwing her clothes and a caged dog into a fire; three children had to barricade themselves in a room (Heersink, 2020).

Children, domestic violence/abuse and the human-animal bond

Domestic violence creates a violent and hostile environment that can have devastating physical and emotional effects on children and is frequently associated with other forms of violence including child abuse (National Coalition Against Domestic Violence, 2015). This impact is not limited to witnessing intimate partner violence; children may also be deeply affected by having witnessed direct harm or indirect threats to their pets. As will be described in greater detail in other chapters of this book, the significance to children's emotional development of their bonds with pets and of their witnessing or committing animal cruelty cannot be overstated. Children in homes marked by domestic violence may be simultaneously attached to their pets and conflicted about the turmoil swirling all around them. The nexus of animal abuse and child maltreatment within a domestic violence environment is exceedingly complex and several key dynamics emerge.

Pets are often a child's best friend, a non-judgmental confidant who can be talked to and share secrets with (Beck, 2011). This social and emotional support takes on additional importance among children who are experiencing traumatic events and even helps compensate for deficits in human bonds (Melson & Fine, 2019).

Having a favourite pet is a positive sign of a child's ability to connect with another living creature – but also makes the child more vulnerable to loss; witnessing abuse of that pet can be a terrifying experience that contributes to a child's feelings of helplessness and guilt (Boat, 2010). Leaving a pet behind when the family escapes an abusive situation can contribute to a child's fear of being similarly abandoned (Boat, 2014).

While bonding with pets may support children's mental health, exposure to animal cruelty may lead to subsequent anxiety, depression and emotional distress (Girardi & Pozzulo, 2015). Children's exposure to animal abuse as well as domestic violence increases the risk of developing compromised socio-emotional well-being (Becker & French, 2004; Merz-Perez & Heide, 2004) and psychological abuse and sexual coercion in adult intimate relationships (Haden and colleagues, 2018). Children who have been exposed to domestic violence are three times more likely to be cruel to animals than children who have not (Currie, 2006). Such exposure should be considered an Adverse Childhood Experience (Boat, 2014). At least nine U.S. states have enhanced criminal penalties for animal abuse offenses committed in the presence of a child (National District Attorneys Association, 2014).

An Australian study (Volant and colleagues, 2008) researched the impact of children witnessing domestic abuse or animal cruelty. Among 204 women surveyed, half of whom were recruited through family violence services and half of whom were sampled from within the larger community, 29% of the family violence sample reported that their children had been exposed to pets being harmed or killed by their partner, with no mothers within the community sample reporting this phenomenon. Additionally, 19% of mothers within the family violence sample reported that their children had harmed or killed a family companion animal, compared to 1% in the community sample.

The largest study on the impact on children experiencing co-occurring domestic violence and animal abuse (McDonald and colleagues, 2015) was a series of interviews with 242 children at 22 domestic violence shelters in Colorado. These children were seen to be simultaneously at risk for emotional and behavioural difficulties and more likely to repeat cycles of violence. Twenty-four percent of children reported threats or actual harm or death of pets by someone in the home. Ninety-five percent of children who witnessed animal abuse said they were upset by the incident. Children who were exposed to animal abuse were five times more likely to have "severe problems" and three times more likely to be "struggling" compared to their more resilient peers. Children were more than twice as likely to harm an animal when the mother's partner harmed an animal (McDonald and colleagues, 2015).

Equally significant, 78% of these children had taken preemptive and protective measures and direct intervention to come to their pets' rescue, which often resulted in their being directly victimised by the abusive partner as well. Their taking steps to protect their pets from abuse suggested that pets are important resiliency agents providing comfort and constancy for children who are exposed to high levels of fear and uncertainty (McDonald and colleagues, 2015).

Some pets were also harmed to punish a child's misbehavior, which the researchers saw as leading to further emotional distress. Animal abuse may also be a component of inter-sibling rivalries which are exacerbated in homes marked by domestic violence and are marked by shifting alliances, competition, empathy deficits regarding sibling mistreatment, and collusion with abusing partners (McDonald and colleagues, 2015).

Responses – legislative

British readers may not be familiar with a fundamental difference between U.S. and U.K. laws. Unlike in the U.K. where national laws govern animal cruelty and domestic violence, in the U.S. these laws are enacted on a state-by-state basis, with 50 individual states each responsible for it's own statutory definitions, judicial interpretations and criminal punishments.

Growing awareness of how animal abuse is a barrier to domestic violence survivors seeking safety has prompted a proliferation of state laws to address these concerns. As of this writing, 38 states allow survivors petitioning for court-ordered protection from abuse to specifically include animals in such protection orders; 19 of these states limit such protection to pets or companion animals, while 19 states include any animals or domestic animals in such coverage. Such orders can order the respondent to not harm or threaten animals, to stay away from them, to not remove them from the premises and to grant sole care and custody of the animal to the petitioner (National Link Coalition, 2021a). Demand for pet-protection orders can be significant once courts and petitioners are aware of these provisions: three years after Minnesota enacted pet protection orders, 1,067 petitioners applied for such protection (National Link Coalition, 2014).

The popularity of these state laws prompted the federal government to enact the PAWS (Pet And Women Safety) Act in December, 2018. This law enables the U.S. government to issue pet protection orders on federal lands and to enforce individual state pet protection orders across state lines should the petitioner leave one jurisdiction for another. The PAWS Act also awards federal grants totalling $2.5 million per year to domestic violence shelters and programs to build housing for residents' companion animals (National Link Coalition, 2019).

When an outcome of domestic violence is divorce or separation, a highly contentious issue is the question of which party gets to keep the family pets. This can be problematic because pets are legally defined as property, and in nine states all property acquired during the marriage is considered communal which must be split equally between the parties. As of this writing, five states specifically allow courts to award custody of pets to the party deemed by the court to be in the animals' best interests – modelling language long employed in settling child custody disputes.

Twelve U.S. states define acts of animal abuse employed as psychological or emotional abuse or coercive controlling behaviour over a spouse or partner as not only an act of cruelty to animals but also within a wider interpretation of domestic violence. Laws in eight U.S. states and the Navajo Nation similarly refer to acts of animal abuse within the statutory definitions of stalking, family violence, emotional abuse or coercion.

The Australian state of Victoria enacted legislation in 2021 that redefined companion animals as "family members" under the 2008 Family Violence Protection Act and called for a new system in which ownership of pets is automatically removed from domestic violence abusers. The state Parliament also approved additional funding for pet-friendly crisis accommodations and for individuals needing help in removing animals from violent homes, and greater scope to family violence leave provisions which will allow women to access family violence leave to help their animals (Meddick, 2021).

Responses – programmatic

Beginning in the late 1990s, animal welfare and domestic violence NGOs began championing ways to better assist those having to decide whether to leave their animals with an abuser or to remain to protect their animals. Ascione (2000) detailed policies and procedures and case evaluation models for survivors with pets at 40 domestic violence shelters that offered off-site foster care through animal shelters, boarding kennels and animal shelters. At the time, no shelters accepted residential pets due to such concerns as lack of space, staff and resident allergies, liability, zoning restrictions and financial constraints.

In response to growing awareness and the need for services, several pro-grammes emerged to assist shelters in becoming pet-friendly. Sheltering Animals and Families Together (SAF-T) became a global initiative helping shelters to create on-site pet housing for families fleeing violence. The SAF-T Start-Up Manual describes four housing styles (separate room, indoor–outdoor kennels, free-standing building or co-living in residents' rooms) and extensively answers administrators' questions about how to safely house pets at a shelter. As of this writing, 243 shelters in 46 states, plus 27 additional shelters in Australia, Canada and the Netherlands are designated as SAF-T; there are an unknown number of other pet-friendly shelters in Spain (Sheltering Animals and Families Together, 2021).

The largest pet-friendly shelter in the U.S. is the Urban Resource Institute's PALS (People and Animals Living Safely) co-living programme in New York City. The agency has the capacity to serve over 40,000 individuals annually with accommodations for 1,200 domestic violence victims every night. 172 co-living apartment units in seven of it's shelters allow pets, including one shelter built specifically for housing people and pets. As of this writing, the PALS programme has sheltered 293 adults and 438 children with 400 pets since 2013 (Urban Resource Institute and National Domestic Violence Hotline, 2021).

As more shelters began to accept pets, the need for funding such facilities grew. Several major sources of financial support are now available. In addition to the PAWS Act grants described above, Purina pet foods has partnered with RedRover, an NGO whose "Safe Escape" grants defray temporary boarding costs for pets while their caregiver is in a shelter, with the "Purple Leash" campaign that funds "Safe Housing" grants for the start-up costs of constructing pet facilities in shelters and off-site locations. Other national corporate and philanthropic funding in the U.S. has been offered by the American Veterinary Medical Foundation, the PetSmart chain of pet supply stores, Bayer veterinary pharmaceuticals and Banfield veterinary hospitals, among others. In Canada, the federal government's Department for Women and Gender Equality's (WAGE) Feminist Response and Recovery Fund has awarded Humane Canada a multi-year grant to address the gap in domestic violence shelters that are able to accommodate pets of survivors (National Link Coalition, 2021b).

While the proliferation of pet-friendly shelters is impressive and growing, these represent only a fraction of the shelters in the U.S., creating a need to enable survivors, in their moment of crisis, to quickly identify which shelters allow pets. In the U.S., Domesticshelters.org, safeplaceforpets.org and the Animal Welfare Institute's Safe Mapping Project are online databases of these facilities. Women's Shelter Canada (2021) created an interactive map identifying 66 on-site and 166 off-site shelters in that country, out of approximately 450 nationwide, that offer pet facilities; a number of these facilities appear to be on First Nations tribal lands.

New frontier for the future: "Domestic violence/abuse and the veterinary profession"

Much as human healthcare professionals have long responded to child abuse and other family violence, veterinarians are now being encouraged to respond to domestic violence as well as to suspected animal abuse. The UK Code of

Professional Conduct for Veterinary Surgeons states, "Given the links between animal, child, and domestic abuse, a veterinary surgeon or veterinary nurse reporting suspected or actual animal abuse should consider whether a child or adult within that home might also be at risk," with recommendations as to how to proceed (Royal College of Veterinary Surgeons, 2016). The Veterinary Council of New Zealand's Code of Professional Conduct for Veterinarians (Veterinary Council of New Zealand, 2020) acknowledges research linking deliberate physical maltreatment of animals with violence against humans and states, "Veterinarians, when confronted with situations of animal abuse, should consider whether people within that home might be at risk."

In 2015, the New Zealand Veterinary Association signed on to a national initiative responding to family violence. The NZVA's submission to the Ministry of Justice described veterinary medicine as a "three-dimensional profession" with a unique voice that transcends animal life, human life and the environment (National Link Coalition, 2015a). Shortly thereafter, the government of Scotland put slightly more than £1,000,000 into a targeted national campaign to train 100,000 professionals deemed most likely to encounter abused women on how to recognise and respond to domestic violence; the three professions identified were hairdressers, dentists and veterinarians (National Link Coalition, 2015b).

Several articles have begun to appear in journals to initiate a discussion of veterinarians' roles and responsibilities when they suspect a client may be experiencing domestic violence. These include articles in the U.S. (Larkin, 2018; Tricarico, 2019; Arkow, 2020), Canada (Gordon & Lathey, 2020; Lathey, 2020a, 2020b), the U.K. (Animal Welfare Foundation & The Links Group, 2016), Australia (Tiplady and colleagues, 2018) and New Zealand (Robertson, 2010; Newland and colleagues, 2019). The Links Group UK's recently updated 3rd edition of *Suspected Abuse of Animals and People: Guidance for the Veterinary Team* (The Links Group 2022) features an extended focus on responding to suspected domestic abuse as well as possible animal abuse.

Implications for practice and conclusions

A growing body of research, augmented by anecdotal experiences and organisational practices, confirms that animal abuse is a particularly pernicious component of domestic violence with potential adverse implications for the human and animal members of families. Given the multi-disciplinary nature of this Link between animal abuse and domestic violence, there are significant implications for numerous professional sectors.

Implications for domestic violence service providers

- There is a need to raise awareness among domestic violence victims about the impact of domestic violence on pets and the availability of resources that can shelter pets to remove a major barrier to safety.

- There is a need for more shelters that accommodate pets. Community domestic violence and animal welfare agencies should create partnerships to support co-sheltering and off-site foster care opportunities. Greater corporate and philanthropic financial support can facilitate shelters establishing pet housing programmes. This support should include initial capital construction and ongoing operational needs such as hiring trauma-informed staffing, maintaining prevention and intervention services and obtaining pet supplies and veterinary care.
- Additional legislation is needed to offer pets legal protection from domestic violence abuse.
- There is a need for more research and evaluation of programmes addressing the intersection of domestic violence and pets.
- Staff, clients and stakeholders should acknowledge the importance of the human-animal bond.
- Questions about pets should be added to screening materials at shelter intake and in ongoing work with clients.
- Agencies should research resources and service providers in their community that can assist survivors with animals.
- Domestic violence shelters should routinely include provisions for pets in safety planning materials.
- Shelters can collaborate with local animal welfare organisations for joint fundraisers.
- Provisions should be made to allow therapy animals to visit residents in the shelter.
- Regional and national domestic violence crisis hotline personnel should be trained to routinely inquire about the welfare, status and housing needs of survivors' pets. Such information removes a key barrier to victims escaping and enables staff to refer survivors to appropriate shelters, rather than having them show up unannounced at a shelter that is not equipped to receive them. It also trains crisis line staff on the highly significant bond between survivors, children and their pets, especially in moments of crisis, and how keeping the entire family together can enhance healing and recovery and protect all vulnerable family members from unsafe environments.

Implications for animal welfare organisations

- Animal welfare organisations need to reach out to local domestic violence resource providers and ask how they can help.
- There needs to be an offer to foster pets temporarily while survivors seek safety.
- Donate pet supplies, food and veterinary care to domestic violence survivors' pets.
- Partner with domestic violence resource providers to raise awareness of The Link between domestic violence and companion animals. Make domestic

violence literature available in shelter lobbies, educational programmes and community events.

- Collaborate with domestic violence agencies to compile a directory of pet-friendly apartments. This can prevent relocating pet owners from having to surrender their pets, and assist domestic violence agencies to find transitional housing for their clients.

Implications for veterinarians

- Veterinarians should reach out to local domestic violence resource providers to ask how they can help survivors with pets.
- Ask these organisations to provide brochures and other literature about domestic violence that can be displayed in the veterinary clinic's lobby.
- Offer to provide free or discounted veterinary care to survivors' pets.
- Train staff on protocols to respond to clients when domestic violence is suspected and help them make referrals to domestic violence service providers.

Implications for social workers and social services

- Encourage the introduction of human-animal studies into the curricula in schools of social work. Currently, only a handful of such schools address clients' relationships with animals, the positive benefits of the human-animal bond and pet-related issues that can be resolved through social workers' problem-solving skills.
- Recognise that many clients have pets and strong emotional attachments to them. Asking questions about pets in their lives builds trust and rapport, amplifies assessments and interventions and provides a window into their home environment and interpersonal relationships.
- Include pets when diagraming families' emotional attachments in geno-grams (Hodgson & Darling, 2011).
- Assist domestic violence survivors with locating pet support services.
- Consider the increasing number of social work career opportunities in veterinary hospitals, victim services units, animal shelters and domestic violence shelters.

Implications for legislators

- Enact laws that aid survivors with pets, such as including pets in orders of protection, defining intimidating animal abuse as an act of domestic violence and allowing courts to award custody of pets in divorce settlements to the party determined to be in the animals' best interests.
- Provide funding for local programmes and service providers that support domestic violence victims with pets.

- Support legislation that helps service providers to develop innovative programmes that increase safety and services for all vulnerable members of the family.

Implications for corporate and philanthropic funders

- Award grants to organisations and service providers to create or expand programmes that address domestic violence and pets. Critical needs include both initial capital construction and remodeling of pet housing facilities, and ongoing funding for supplies and materials, staffing, training and awareness campaigns for internal and external stakeholders on the intersection of domestic violence and pets.

Implications for individuals

- Donate to domestic violence and animal welfare organisations working to protect all vulnerable members of families.
- Encourage legislators to enact laws that address issues of pets affected by domestic violence.
- Start a conversation with friends, family members and community influencers about pets and domestic violence.
- Make a safety plan for your pets' care in case of a crisis or emergency.
- Join the National Link Coalition (The National Resource Center on The Link between Animal Abuse and Human Violence) in the U.S., the Links Group UK, the Canadian Violence Link Coalition and similar Link coalitions including: L'Association contre la Maltraitance Animale et Humaine (France), Link Italia (Italy), Observatorio de Violencia Hacia los Animales (Spain) and Se Sambandet and Veterinär Omtanke Om Våldsutsatta (Sweden). Help organise a local multi-disciplinary Link coalition in your community.

Questions to consider

1   What role would you/your profession play if faced with a domestic abuse case that involved an animal?
2   Would you be comfortable knowing who should be working with whom and what support is available in your area for victims including animal victims?
3   Do you think there is enough protection and support in your country for those looking to flee domestic abuse with animal victims?

Key Points

1   Domestic violence and animal protection agencies must recognise that fear of leaving animals behind with abusers is a significant barrier to human victims seeking safety.
2   Animal abuse is a particularly pernicious component of domestic violence with potential adverse implications for the human and animal members of families.
3   Veterinarians have a critical role in responding to domestic violence as well as to suspected animal abuse and more veterinarians need to be made aware of this.
4   There is a need for more research and evaluation of programs addressing the intersection of domestic violence and pets.
5   There is a need for more shelters and opportunities for foster placements that accommodate pets so that individuals and families can flee domestic violence as soon as they are ready to do so.

References

American Veterinary Medical Association (2007). *U.S. pet ownership and demographics sourcebook*.
American Veterinary Medical Association (2012). *U.S. pet ownership and demographics sourcebook*.
Animal Welfare Foundation and The Links Group (2016). *Recognising abuse in animals and humans: Comprehensive guidance for the veterinary team*. British Veterinary Association.
Arkow, P. (2019). *Breaking the cycles of violence: A guide to multi-disciplinary responses for domestic violence, child protection, adult protection, and animal care & control agencies*. Alameda: Latham Foundation.
Arkow, P. (2020). Human–animal relationships and social work: opportunities beyond the veterinary environment. *Child and Adolescent Social Work Journal, 37*(6), 573–588.
Ascione, F. R. (2000). *Safe havens for pets: Guidelines for programs sheltering pets for women who are battered*. FR Ascione.
Barrett, B. J., Fitzgerald, A., Peirone, A., Stevenson, R., & Cheung, C. H. (2018). Help-seeking among abused women with pets: Evidence from a Canadian sample. *Violence and Victims, 33*, 604–62610.1891/0886-6708.vv-d-17-00072.
Brennan, C. L., Borgman, R. A., Watts, S. S., Wilson, R. A., & Swartout, K. M. (2021). Childhood neglect history, depressive symptoms, and intimate partner violence perpetration by college students. *Journal of Interpersonal Violence, 36*(23-24), NP12576–NP12599.
Beck, A. M. (2011). Animals and child health and development. In P. McCardle, S. McCune, J. A. Griffin, L. Esposito, & L. S. Freund (Eds.), *Animals in our lives: Human-animal interaction in family, community, and therapeutic settings*. Paul H. Brookes Publishing Co.
Becker, F., & French, L. (2004). Making the links: Child abuse, animal cruelty and domestic violence. *Child Abuse Review: Journal of the British Association for the Study and Prevention of Child Abuse and Neglect, 13*(6), 399–414.

Boat, B. W. (2010). Understanding the role of animals in the family; Insights and strategies for clinicians. In A. H. Fine (Ed.), *Handbook on animal-assisted therapy: Theoretical foundations and guidelines for practice*. (3rd ed., pp. 265–282). Academic Press.

Boat, B. W. (2014). Connections among adverse childhood experiences, exposure to animal cruelty and toxic stress: What do professionals need to consider. *National Center for Prosecution of Child Abuse Update, 24*(4), 1–3.

Campbell, A. M. (2021). Behind the mask: Animal abuse perpetration as an indicator of risk for first responders to domestic violence. *Forensic Science International: Animals and Environments, 1*, 100003.

Currie, C. L. (2006). Animal cruelty by children exposed to domestic violence. *Child Abuse & Neglect, 30*(4), 425–435.

Dogs Trust Freedom Project (2021, April 28). Our findings from our research carried out into domestic abuse and pets. https://www/moretodogstrust.org.uk/freedom-project-parent/news-and-updates

Domestic Abuse Intervention Project (2021, April 28). Wheel information center. https://www.theduluthmodel.org/wheels/

Feely, P. (2021, Feb. 17). Man accused of leaving severed rabbit heads on Manchester woman's car surrenders to police. *New Hampshire Union Leader*. https://www.unionleader.com/news/crime/man-accused-of-leaving-severed-rabbit-heads-on-manchester-woman-s-car-surrenders-to-police/article_48b7f5c2-3f02-5d57-9af1-b4680c30a2fe.html

Fitzgerald, A. J., Barrett, B. J., Gray, A., & Cheung, C. H. (2022). The connection between animal abuse, emotional abuse, and financial abuse in intimate relationships: Evidence from a nationally representative sample of the general public. *Journal of Interpersonal Violence, 37*(5-6), 2331–2353.

Garcia, T. (2021, January 5). Police: Man killed girlfriend's dog after gambling setback. *Las Vegas Review-Journal*. https://www.reviewjournal.com/crime/police-man-killed-girlfriends-dog-after-gambling-setback-2243037/

Girardi, A., & Pozzulo, J. D. (2015). Childhood experiences with family pets and internalizing symptoms in early adulthood. *Anthrozoös, 28*(3), 421–436.

Gordon, E., & Lathey, L. (2020, June). Domestic violence and animal abuse during COVID-19: The role of the veterinarian. *West Coast Veterinarian, 39*, 18–19.

Haden, S. C., McDonald, S. E., Booth, L. J., Ascione, F. R., & Blakelock, H. (2018). An exploratory study of domestic violence: Perpetrators' reports of violence against animals. *Anthrozoös, 31*(3), 337–352.

Heersink, O. (2020, June 3). Man accused of assault, arson and animal cruelty; held on $750K bond in 2C jail. *Idaho Press*. https://www.idahopress.com/news/local/man-accused-of-assault-arson-and-animal-cruelty-held-on-750k-bond-in-2c-jail/article_17d466b3-48d1-5fe4-8d92-196fd02c566a.html

Hodgson, K., & Darling, M. (2011). Pets in the family: practical approaches. *Journal of the American Animal Hospital Association, 47*(5), 299–305.

Krienert, J. L., Walsh, J. A., Matthews, K., & McConkey, K. (2012). Examining the nexus between domestic violence and animal abuse in a national sample of service providers. *Violence and Victims, 27*(2), 280–296.

Larkin, M. (2018, Sept. 15). When domestic violence arrives at the clinic door. How veterinary staff can respond to abused clients and patients. *Java-Journal of the American Veterinary Medical Association, 253*(6), 656–660.

Lathey, L. (2020a, September). Recognizing domestic violence in clients and their pets. *West Coast Veterinarian, 40*, 44–45.

Lathey, L. (2020b, December). Helping people with animals who are fleeing domestic violence. *West Coast Veterinarian, 41,* 17.

The Links Group UK (2022). *Suspected abuse of animals and people: Guidance for the veterinary team* (3rd ed.).

McDonald, S. E., Collins, E. A., Nicotera, N., Hageman, T. O., Ascione, F. R., Williams, J. H., & Graham-Bermann, S. A. (2015). Children's experiences of companion animal maltreatment in households characterized by intimate partner violence. *Child Abuse & Neglect, 50,* 116–127.

Meddick, A. (2021, March 3). *Victorian Parliament votes for animals to be considered victims of family violence.* https://andymeddick.com.au/2021/03/03/victorian-parliament-votes-for-animals-to-be-considered-victims-of-family-violence/

Melson, G. F., & Fine, A. H. (2019). Animals in the lives of children. In A. H. Fine (Ed.), *Handbook on animal-assisted therapy: Foundations and guidelines for animal-assisted interventions,* (5th ed., pp. 249–270). Academic Press.

Merz-Perez, L. & Heide, K. M. (2004). *Animal cruelty: Pathway to violence against people.* AltaMira Press.

National Coalition Against Domestic Violence (2020). *Domestic violence* [Fact sheet]. https://assets.speakcdn.com/assets/2497/domestic_violence-2020080709350855.pdf?1596828650457

National Coalition Against Domestic Violence (2015). *Domestic violence and children* [Fact sheet]. https://assets.speakcdn.com/assets/2497/children_and_dv.pdf

National District Attorneys Association (2014). *Criminal penalties for exposing children to animal abuse.* https://ndaa.org/wp-content/uploads/Criminal-Penalties-for-Exposing-Children-to-Animal-Abuse-1.pdf

National Domestic Violence Hotline (2021, April 28). *Power and control.* https://www.thehotline.org/identify-abuse/power-and-control/

National Link Coalition (2014, January). Pet protective order statistics reported in Minnesota. *The LINK-Letter, 7*(1), 5.

National Link Coalition (2015a, October). "Three-dimensional" New Zealand veterinarians respond to domestic violence. *The LINK-Letter, 8*(10), 5.

National Link Coalition (2015b, October). Scottish veterinarians enlisted to stop domestic violence. *The LINK-Letter, 8*(10), 4.

National Link Coalition (2019, January). Congress passes pet and women safety (PAWS) act to fund pet care and pet protection orders for survivors. *The LINK-Letter, 12*(1), 1–2.

National Link Coalition (2021a). *Pets in protection orders by state.* https://nationallinkcoalition.org/wp-content/uploads/2021/06/PPO-Summary-by-State-2021-5.pdf

National Link Coalition (2021b). National initiative in Canada to address gap in pet-friendly sheltering opportunities. *The LINK-Letter, 14*(9), 2.

National Network to End Domestic Violence (2021, April 28). *Frequently asked questions about domestic violence.* https://nnedv.org/content/frequently-asked-questions-about-domestic-violence/#whyreturn

Nelson, S. (2020, August 27). Malmo murder suspect held without bond. *Fremont Tribune.* https://fremonttribune.com/news/local/crime-and-courts/malmo-murder-suspect-held-without-bond/article_872783f2-2775-50ae-a568-89cb000ad06b.html

Newberry, M. (2017). Pets in danger: Exploring the link between domestic violence and animal abuse. *Aggression and Violent Behavior, 34,* 273–281.

Newland, X., Boller, M., & Boller, E. (2019). Considering the relationship between domestic violence and pet abuse and it's significance in the veterinary clinical and educational contexts. *New Zealand Veterinary Journal, 67*(2), 55–65.

Pennsylvania Coalition Against Domestic Violence (2021, April 28). About abuse. https://www.pcadv.org/about-abuse/

Ponder, C., & Lockwood, R. (2000). *Cruelty to animals and family violence*. International Association of Chiefs of Police Training Key #526.

Quinlisk, J. A. (1999). Animal abuse and family violence. In F. R. Ascione & P. Arkow (Eds.), *Child abuse, domestic violence, and animal abuse: Linking the circles of compassion for prevention and intervention* (pp. 168–175). Purdue University Press.

Reavy, P. (2021, March 2). West Valley man accused of stealing ex-girlfriend's dog, setting it on fire. *The Deseret News*. https://www.deseret.com/utah/2021/3/2/22309046/dog-set-on-fire-found-wandering-near-freeway-police-seeking-suspect-abuse-magna

Robertson, I. A. (2010). Legally protecting and compelling veterinarians in issues of animal abuse and domestic violence. *New Zealand Veterinary Journal, 58*(3), 114–120.

Roguski, M. (2012). *Pets as pawns: The co-existence of animal cruelty and family violence*. Royal New Zealand Society for the Prevention of Cruelty to Animals.

Royal College of Veterinary Surgeons (2016): *Code of Professional Conduct for Veterinary Surgeons, Supporting Guidance No. 14 (Client Confidentiality)*.

Sheltering Animals and Families Together (2021). *Pet friendly domestic violence shelters*. https://saftprogram.org/sheltering-animals-and-families-together-2/pet-friendly-domestic-violence-shelters/

Simmons, C. A., & Lehmann, P. (2007). Exploring the link between pet abuse and controlling behaviors in violent relationships. *Journal of Interpersonal Violence, 22*(9), 1211–1222.

Tiplady, C. M., Walsh, D. B., & Phillips, C. J. C. (2018). "The animals are all I have": Domestic violence, companion animals, and veterinarians. *Society & Animals, 26*(5), 490–514.

Tricarico, E. (2019, Dec. 23). A refuge from violence for pets and people. dvm360.

Urban Resource Institute and National Domestic Violence Hotline (2021). *PALS report and survey: Domestic violence and pets: Breaking barriers to safety and healing*. Urban Resource Institute.

Veterinary Council of New Zealand (2020). *Code of professional conduct for veterinarians*. Wellington: Veterinary Council of New Zealand.

Volant, A. M., Johnson, J. A., Gullone, E., & Coleman, G. J. (2008). The relationship between domestic violence and animal abuse: An Australian study. *Journal of Interpersonal Violence, 23*(9), 1277–1295.

Walton-Moss, B. J., Manganello, J., Frye, V., & Campbell, J. C. (2005). Risk factors for intimate partner violence and associated injury among urban women. *Journal of Community Health, 30*(5), 377–389.

Women's Shelter Canada (2021). *Sheltersafe*. https://sheltersafe.ca/

4 Defining animal cruelty within an international framework

Angus Nurse

Nottingham Trent University

Aims of this chapter

Most jurisdictions now have laws that make animal abuse an offence; albeit some variation exists in how offences are framed. At a basic level, laws generally provide protection for companion animals in the form of anti-cruelty statutes that govern the relationship between humans and their non-human animal companions. While there is a lack of coherent international animal protection laws, domestic laws often create animal abuse crimes in respect of causing unnecessary suffering and by specifying prohibited acts.

This chapter's focus is on animal protection and welfare law as the area of animal law that engages directly with issues of animal abuse and the manner in which animal abuse is defined in law. It considers key terminology used in animal law and also examines how animal protection measures are put in place via legal systems. Historically animal protection law has arguably been primarily negative in nature, achieving protection by enshrining in law prohibitions of the 'thou shalt not' variety. However, this chapter's analysis identifies that in some areas there has been a shift in animal protection towards imposing a positive duty to protect animals and a widening of the scope of animal protection and welfare considerations to include positive protection for animals and the creation of animal welfare duties via domestic law.

Introduction

Animal abuse has been defined in many ways over the years although there is arguably an emerging consensus on some core aspects of the legal definition of animal abuse.

International perspectives allow continued use and exploitation of animals with the proviso that such use should be sustainable. Even where this does result in animal killing, there is a general presumption in law that any suffering

DOI: 10.4324/9781003165552-4

should be the minimum necessary in respect of the permissible act. But this also means that there are variations in the level of suffering or pain that are legally permissible in different practices that may involve harm to animals. Thus, notions of what constitutes abuse are arguably socially constructed and vary across jurisdictions.

This chapter explores key terminology used in definitions of animal abuse. It aims to provide an overview of the framework contained in legal terminology to recognise and classify intentional (non-accidental cruelty) and unintentional animal cruelty. It will also explore the legal frameworks relevant to animal abuse in different national contexts.

The basics of animal law

Most jurisdictions now have laws that make animal abuse an offence; albeit some variation exists in how offences are framed. At a basic level, laws generally provide protection for companion animals in the form of anti-cruelty statutes that govern the relationship between humans and their non-human animal companions. As a minimum, these statutes prohibit the deliberate, intentional and arbitrary inflicting of pain. In respect of livestock and animals that are exploited for human consumption in the food industry, animal welfare laws provide a regulatory function, ensuring or attempting to ensure that animals are reared and slaughtered in a humane manner and that the suffering experienced by animals is minimised so far as is possible. In respect of wildlife, laws provide for the conservation, management, protection and prohibition on certain methods of killing wildlife (Nurse, 2013; Vincent, 2014). But arguably wildlife living outside of human control is protected less than non-human companions and is protected only so far as the interests of when wildlife coincides with human interests (Schaffner, 2011; Nurse & Ryland, 2014; Nurse & Wyatt, 2020). An underlying principle is that wildlife is arguably defined as a natural resource available for human exploitation, particularly in those countries that rely on revenues from animal tourism and sport killing (game and trophy hunting). Other laws may also regulate the transport of animals, the use of animals for clothing, the use of animals in scientific experiments and the possession of animal parts or derivatives including those derived from hunting and game activities. Laws may also distinguish between different types of wildlife; for example, between animals naturally occurring in the wild and living free and wildlife managed for game purposes.

Animal law thus attempts to do various things and offers different levels of protection to animals dependent on their status and the intended human use or relationship to animals. Accordingly, "the law criminalizes deliberate individual acts of gratuitous cruelty towards most animals, yet allows and even supports institutional cruelty of animals" (Schaffner, 2011, p.3). Animal law thus has to contend with a range of issues concerning the legal social and biological nature of non-human animals. The status of animals, which generally determines domesticated animals as the private property of their human or corporate owners, is important (Deckha, 2021). Thus, while laws such as the UK's Animal Welfare Acts 2006 provide for a duty of care towards animals, which includes a requirement to consider the needs of the individual animal, they remain property. As a consequence, the harm suffered by animals is largely a harm visited on the 'owner' or person responsible for that animal. Thus, while laws may construct harm caused to animals or the illegal exploitation and killing outside of the exploitation permissible by law as a crime, such laws generally construct these harms as property crimes (including theft of state property in the context of trophies) or in respect of the commission of a prohibited act, rather than a crime in respect of the animal victim. Indeed, in many jurisdictions, an animal cannot be legally defined as a crime victim due to not having legal personhood and as lawyer Stephen Wise states 'without legal personhood, one is invisible to civil law. One has no civil rights. One might as well be dead' (Wise, 2000, p.4).[1] Animal law is accordingly 'quite diverse and cuts across every substantive area of the law including property, tort, contract, criminal, family and trusts; all jurisdictional boundaries – federal, state and international; and every source of law – constitutional, statutory, regulatory and common law' (Schaffner, 2011, p.5).

This chapter's focus is on animal protection and welfare law as the area of animal law that engages directly with issues of animal abuse and the manner in which animal abuse is defined in law and protection measures are put in place. Historically, animal protection law has arguably been negative in nature, by enshrining in law prohibitions of the 'though shalt not' variety, for example making it unlawful to use poison to kill protected animals. However, this chapter's analysis identifies that in some areas there has been a shift in animal protection towards imposing a positive duty to protect animals and a widening of the scope of animal protections and welfare considerations. However, this is a variable feature of domestic legislation rather than being clearly defined via international law.

International animal law

International law defines the obligations of states to meet and apply certain legal standards, mostly through treaties and conventions as the main 'hard law' instruments. Thus, in order to establish the core requirements for animal protection in international law, examination of the relevant legal documents would normally be the first step. However, at present there is no binding international treaty for the protection of animals and thus no clear international legal standard in respect of animal protection and anti-cruelty. Instead, it is broadly down to individual states to determine how best to provide animal protection and anti-cruelty through domestic law. Thus, anti-cruelty and animal protection statutes are largely a social construction reflecting each state's determinations on how best to achieve animal protection through the appropriate public or private law mechanisms. Accordingly, "levels of animal protection vary from country to country or even on a regional basis … dependent on the legislative approach taken and the extent to which cultural perspectives on animal harm are incorporated into legislation" (Nurse, 2013, p.7).[2]

There have been attempts to enshrine animal abuse in international law. First, a Universal Declaration of Animal Rights (UDAR) was presented to the United Nations Educational, Scientific and Cultural Organization (UNESCO) in 1978. The proposed declaration included measures that would provide for:

1   The introduction of legal animal rights similar to human rights principles including the right to live, the right to freedom, the right to home (for wild animals), freedom from cruel or inhumane treatment and freedom of expression rights.
2   Minimum standards of animal welfare and freedom from cruelty for companion animals.
3   Governmental Responsibilities for animal rights and animal welfare
4   The outlawing of animal experimentation.

(Nurse, 2013, p. 8)[3]

While the Declaration failed to achieve widespread international agreement and so did not become legally binding or a formalised part of international law, subsequently World Animal Protection (formerly the World Society for the Protection of Animals, WSPA) supported by other NGOs pursued a proposal for a Universal Declaration on Animal Welfare (UDAW) to be adopted by the United Nations. The UDAW seeks recognition that animals are sentient and aims to prevent cruelty to animals whilst also promoting binding standards of animal welfare in respect of companion animals, farm animals, animals used in scientific research, wildlife and animals in recreation (WSPA, 2007). The UDAW has also yet to be adopted.

Key aspects of both the UDAR and UDAW are arguably incorporated into the Five Freedoms for animal welfare relating to animals under human control. The concept of Five Freedoms originated with the 1965 Brambell Report (the report of the Technical Committee to Enquire into the Welfare of Animals kept under Intensive Livestock Husbandry Systems) and was subsequently adopted by the Farm Animal Welfare Council around 1979 (FAWC, 1979), by the RSPCA in 1993 (RSPCA Australia, 2021) and by the Federation of Veterinarians of Europe in approximately 2016. Subsequently, the Five Freedoms have gained currency in discussions around appropriate animal welfare standards and as currently expressed, the five freedoms are as follows:

1   *Freedom from hunger and thirst:* by ready access to fresh water and a diet to maintain full health and vigour.
2   *Freedom from discomfort:* by providing an appropriate environment including shelter and a comfortable resting area.

3 *Freedom from pain, injury or disease:* by prevention through rapid diagnosis and treatment.
4 *Freedom to express normal behaviour:* by providing sufficient space, proper facilities and company of the animal's own kind.
5 *Freedom from fear and distress:* by ensuring conditions and treatment which avoid mental suffering.

Arguably the failure to comply with these principles could constitute animal abuse whether by act or omission. As this chapter's discussion identifies, even though the Five Freedoms may not be directly written into law as binding legal principles, and despite the lack of general international protection for animals and a specific international anti-cruelty statute, there are several provisions in international law relating to the conservation, management and trade in animals. These and treaties that provide general protection for animals during international transport and when transported for slaughter, and protection for animals kept as farm animals (livestock) and as companion animals articulate some of the principles of the Universal Declaration and the Five Freedoms. These principles are also implemented in domestic legislation such as the UK's Animal Welfare Acts 2006. The legal terminology used and the manner in which animal abuse is socially constructed is important in providing for how animal abuse is understood and codified.

A useful starting point is how animal harm is generally regarded in law. EU law, for example, recognises animals as sentient beings within it's foundational treaties and indicates that Member State government policies need to implement appropriate legal protections for animal welfare to reflect the concept of animals as sentient beings requiring legal protection. Article 13 of the Treaty on the Functioning of the European Union (the Lisbon Treaty) states:

> In formulating and implementing the Union's agriculture, fisheries, transport, internal market, research and technological development and space policies, the Union and the Member States shall, since animals are sentient beings, pay full regard to the welfare requirements of animals, while respecting the legislative or administrative provisions and customs of the Member States relating in particular to religious rites, cultural traditions and regional heritage.[4]

The fact that the promotion of animal welfare is mentioned in the "constitutional" provisions of the EU Treaties[5] signifies the elevation of animal welfare[6] as a priority issue in the EU, alongside other key objectives, such as environmental protection and promoting sustainable development (Ryland & Nurse, 2013). Arguably, the Lisbon Treaty as a part of EU law by explicitly identifying animals as sentient beings provides for EU recognition that animals have feelings, interests and should be fully protected under the law. Because of this, a principle could be said to exist that animal cruelty statutes should be implemented by EU states. However, whilst recognition of sentience is undoubtedly important in providing a legal framework for animal protection within the EU and is sometimes used as the basis for extending the protection, it falls short of providing animals with absolute protection from harm or providing them with a distinct form of rights that dictates that animal welfare takes priority in policy considerations (Nurse, 2013). However, separate from Article 13 of the Lisbon Treaty EU law contains other animal welfare provisions such as the EU's Council Directive 98/58/EC of 20 July 1998 concerning the protection of animals kept for farming purposes which is based on the European Convention for the Protection of Animals kept for Farming Purposes which incorporates the 'Five Freedoms' animal welfare and protection measures. Article 3 of the Protection of Animals Convention specifies that animals shall be housed and provided with food, water and care in a manner which – having regard to their species and to their degree of development, adaptation and do-mestication – is appropriate to their physiological and ethological needs in accordance with established experience and scientific knowledge. Thus, the Convention (and the EU Council Directive) requires recognition of the individual nature of animal species rather than a homogenised approach to animal welfare. Whilst sentience is not specifically mentioned in the Convention, it's provisions arguably amount to recognition of animals' capacity to feel and experience discomfort, commensurate with notions of sentience. Failure to comply with these provisions could constitute abuse.

EU law on the protection of animals used for scientific purposes also sets out measures for the protection of animals used for scientific purposes within European Directive 2010/63/EU. With this directive, the EU specifies that since it's original 1986 law (Directive 86/609/EEC) new scientific knowledge had become available in respect of factors influencing animal welfare as well as the capacity of animals to sense and express pain, suffering, distress and lasting harm. The EU therefore considered it necessary to improve the welfare of animals used in scientific procedures by raising the minimum standards for their protection in line with the latest scientific developments. Accordingly, the new EU Directive expanded the scope of the animals covered by EU laws on animal experimentation. In addition to vertebrate animals, the new law specified that cyclostomes (jawless fishes) and cephalopods (molluscs such as octopus or squid) should also be included in the scope of the Directive, "as there is scientific evidence of their ability to experience pain, suffering, distress and lasting harm" (European Directive 2010/63/EU).

Legal terminology on cruelty and animal abuse

Before discussing the detail of legal definitions of cruelty and animal abuse it is worth noting that the legal definition of 'animal' requiring protection con-tained within legislation may vary between jurisdictions and even between different pieces of legislation. So too can the use of various terms within animal legislation. However, several common terms are found within animal protection laws drawn from some of the international principles outlined earlier in this chapter. The following discussion aims to explore the key terms.

Anti-Cruelty Statutes are a core feature of legal conceptions on what constitutes abuse, but the reality of anti-cruelty statutes is that most only include sentient animals within their scheme of protection. Arguably this reflects the notion that "cruelty, the intentional infliction of pain on another being presupposes that the victim is capable of feeling and perceiving pain" (Schaffner, 2011, p.10). For example, the UK's Animal Welfare Act 2006 applies only to 'protected animals' which broadly means a vertebrate other than man (Section 1(1) of the Act). There is a provision in the Act to extend the definition of animal to include invertebrates and thus extend protection to other species. However, the power "may only be exercised if the appropriate national authority is satisfied, on the basis of scientific evidence, that animals of the kind concerned are capable of experiencing pain or suffering" (Section 1(4) of the Act). Thus, the Act is clear in that it only extends protection to animals that are considered to be sentient and arguably is clear in indicating that anti-cruelty laws are limited in their scope and application, whilst also indicating that some animals are considered more deserving of protection from cruelty than others.

Otto (2005, pp. 134–138) analysed recent felony laws to identify how animal abuse was constructed within the meaning of these laws. Of interest to this chapter's discussion of terminology in animal laws is how commonly used terms in animal abuse law are defined and how the seriousness of offences might be characterised. Otto (2005) concluded that "with few exceptions, states are currently reserving felony status for the most egregious, affirmative acts of abuse, and are requiring a high degree of criminal culpability" (2005, p.137). Thus, animal abuse law is selective in how it defines and punishes cruelty.

Animal abuse

Anti-cruelty statutes generally attempt to define animal abuse by specifying which activities are prohibited and providing guidance to animal owners, investigators and prosecutors alike by explicitly categorizing animal abuse activities within the context of specific descriptors and definitions within the legislation. There is, however, considerable variation even between different regions of the U.S. where state anti-cruelty acts adopt different definitions reflecting legislators' preferences or intentions towards animal protection. For example, Alaska's Anti-Cruelty Statute 11.61.140 defines animal cruelty as when a person "knowingly inflict[s] severe physical pain or suffering; or with criminal negligence fails to care for an animal and causes it's death or severe pain or prolonged suffering', while Massachusetts" General Laws Chapter 272–77 more expansively specifies cruelty to animals as when a person:

> overdrives, overloads, drives when overloaded, overworks, tortures, torments, deprives of necessary sustenance, cruelly beats, mutilates or kills an

animal, or causes or procures such; and whoever uses in a cruel or inhuman manner in a race, game, or contest, or in training therefore, as lure or bait a live animal; inflicts unnecessary cruelty upon it, or unnecessarily fails to provide it with proper food, drink, shelter, sanitary environment, or protection from the weather, or cruelly drives or works it when unfit for labor, or wilfully abandons it, or carries it or causes it to be carried in or upon a vehicle, or otherwise, in an unnecessarily cruel or inhuman; or knowingly and wilfully authorizes or permits it to be subjected to unnecessary torture, suffering or cruelty of any kind.

In addition, Massachusetts has separate provisions relating to the *malicious* killing of an animal, which by implication does not include the above acts. In this case, the law specifically makes it an offence where any person "wilfully and maliciously kills, maims or disfigures any horse, cattle or other animal of another person, or wilfully and maliciously administers or exposes poison with the intent that it shall be taken or swallowed by any such animal" and provides for a potential seven-year prison term (Massachusetts' Gen Laws Ch. 266-112). Other U.S. states also distinguish between 'ordinary' animal abuse and malicious or wanton animal abuse which implies a greater level of severity in the abuse (Nurse, 2013).

Thus, the definitions contained within anti-cruelty legislation often identify *deliberate* physical harm as the essential element in animal abuse as defined by legislation. Schaffner (2011, p.22) comments that U.S. anti-cruelty laws are primarily designed to "protect animals from the intentional and gratuitous infliction of pain and suffering at the hands of humans". This is true of other jurisdictions where the law is concerned not just with intent or accident but with the nature of that intent and contextualisation of the nature of deviance. Thus, phrases like 'wilfully and maliciously', 'knowingly and recklessly' or 'intentionally' are commonly found in Global North wildlife and animal welfare legislation, reflecting legislators' focus on deliberate acts of violence towards animals which has also dominated criminological attention in species justice discourse. This reflects theoretical debates about both the exercise of power over animals by man (Rollin, 2006; Linzey, 2009) and animal rights discourse concerning not only animals' rights not to suffer pain, but also the moral wrong of deliberate exploitation of animals by humans.

Thus, the term 'unnecessary suffering' is one of the key terms used in animal abuse and anti-cruelty legislation to define the nature of suffering caused to animals and legislative goals to minimise it if not eliminate suffering (Radford, 1999). Arguably the notion of *unnecessary* suffering implies that there is an agreed conception of 'necessary' suffering or at least (legally) acceptable suffering that may be caused to non-human animals. For example, animal welfare standards have been applied to industrial food processing operations and are generally required to be followed by slaughterhouses and other food processing operations. But the reality of such operations is that they still result in the death of a non-human animal. While the ideal may be that death occurs instantaneously and with no suffering at all within the context of a regulated animal killing operation, the reality is that animal law requires minimising any suffering rather than entirely eliminating it (see later discussion of humane killing). Evidence also exists that neglect of animals and inhumane practices have been a feature of the slaughterhouse industry (Eisnitz, 2006; Muller, 2018). It is also worth noting that evidence exists to suggest that those involved in the animal slaughter industry are also caused harm by the acts of killing and workplace practices in animal killing industries (Dillard, 2008).

By contrast, the UK's Animal Welfare Act 2006 arguably provides for a more expansive definition of animal cruelty that goes further, for example, than Ascione's definition which identified animal abuse and cruelty as being "socially unacceptable behaviour that intentionally causes unnecessary pain, suffering, or distress to and/or death of an animal" (Ascione, 1993, p.228). While this definition importantly incorporates the concept of 'distress' which, broadly construed, includes non-physical harm, it's focus is still on *intentional* animal abuse which this chapter contends is only a limited part of animal harm, and the legal codification of abuse, albeit an important one. Of equal importance are the unintentional or incidental animal harm activities that are, nevertheless, unlawful and require criminological attention. Neglect causing animal harm still has the potential to cause significant injury to animals and may be linked to other aspects of criminality that are worthy of attention. Animal laws also consider acts of omission or a failure to act that may result in animal harm. But there is some complexity in establishing when a failure to act provides liability for animal abuse.

Duty of care

Whilst animals generally remain property within legal systems, in respect of companion animals, the UK Animal Welfare Acts[7] impose a duty to ensure the welfare of protected animals (which broadly means animals under human control). Thus, an important element of the Acts' legal principles is the requirement for an 'owner' or 'responsible person' to ensure that a protected animal's needs are met. Arguably, the Acts extend "beyond historical notions of ownership, animals as property and preventing cruelty whether by act or omission to provide for *a positive* obligation to ensure animal welfare" (Nurse & Ryland, 2014, p.1). This requires that those responsible for protected animals must do more than just refrain from causing harm as is usually defined by anti-cruelty statutes, they must actively observe and implement good standards of animal welfare. This requires owners or those responsible for protected animals to provide for each of their animal's basic needs, which includes: providing adequate food and water; veterinary treatment; and an appropriate environment in which to live. The duty to ensure welfare had previously only existed for farm animals, although the Protection of Animals Act 1911 (as subsequently amended) contained the offence of causing unnecessary suffering to an animal.[8] The Animal Welfare Acts, however, extend the definition of unnecessary suffering to include psychological distress caused to an animal by virtue of exposing it to stressful activity or any failure to allow it to exhibit normal behaviours.

Humane killing

The term 'refinement' is used to describe the use of methods that help to minimise animal suffering in the laboratory (Herrmann & Flecknell, 2018). The UK's Welfare of Animals (Slaughter or Killing) Regulations 1995 requires that "no person engaged in the movement, lairaging, restraint, stunning, slaughter or killing of animals shall: (a) cause any avoidable excitement, pain or suffering to any animal; or (b) permit any animal to sustain any avoidable excitement, pain or suffering. The act further makes reference to 'rapid and effective killing or stunning" and to killing 'without delay' (Schedule 5). The principle to be applied in most animal killing situations is that where necessary, animal killing should be carried out humanely and 'to ensure that animals are killed without avoidable pain and distress' (Thornber and colleagues, 2014, p. 304). Underlying these provisions is the principle that there should be a short period of time between the act that is intended to stun or kill the animal and it's irreversible loss of consciousness. The Agreement on international humane trapping standards between the European Community, Canada and the Russian Federation specifies times for the occurrence of unconsciousness and insensibility produced by killing techniques varying from 45 seconds in the case of *Mustela erminea* (the stoat or short-tailed weasel) through to 300 seconds for a range of other species that includes the coyote, beaver, wolf, otter and badger. Accordingly, the killing of animals outside of these times, even if carried out in the course of an otherwise lawful action would constitute unnecessary suffering and would be classed as abuse.

Intentional and unintentional animal abuse

The question of whether animal abuse is intentional can sometimes be problematic. The Law Commission in it's 2014 analysis of UK wildlife law assessed how animal protection law defined what is 'deliberate' in respect of harm caused to animals. This issue was previously considered by the Court of Justice of the European Union (CJEU) who concluded as follows:

> Deliberate harm to protected species of fauna is therefore to be assumed if the harm is the result of an act whereby the perpetrator was aware of the risk to the protected species and also accepted that risk.
> (Opinion of Advocate General Kokott, Case C-221/04,
> *Commission v Spain* [2005] ECR I-4518 at [54]

Based on the case law, the Law Commission concluded that acceptance of a risk went beyond mere appreciation that a risk existed and also incorporated 'conscious acceptance' of the risk (Law Commission, 2014, p.71). As a result, the law arguably considered the level of knowledge that a perpetrator had and whether armed with that knowledge they still took a decision to act. In doing so, this is clearly a 'deliberate' and intentional act. But the law also considers circumstances where a person may act with a lower threshold of potentially ignoring the risk.

Knowingly or recklessly

Wildlife and animal protection law frequently includes the words 'knowingly' or 'recklessly' to discuss the extent to which a person knew or ought to have known that the actions they undertook would have harmed animals. UK law defines recklessness in respect of:

1   a circumstance when they are aware of a risk that it exists or will exist; [or]
2   a result when they are aware of a risk that it will occur;

and then in the circumstances known to them, it is unreasonable for them to take the risk (R v G [2003] UKHL 50, [2004] 1 AC 1034, at [41]. The Law Commission in it's 2014 analysis of wildlife law identified that "the concept of "recklessness" covers a wider range of knowledge and attitudes than the term "deliberate" as defined by the Court of Justice in Commission v Spain" (Law Commission, 2014, p.68). The Commission identified that one reading of 'recklessness' could be that the concept criminalises *all* instances where "it is established that the defendant knew about a risk of harm to a species and carried out the activity despite that knowledge (in circumstances where the court considers that it was unreasonable for the defendant to do so)" (ibid.). As a result, any harm to animals where there was some knowledge of the potential harm could create a risk of a court deciding that it was unreasonable to take the risk of harm. Indeed, the term 'knowingly or recklessly' is also included in some legislation as a phrase that reflects the fact that animal harm can be a result of either type of activity; something carried out by somebody in full knowledge of their actions and how they might harm animals, or an act that is carried out in a manner that is reckless as to the risks.

The question of knowledge in relation to animal abuse was clarified by the courts in the case R (on the application of Gray and Another) v Aylesbury Crown Court [2013] EWHC 500 (Admin). Gray, a horse farm trader was convicted of causing unnecessary suffering to animals when the police seized 115 equines from his premises. Gray appealed against his convictions and argued that section 4(1)(bb) of the Animal Welfare Act 2006 required either proof of knowledge that the animal was in a condition causing it unnecessary suffering or proof that it was showing signs of suffering which could not be missed by a reasonable, caring owner. The crux of Gray's argument was that for him to be convicted of the offence of causing unnecessary suffering required either actual knowledge or a form of constructive knowledge that the animal was showing signs of unnecessary suffering. He argued that negligence (his failure to care for the animals so that they did actually suffer) was not sufficient.[9] The Court disagreed with Gray's arguments and identified that Section 4(1)(bb) of the Animal Welfare Act 2006 had as it's purpose the imposition of criminal liability for unnecessary suffering caused to an animal whether by act or omission and which the person responsible for the animal either had known or should have known was likely to cause unnecessary suffering whether by negligent act or omission. The Court concluded that Section 9(1) of the 2006 Act also sets an objective standard of care which a responsible person is required to provide for the animal. As a result, the issue is whether the animal has suffered unnecessarily, not the mental state (i.e., level of knowledge or intent) of the person concerned.

Implications for practice and conclusions

As the analysis of this chapter shows, varied conceptions on what constitutes animal abuse are presented within legal terminology. In assessing what constitutes abuse we should consider both direct and indirect abuse and intentional and unintentional acts. Understanding of abuse also requires examining the nature of the harm or acts involved. Legal systems distinguish between intentional and unintentional abuse in part by assessing the nature of the act, but also by assessing the understanding of the person committing the act. The law thus considers the extent to which 'deliberate' acts are focussed upon an animal or whether a person whose actions harm an animal has somehow failed to appreciate the risks inherent in their actions.

Abuse can occur through both intentional acts or failure to act, it can also occur by accident or through neglect. As a result, recognising abuse can sometimes be complex, but a starting point is often whether it should be obvious both to the person committing the act and a 'reasonable' (i.e., non-expert) observer that animal harm is the likely outcome.

There is a growing body of research, legislative analysis and enforcement practice evidence that identifies that while strong animal protection and animal welfare law exists on the statute books, it is in the enforcement of this legislation that problems often occur. In addition, while animal abuse is frequently a component in or allied to intimate partner violence and is recognized as a possible predictor of future human violence, it is still largely dealt with as an animal welfare problem rather than as a core criminal justice issue. Given the nature of companion animal abuse as a crime in it's own right, and the evidence of a link between animal abuse and human violence, there are implications for several professional sectors and for law enforcement policy and practice.

Implications for veterinarians

- Consider whether injuries caused to animals requiring treatment are the type of abuse that might be classed as unnecessary suffering which could constitute a crime.

- Train staff on local arrangements and protocols for referring injuries and animal harm for investigation as animal abuse.
- Consider training staff in providing evidence of animal abuse for investigations and court proceedings.

Implications for social workers and social services

- Consider providing training in animal abuse law as part of the toolkit for social workers and health visitors.
- Encourage staff to be alert for signs of animal abuse including deliberate harm, the causing of unnecessary suffering and neglect. These are potential signs that domestic abuse and intimate partner violence may be occurring.
- Establish multi-agency partnerships and protocols to deal with animal abuse and domestic violence as integrated problems and to consider animal abuse as part of the cycle of violence, abuse and coercive control occurring within family situations.

Implications for legislators and policymakers

- Enact laws that provide for the duty of animal welfare, similar to those contained in UK law that provide for an animals' individual needs.
- Provide guidance for enforcers on animal abuse and animal cruelty to address any gaps in knowledge on the criminal law aspects of animal abuse. Such guidance should be clear on the nature and specifics of offences and how animal abuse is defined in law; powers of arrest, levels of sentencing and possibilities for introducing or applying for banning orders in the event of conviction.
- Provide easily accessible 'plain English' guidance for animal owners (and those responsible for animals) on their obligations towards animals and the types of offences that are included in law.
- Provide appropriate resources and support for enforcement activities and for multi-agency working to address animal abuse and animal cruelty.
- Support legislation and policy that provides for the recording of animal abuse and cruelty as part of crime statistics.

Implications for prosecutors and the judiciary

- Produce prosecutorial guidance on animal abuse and animal welfare law which takes into account the harm caused to animals and the seriousness of offences (e.g., level of intent and level of harm).
- Ensure sentencing guidelines are produced, maintained and up to date to allow magistrates and other jurists to consider animal abuse in it's international and domestic context and to provide for effective prevention of future offending as well as for punitive and rehabilitative aspects of offending.

Questions to consider

1 Do you think there are enough protections for animals in legislation in your country?
2 Do you think all animals should be protected legally, regardless of whether they are viewed as sentient (can experience feelings and emotions) beings or not?
3 Do you think legislation that is there to protect animals is adequately enforced in your country?

Key Messages

1 In assessing what constitutes abuse we should consider both direct and indirect abuse and intentional and unintentional acts.
2 Legal systems distinguish between intentional and unintentional abuse in part by assessing the nature of the act, but also by assessing the understanding of the person committing the act.
3 Veterinarians should consider whether injuries caused to animals requiring treatment are the type of abuse that might be classed as unnecessary suffering which could constitute a crime.
4 Multi-agency partnerships and protocols need to be established to deal with animal abuse and domestic violence as integrated problems and to consider animal abuse as part of the cycle of violence, abuse and coercive control occurring within family situations.
5 Ensure sentencing guidelines are produced, maintained and up to date to allow magistrates and other jurists to consider animal abuse in it's international and domestic context and to provide for effective prevention of future offending as well as for punitive and rehabilitative aspects of offending.

Notes

1 The idea of legal personhood is essentially the concept that an entity should be treated as if it were a person and so is given rights that a person might claim. The idea has been applied to artificial and fictitious persons such as corporations. Legal personhood is not quite the same thing as human rights although there have been legal arguments raised in some court cases that non-human animals should be treated as legal persons in order to provide them with some benefits such as freedom from imprisonment and the right not to be kept in cages.
2 It should be noted that there are regional measures such as the Council of Europe's European Convention for the Protection of Pet Animals, and the European Convention for the Protection of Animals Kept for Farming.

3 A copy of the declaration's text can be found online at: http://www.esdaw.eu/unesco. html#:~:text=%20UNESCO%20-%20Universal%20Declaration%20of%20Animal %20Rights,on%20man%20has%20the%20right%20to...%20More%20

4 *Consolidated version of the Treaty on the Functioning of the European Union.* Official Journal of the European Union art.13, October 26, 2012, 2012 O.J. (C326) 47. https://eur-lex. europa.eu/legal-content/EN/TXT/PDF/?uri=CELEX:12012E/TXT&from=EN

5 See the narrow interpretation accorded to animal welfare under the Amsterdam nego-tiated Protocol of 1997 by the Court of Justice of the European Union previously in Case C-189/01 *H. Jippes, et al. v.Minister van Landbouw, Natuurbeheer en Visserij* [2001] ECR I-5689; cited in Rasso Ludwig & Roderic O'Gorman R, *A cock and bull story? Problems with the protection of animal welfare in EU law and some proposed solutions,* 20 jel 363 (2008).

6 T. Camm & David Bowles, *Animal welfare and the Treaty of Rome—a legal analysis of the protocol on animal welfare and welfare standards in the European Union,* 12 jel 197 (2000).

7 There is country-specific legislation in Scotland and Northern Ireland; the *Animal Health & Welfare (Scotland) Act 2006* and the *Welfare of Animals Act (Northern Ireland) 2011.* The three Animal Welfare Acts have similar aims of preventing harm and promoting animal welfare although there are some differences in the respective *Acts.* The discussion within this chapter is primarily concerned with the Animal Welfare Act 2006 and it's application in England and Wales although it's principles apply in the devolved legislation.

8 The Department for Environment Food and Rural Affairs (Defra) has published several codes of practice setting out the appropriate standard of care for various animals kept under human control.

9 Gray also raised arguments that his convictions under section 9 of the Act amounted to duplication because they were based on the same issues and findings of fact relating to his convictions under Section 4. These arguments were essentially dismissed, and the appeal judge concluded that there was not complete duplication as some of the animals that had been the subject of charges under section 9 had not also been the subject of charges under section 4.

References

Ascione, F. R. (1993). Children who are cruel to animals: A review of research and im-plications for developmental psychopathology. *Anthrozoös, 6*(4), 226–247.

Deckha, M. (2021). 1 No Escape: Anti-cruelty Laws' property foundations. In *Animals as Legal Beings* (pp. 39–78). University of Toronto Press.

Dillard, J. (2008). A slaughterhouse nightmare: Psychological harm suffered by slaughter-house employees and the possibility of redress through legal reform. *Georgetown Journal on Poverty Law & Policy, 15,* 391.

Eisnitz, G. (2006). *Slaughterhouse: The shocking story of greed, neglect, and inhumane treatment inside the US meat industry.* Amherst, NY: Prometheus.

FAWC (1979, September 2021). Press Release. Available at: https://webarchive. nationalarchives.gov.uk/ukgwa/20121010012428mp_/http://www.fawc.org.uk/pdf/ fivefreedoms1979.pdf

Herrmann, K., & Flecknell, P. (2018). The application of humane endpoints and humane killing methods in animal research proposals: A retrospective review. *Alternatives to Laboratory Animals, 46*(6), 317–333.

Law Commission (2014). Wildlife Law, Volume 1: Report. Available at: https://s3-eu-west-2.amazonaws.com/lawcom-prod-storage-11jsxou24uy7q/uploads/2015/11/ lc362_wildlife_vol-1.pdf

Linzey, A. (ed) (2009). *The link between animal abuse and human violence.* Brighton: Sussex Academic Press, 1–10.

Muller, S. M. (2018). Zombification, social death, and the slaughterhouse: US industrial practices of livestock slaughter. *American Studies, 57*(3), 81–101.

Nurse, A. (2013). *Animal Harm.* Farnham: Ashgate.

Nurse, A., & Ryland, D. (2014). Cats and the law: Evolving protection for cats and owners. *Journal of Animal Welfare Law,* 1–6.

Nurse, A., & Wyatt, T. (2020). *Wildlife criminology.* Bristol University Press.

Otto, S. K. (2005). State animal protection laws-the next generation. *Animal Law, 11,* 131.

Radford, M. (1999). "Unnecessary suffering": The cornerstone of animal protection legislation considered. *Criminal law Review (London, England),* 702–713.

Rollin, B.E. (2006). *Animal rights & human morality* (3rd Edition), Amherst: Prometheus Books, pp. 46–48.

Ryland, D., & Nurse, A. (2013). Mainstreaming after Lisbon: Advancing animal welfare in the EU internal market. *European Energy and Environmental Law Review, 22*(3), 101–115.

RSPCA Australia (2021, September 28). *What are the Five Freedoms of animal welfare?* Available at: https://kb.rspca.org.au/knowledge-base/what-are-the-five-freedoms-of-animal-welfare/

Schaffner, J. (2011). *An introduction to animals and the law.* New York: Palgrave Macmillan.

Thornber, P. M., Rubira, R. J., & Styles, D. K. (2014). Humane killing of animals for disease control purposes. *Revue scientifique et technique (International Office of Epizootics), 33*(1), 303–310.

Vincent, K. (2014). Reforming wildlife law: Proposals by the Law Commission for England and Wales. *International Journal for Crime, Justice and Social Democracy, 3*(2), 67–80.

WSPA (2007). Universal Declaration on Animal Welfare. Available at: https://www.worldanimalprotection.ca/sites/default/files/media/ca_-_en_files/case_for_a_udaw_tcm22-8305.pdf

Wise, S. (2000). *Rattling the cage: Towards legal rights for animals.* London: Profile Books Ltd.

5 Investigating animal abuse and the importance of sharing intelligence

Mike Flynn and Gilly Mendes Ferreira
Scottish SPCA

Aims of this chapter

There are many Society for the Prevention of Cruelty towards Animals (SPCAs) around the world with the core aim of safeguarding animal welfare and preventing cruelty towards all animals. These Society's look to protect all species within the area they work. This chapter focuses predominantly on the work of the Scottish Society for the Prevention of Cruelty to Animals (Scottish SPCA), but also includes case examples from the Royal Society for the Prevention of Cruelty to Animals (RSPCA), which highlight clear links between those who have harmed animals and who are also involved in other serious crimes. Chapter 4 has already covered the wider legal framework and definitions of animal abuse and cruelty within an international context. This chapter therefore includes the most commonly used legislative frameworks by the Scottish SPCA and RSPCA to showcase the process of how an investigation is conducted and subsequently submitted for prosecution. The chapter also outlines how cases are evidenced, how the prosecution system works, and highlights the importance of intelligence sharing. It provides recommended practice for taking a multi-agency approach to protecting human and animal welfare.

The history of SPCAs

The Royal Society for the Prevention of Cruelty to Animals (RSPCA) was founded in 1824. They started the global movement towards having better protection for animals. They actually inspired the creation of Societies for the Prevention of Cruelty towards Animals (SPCAs) around the globe, including in the USA in 1860, Australia in 1872, New Zealand in 1882, and Hong Kong in 1903. Today there are more than 200 SPCAs around the world (RSPCA, 2022). The RSPCA's (2022) vision is a *world where all animals are respected and*

DOI: 10.4324/9781003165552-5

treated with kindness and compassion. Their mission is *to ensure animals have a good life by rescuing and caring for those in need, by advocating on behalf of all animals and by inspiring everyone to treat them with compassion and respect.*

The Scottish Society for the Prevention of Cruelty to Animals (Scottish SPCA) was set up in 1839 and even though much of the work that is done today has evolved, the Society's core purpose has remained the same. It's vision is that *"every animal has a good life. Every person embraces the joy and value animals add to our lives, and recognises they have feelings and needs which should be met"*. The Scottish SPCA's purpose is to '*champion animal welfare in Scotland and ensure animals are treated with respect and kindness. To provide the support and knowledge people need to protect the welfare of the companion, wild and farmed animals in their lives*' (Scottish SPCA, 2022).

When you look at other SPCAs around the world the visions and missions or purposes are consistently linked to words such as protection, kindness and respect (see Box 5.1).

Box 5.1   Examples of SPCA's visions and missions

ASPCA (2022)
Vision – The vision of the ASPCA is that the United States is a humane community in which all animals are treated with respect and kindness.

Mission – to provide effective means for the prevention of cruelty to animals throughout the United States.

RSPCA Australia (2022)
Vision – To be the leading authority in animal care and protection.

Mission – To prevent cruelty to animals by actively promoting their care and protection.

SPCA Hong Kong (2022)
Aims – To promote kindness and to confront and prevent cruelty to animals.

Mission – To promote kindness to animals, to protect their health and welfare, to prevent cruelty and alleviate suffering, and through education to cultivate a deep respect for life in the community so that all living creatures may live together in harmony.

World Federation for Animals (2022)
Vision – Our vision is for all animals to live a life free of cruelty and suffering.

Mission – To advance the safety and well-being of animals.

> **British Columbia SPCA (2022)**
>
> Vision – To inspire and mobilize society to create a world in which all animals enjoy as a minimum, five essential freedoms: Freedom from hunger and thirst; Freedom from pain, injury, and disease; Freedom from distress; Freedom from discomfort; Freedom to express behaviours that promote well-being.
>
> Mission – To protect and enhance the quality of life for domestic, farm and wild animals in British Columbia.

Animal offences in the UK, how are these dealt with?

Although separate organisations the RSPCA (which operates in England and Wales) and the Scottish SPCA (which operates in Scotland) support the public in similar ways and work very closely together. The main difference is the Scottish SPCA is a reporting agency meaning it is authorised by the Scottish Ministers to enforce the Animal Health and Welfare (Scotland) Act 2006 without the need for police assistance. Scottish SPCA inspectors can investigate, gather evidence and submit a report directly to the Crown Office Procurator Fiscal Service (COPFS). It is then COPFS who decides whether that case is taken forward for prosecution. As stated by the Scottish Government the requirement for corroboration has been a unique feature of criminal law in Scotland for hundreds of years. The basic principle of the corroboration rule is that an accused cannot be convicted of a crime unless the essential facts of the crime are able to be established by evidence from at least two independent sources. The essential facts are: (1) that the crime was committed and (2) that the accused was the person who committed the crime. Therefore, any cases submitted to COPFS must ensure the required number of sources are presented (Scottish Government, 2021).

The majority of animal welfare prosecutions in Scotland are handled by the Scottish SPCA. Breach of animal welfare legislation can result in a custodial sentence, a community payback order, a fine and/or a ban from keeping animals (which could be for a fixed term period or for life). Animals would have usually been removed from the owner and following veterinary advice either commence a rehabilitative programme within a rescue centre whilst the court case proceeds or in sadly some cases it is recommended that the animal is humanely destroyed. Up until the end of 2021, animals would need to wait until the court case had been concluded before they could be rehomed or in rare cases returned to their owner. Through the introduction of the Animals and Wildlife (Penalties, Protections and Powers) (Scotland) Act 2020 if someone has not agreed to sign the animal over, the animal can now be rehomed in as little as three weeks, subject to veterinary advice. If the owner subsequently wins their case, they are eligible to receive compensation for their animal(s) but would not retain ownership of any animal that had been subject to the case itself.

As part of a Scottish Government internship an audit of the Scottish SPCA's animal welfare prosecutions was conducted. In the report that was produced it was noted that from January 2011 to July 2019 the Scottish SPCA reported over 1,500 charges to COPFS. These charges came from over 800 cases and involved over 1,000 accused (Scottish Government, 2020). Animal welfare cases can often be quite complex. For example, a case may involve multiple charges against one person, multiple charges involving just one animal, or multiple people involved in one case and sometimes multiple animals, linked to multiple people. The most common charge type during this seven-year period were those covered by Section 19 of the Animal Health and Welfare (Scotland) 2006 Act for unnecessary suffering (59.5%). This was followed by charges under Section 24 (18.5%) of the same Act for failures to ensure the welfare of animals (Scottish Government, 2020). This report highlighted that the most common type of offence was to omit to provide veterinary attention. This represented 29% of all charges. A further 20% of charges were for offences for omission of both veterinary attention and adequate nutrition, whilst 18.4% of offences were for failings to meet the needs of an animal. These three most common offence types made up over two-thirds of all charges (68.2%). The report went on to state that dogs were identified as at least one of the types of animals involved in 60.3% of all charges. Cats were listed in 10.1% of charges. For most offences under the Animal Health and Welfare (Scotland) 2006 Act the most common animal type involved was dogs. However, for Section 29 offences (abandonment) more charges involved cats than dogs.

The report also highlighted the range of sentencing options that were available to the courts and how these were applied to the charges brought forward during this time period. Following analysis, the Scottish Government (2020) found that over half (56.4%) of all charges reported between January 2011 and July 2019 resulted in a conviction. Accounting for only charges proceeded against (and excluding charges dealt with using fiscal measures), the conviction rate was 84.4%. Just over a fifth (21.7%) of all charges did not lead to proceedings and 11.4% resulted in Procurator Fiscal (PF) measures. There was a verdict of not guilty for 7.1% of charges, the case was dropped for 2.3% and a small number received a verdict of not proven (0.8%). Of charges where a disposal is expected (guilty result in court or receiving a fiscal measure), the PF gave a warning in 12.2% of charges and a fine for 4.6%. Of charges with a guilty result in court only, nearly two-thirds (64.2%) received a disqualification order and 41.2% were given a fine. Just over a fifth (21.7%) of these received a community payback order (CPO). Many charges resulted in an outcome of more than one disposal type. The most common outcome for charges with a disposal was a disqualification order and a court fine (19.1%). The average (median) fine amount was £300 overall, or £360 for those given in court and £200 for those given by the PF. The average (median) length of a disqualification order was 60 months and the median custodial sentence was eight months.

In contrast, Loraszko and colleagues (2021) surveyed 184 prosecutors' experiences of court cases involving animal cruelty in Hungary. They found that 44% of the offences were attributable to neglect and 56% to physical abuse. They also found that 97% of cases resulted in a conviction and 3% of the accused persons were acquitted. Similarly, to Scotland, the majority of offences related to dogs (73%) followed by cats (10%), horses (4%), other domestic species (9%) and wild animals (4%).

In Brazil, Gomes and colleagues (2021) in a study of animal abuse found that again dogs were the most affected animals (59.7%), followed by cats (14.9%) and then horses (5.4%). The age of animals who were victims of abuse tended to be when they were adults (55.2%) with cats having the highest chance of death and they were also the species that suffered most from intoxication abuse. The perpetrators of abuse were predominantly male (66.8%) aged between 40 and 59 years old. They went on to state that perpetrators of animal abuse were 3.57 times more likely to be male and 2.5 times more likely to have no college education. Interestingly Gomes and colleagues (2021) found that the perpetrators of animal abandonment had a 25 times greater chance of being between 18 and 24 years old and perpetrators of animal intoxication had five times greater chance of also being 18 and 24 years old.

Recently, the Scottish Government commissioned research into restorative justice and empathy training for animal welfare and wildlife offences (Scottish Government, 2022). The report states that the direct application of restorative justice and empathy-based interventions for animal welfare and/or wildlife offences is limited. It goes on to state that one of the barriers that could hinder the use of restorative justice in this context would be who would speak for the animal? Running empathy-based rehabilitative programmes is very different from delivering educational programmes that encourage empathy and compassionate behaviours towards animals. The use of interventions to tackle intentional and unintentional animal abuse is explored further in Chapter 8.

The introduction of the Animals and Wildlife (Penalties, Protections and Powers) (Scotland) Act 2020 has provided the courts with the opportunity to utilise 5-year custodial sentencing for the most serious animal welfare and wildlife offences. Inconsistency in sentencing for animal welfare offences is something the Scottish SPCA is working hard to rectify with partners in Scotland. The Scottish SPCA wants to ensure that knowledge of what good animal welfare actually is, definitions and indicators of poor animal welfare, the links between animal welfare offences and serious organised crime, and the legislation that is available to deal with such offences are all connected. Similar discussions are taking place between other SPCAs and their respective governments and partners around the world.

When considering how animal welfare offences are dealt with in England and Wales it is important to note that the RSPCA are only able to take out private prosecutions and are not currently a recognised enforcement agency in the eyes of the law. At the time of writing the RSPCA are working hard to obtain similar authorisation to the Scottish SPCA and become a recognised reporting agency to the Crown Prosecution Service in England and Wales. Both the RSPCA and Scottish SPCA are working closely together to analyse the types of offences that are committed across the UK, recognising the increasing complexity that surrounds these types of cases and in particular how animal welfare offences are often linked to societal issues. Figure 5.1 shows how an animal welfare investigation would be conducted in Scotland by the Scottish SPCA and certainly, the RSPCA would conduct a similar process.

Key legislative frameworks used by the Scottish SPCA and RSPCA

As already noted in this chapter there is specific legislation that is available in the UK to tackle the issue of animal abuse and neglect. The Scottish SPCA and RSPCA tend to use the following in the majority of cases:

* The Animal Health and Welfare (Scotland) Act 2006 – *Scottish SPCA*
  This Act places a duty of care on pet owners and others responsible for animals to ensure that the welfare needs of the animals are met. It was designed to prevent animal abuse, promote animal welfare and protect animals in distress. Anyone causing a protected animal unnecessary suffering would be committing an offence under the Act. The Act also brought in regulations around the age someone could purchase an animal, tackled the issue of abandonment, and enabled an inspector or constable to take possession of an animal that is suffering or is likely to suffer. When first introduced it was a real milestone for protecting animal welfare in Scotland. Breaching this Act could result in a custodial sentence of up to one year, a fine (up to £5,000 for abandonment or £20,000 for offences relating to unnecessary suffering) and a fixed term or life ban for keeping an animal (or animals) (Scottish Government, 2006).
* The Animals and Wildlife (Penalties, Protections and Powers) (Scotland) Act 2020 – *Scottish SPCA*
  The implementation of this new Act has been a monumental change in Animal Welfare legislation in Scotland. It sought to address loopholes identified in the 2006 Act and has provided courts with the ability to pass tougher sentencing for the most serious of offences. Those convicted of a serious animal welfare offence can now be handed a five-year custodial sentence or an unlimited fine or both. It also places greater protection for service animals (known as Finn's Law), and increases penalties for wildlife offences to five years imprisonment and or an unlimited fine with additional penalties for other wildlife offences. One of the most significant provisions included is that authorised persons (including certain inspectors and constables) who have seized an animal as part of an animal welfare investigation are now able to transfer, sell, treat or, in limited circumstances, humanely destroy those animals prior to the case reaching the courts (Legislation, 2022[1]).

In response to a complaint	Received when/by whom?	

Accompanied by whom?

You went | Where? Address of Locus

Animal involved in allegation

Who? Owner or person in charge / Independent witness

You saw | Condition of the animal, note injuries/condition

Animals living conditions (clean-dirty) overall house

You did | In case of abandonment

Interview potential witnesses – obtain statements

Remove animal | Initial check, property un-occupied

Arrange veterinary examination and photographs | Arrange further treatment | Tape all entrances

Involve and work with other agencies as neccesary

Arrange secure accommodation | Monitor animal's progress | Notify police and housing

Leave notification for householder

If urgent (medically or in poor conditions) gain entry and remove animals

Collect evidence i.e. statements | 24 hours later, gain entry and remove animal

Seek vet examination and care for animal

©Scottish SPCA

Submission of SCRO within 14 days of charge

Prepare report for Procurator Fiscal – copy to Regional Chief Inspector within 6 weeks of charge | Trace owner

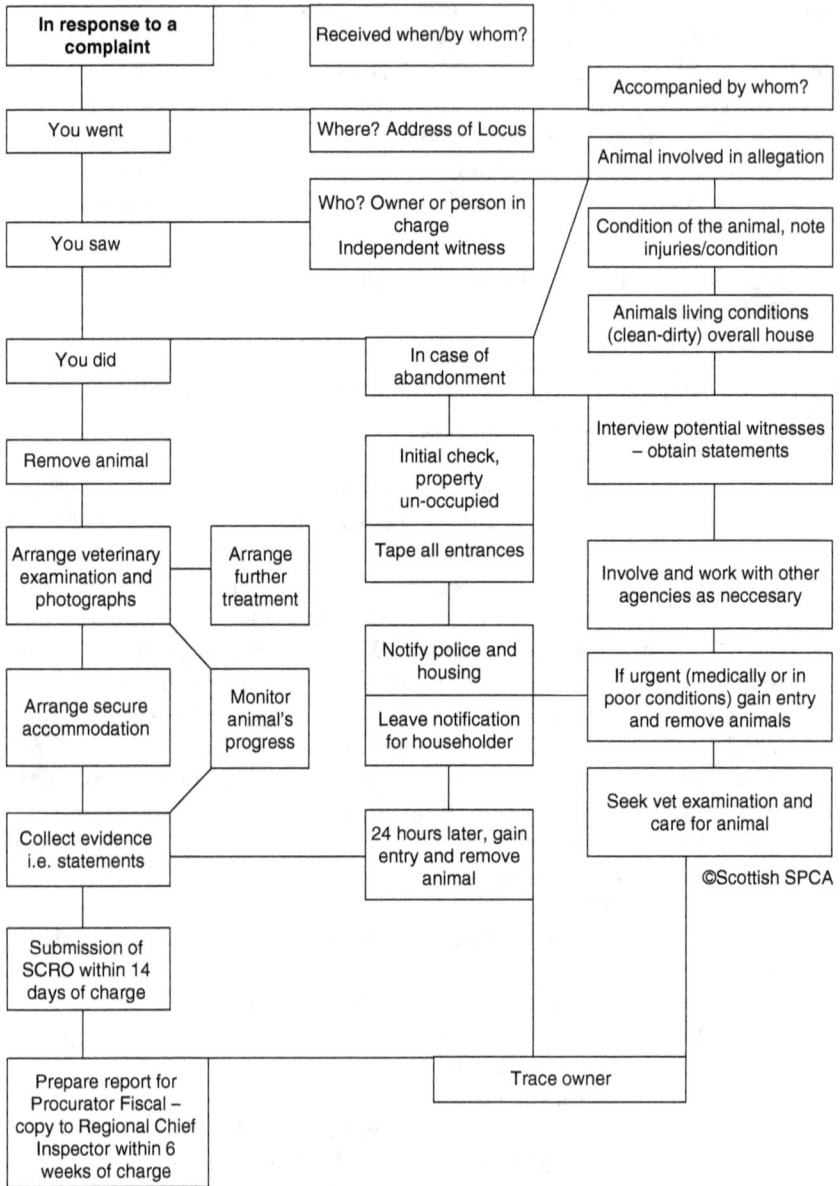

Process of conducting an animal welfare investigation

Figure 5.1 Process of conducting an animal welfare investigation.
Source: © Scottish SPCA.

- The Animal Welfare Act 2006 (England and Wales) – *RSPCA*

  This Act is very similar to the Animal Health and Welfare (Scotland) Act 2006 in that it places a duty of care on people to ensure they are meeting their animal's needs (S9) and has a specific offence for causing unnecessary suffering (S4). There are provisions for Regulations to be placed under this Act such as for licensing those that sell or breed certain animals (Licensing Activities Involving Animals (England) Regulations 2018. The Animal Welfare (Sentencing) Act 2021 increased the penalties for the most serious animal welfare offences to five years imprisonment. In 2021 the RSPCA undertook 94% of it's investigation and prosecution work under this Act. 62% of offences were under Section 4 and 31% under Section 9. Similar to the Scottish SPCA, nearly half (48%) of prosecutions were for offences committed against dogs.

Animal welfare is primarily devolved and at the time of writing, a number of new animal welfare bills are being debated in the four different devolved legislatures within the UK. A bill that recognises animals as sentient beings following the UK's withdrawal from the European Union has now become law (Animal Welfare (Sentience) Act 2022). This sets up a Committee to assess how policy was formulated whilst taking into account animal sentience, which will apply to non-devolved legislation in the UK and to devolved legislation in England. The Kept Animals Bill looks to strengthen the welfare of certain kept animals that are imported into, or exported from Great Britain (UK Parliament, 2022). In addition, a number of Regulations have been introduced in Scotland that tighten guidance and regulate activities when it comes to breeding certain animals such as dogs, cats and rabbits and regulating those who rehome animals or run animal sanctuaries (for example The Animal Welfare (Licensing of Activities Involving Animals) (Scotland) Regulations 2021). There are now similar laws in Scotland, Wales and England regulating those that are involved in the sale of pets.

It has been said that there can sometimes be an 'enforcement gap' where there are issues between the legislation that is in place and how this translates to the real-world enforcement of that legislation. Morton and colleagues (2020) looked at the enforcement gap in how animal welfare legislation is used in Australia. They argued that the 'gap' is caused by numerous factors derived from all stages of the enforcement process: (1) reporting acts of animal cruelty; (2) ambiguity and shortcomings derived from the language used in animal welfare legislation; (3) the nature of enforcement authorities; and (4) court determination on the matter. They state that the causes of the enforcement gap are multifactorial and derived from all stages of the enforcement process. They argue that further research is required with regards to the enforcement model itself, combined with public education, and legislative reform. Similarly, in Poland there has been a growing number of recorded cases of animal abuse but offenders are rarely prosecuted and when they are, they seldom face severe penalties. Animal abuse prosecutions in Poland are hindered by a delayed response from law enforcement agencies as well as investigative failures and errors in collecting evidence (Solodov, 2021).

It is important to note that legislation is very much compartmentalised into human and animal welfare law. For example, the animal welfare acts only relate to animals and the Domestic Abuse (Scotland) Act 2018 only relates to humans (although does recognise the behaviour over 'property' with animals falling into this category). The Online Safety Bill which at the time of writing is currently going through the UK Parliament aims to introduce a regulatory framework for internet services and there is a call that viewing animal abuse content should be included in this bill.

The legislative frameworks that are in place in other countries around the world do seek to protect animals from harm in a variety of ways with some countries having stronger legislation in place than others (see Chapter 4). A unique tool that helps identify the differences in animal welfare protection around the globe is the Animal Protection Index (API). World Animal Protection created an Animal Protection Index (API) back in 2014 and released a second edition in 2020. The API ranks 50 countries around the world according to their animal welfare policy and legislation. Countries are assessed by 10 indicators that are grouped into four goals. These goals are: 1) recognition of animal sentience and prohibition of animal suffering; 2) presence of animal welfare legislation; 3) establishment of supportive government bodies; and 4) support for international animal welfare standards (World Animal Protection, 2022). It is certainly a great tool for gaining a better understanding of the challenges that countries face and the opportunities that are available for raising the standards of animal welfare globally.

Animal welfare legislation in many countries has traditionally been based around the 'five freedoms' of animal welfare. That is animals should be free from hunger and thirst; free from discomfort; free from pain, injury and disease; free to express normal behaviour; and free from fear and distress (FAWC, 2009). In recent years there has been a call for legislation to adopt the five domains approach. The five domains model has existed for the past 25 years and has been regularly updated in line with latest scientific evidence. Mellor and colleagues (2020) initially created the five-domains model as an assessment tool that centres around the fact that animals can have both positive and negative experiences that will affect them physically, functionally and mentally. This differs from the five freedoms which have focused very much on minimising the negative welfare experiences and harm. In the latest version of the five domains model Mellor and colleagues (2020) continue to list the domains as: 1) Nutrition; 2) Physical Environment; 3) Health; 4) Behavioural Interactions and 5) Mental State. Nutrition, physical environment, health and behaviour are all linked to the biological and/or physical function of that animal whereas the mental state connects with the psychological well-being of that animal. This links to current discussions around ensuring that animals have a good 'quality of life' or a 'life worth living'. Adopting the five domains approach as legislation is updated would support those challenging cases where it's not just the basic needs that have not been met but that the animal has also been deprived of it's mental state needs, affecting it's quality of life, which should be taken into account when considering sentencing outcomes.

Key terms used in prosecutions:

There are many terms that have been used over the years either in addition to or instead of the term 'cruelty' (see Chapter 1 and Chapter 4). When it comes to prosecutions the following terms are commonly used in witness reports as part of the evidence presented with the following questions being applied in relation to each term during an investigation:

Unnecessary suffering

- Could the suffering reasonably have been avoided or reduced?
- Could the person have known, or ought reasonably to have known, that what they did would have caused the suffering or be likely to cause suffering to the animal?
- Did the person commit the offence for a legitimate purpose, for example benefiting the animal or protecting a person, property or another animal?

Neglect

- Did the person know and is capable of knowing what that animal needs to have a good quality of life?

Abuse

- Did the person intentionally harm that animal?
- Was there motivation behind the act that has taken place?

What is classed as evidence?

In order to answer the questions above and confirm if an animal has suffered unnecessarily, has been neglected and/or has been abused a thorough animal welfare investigation needs to be conducted which relies on multiple sources of evidence. In addition, evidence seized may also link to other human-related crimes which very much links to the concept of 'The Link' as already discussed in Chapter 3. Evidence that is captured during an investigation include:

- Photography – of scene, of subject (animal(s)), in some cases of accused
- Videography – of scene, of subject (animal(s)), in some cases of accused
- Veterinary Forensics – diagnostics results (e.g., bloodwork, scans, x-rays, post-mortem reports)
- Digital Forensics – computer, phone, and technological devices used

- Witness statements – Might be from an expert with relevant expertise in the field of animal welfare (such as a Veterinary Surgeon) or indeed someone who witnessed the event taking place (member of the public)

Lockwood and colleagues (2019) conducted a study in the US that looked at the priorities of attorneys when taking on animal cruelty cases and the factors that help or hinder prosecuting such cases. Two hundred prosecuting attorneys completed a survey. Results showed that the most frequently relied upon evidence were traditional sources of evidence such as detailed medical and crime scene reports and good-quality photographic evidence. Forensic evidence such as DNA, computer forensics, blood and trace evidence were rarely employed. Lockwood and colleagues (2019) went on to state that veterinary forensic evidence was viewed as an important factor by a majority of prosecutors in deciding whether to accept a case for prosecution and in achieving a successful outcome. Photographic evidence, particularly those that highlighted injuries and living conditions, were thought to be the most persuasive with both the judge and the juries and were thought to lead to favourable outcomes.

Additional forensic techniques that could prove useful as part of the evidence chain in animal welfare prosecutions include using hair cortisol as an indicator of stress (Heimbürge and colleagues, 2019). Using techniques such as this as evidence, should be explored further to help answer questions such as 'how long has this animal been suffering?'

Case examples

To give examples of the types of animal welfare cases that have links to other forms of crime, four cases that either the Scottish SPCA or RSPCA have dealt with are highlighted here. It is important to note that these cases have been amended purely to protect anonymity. When reading through each case think about the following:

- What evidence do you think should be collected as part of the investigation?
- Do you think the sentence that was given matches the severity of the crime?
- Try applying the Scottish SPCA's **ANIMAL** approach (Chapter 1) to each case.

Case 1

A man (mid-20s) was charged with 25 offences relating to the breach of the Dangerous Wild Animals Act 1976 and the Animal Health and Welfare (Scotland) Act 2006. The accused had a large number of snakes (many of which were venomous), lizards, scorpions and turtles in his flat.

They were being kept in appalling conditions and many of the animals were on the verge of starvation. One animal had to be put to sleep on site. The accused should also have had a dangerous wild animals licence for some of the animals in his care, which would require him to house them in specific conditions to ensure they pose no threat to others. The accused did not have the required licences for 13 snakes and two scorpions. When his property was being searched a venomous snake was found on the loose and had to be caught by specialist handlers. The accused used some of his exotics as part of his children's party's business. The property smelt strongly of urine and faeces which came from the Vivarium's that were housing these exotics in the one-bedroom flat. Equipment was seized from the premises at a later date as evidence, and links to Child Pornography was discovered.

The accused received an 18-month custodial sentence and a 10-year disqualification from keeping animals. He was released early from prison but was then rearrested in relation to possession of indecent images. He was handed a three-year custodial sentence for these additional offences. All animals involved were found suitable homes with specialist exotics collectors known to the Scottish SPCA. This was a multiagency operation led by the Scottish SPCA with support from partners such as Police Scotland, Veterinary Surgeons and Exotic Specialists (Image 5.1).

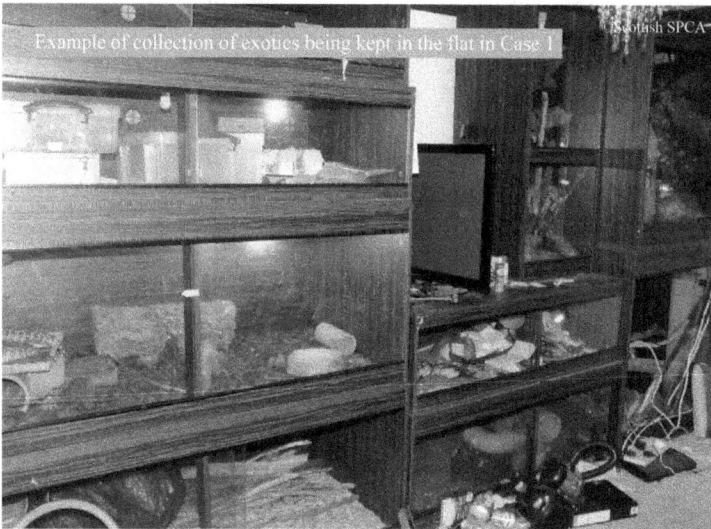

Image 5.1 Example of collection of exotics being kept in flat in Case 1.

Case 2

A man (early 50s) and a woman (late 20s) were charged with a total of five offences under the Animal Health and Welfare (Scotland) Act 2006. The offences related to the care of over 60 dogs aged 8 weeks upwards and more than 20 puppies under 8 weeks old. The accused failed to provide the dogs and puppies with sufficient ventilation, lighting, suitable and comfortable resting areas or housing appropriate to their needs. Appropriate food and water was not provided, the environment was not clean and there were no provisions in place to protect the animals from disease, illness, suffering or injury. A burnt-out van containing dog carcasses was also found on the premises.

Over 70 dogs had been seized from the property four years previously after being discovered packed into a cattle shed, with breeding bitches and dogs suffering from lice, skin sores, matted hair and cysts. One of the accused who pled guilty at the time received a ban from keeping more than two dogs for the next three years. The accused were selling these puppies and became known to agencies due to members of the public phoning to say their puppies were sick and in some cases had died. The accused had secured a significant amount of money over the years from putting profit over welfare and were of interest to other agencies due to not declaring income and links to other crimes.

The main accused (man) received nine months in prison and was disqualified from owning or keeping dogs, rabbits or ferrets for life. The co-accused (woman) was sentenced to 300 hours of community service and disqualified from keeping or owning dogs, rabbits or ferrets for ten years. All surviving animals underwent extensive rehabilitation and were eventually rehomed (Image 5.2).

Image 5.2 One of the many dogs seized in Case 2.

Case 3

A man (40-year-old) was charged and pleaded guilty to three offences under the Animal Welfare Act 2006. The RSPCA were asked to investigate when suspicions were raised after a young puppy sustained six fractured ribs. Despite the young dog developing breathing difficulties, a raised temperature and being hunched up when walking the accused did not take him to a vet for two days. X-rays showed the puppy had trauma to the chest area along with six recent rib fractures causing him significant pain. It was also revealed that the pup had sustained a further 24 fractured ribs on both sides of his chest on an earlier occasion and these were at differing stages of healing. Vets felt the fractures were likely to have been caused by blunt force trauma. When questioned by the vet the accused was not aware of any circumstances that may have caused the pup to have sustained such severe injuries. However, during further questioning by the RSPCA the accused had suggested that the pup may have become injured as a result of a bin liner full of books having fallen on him.

The RSPCA Inspector who led the investigation, arranged for police to seize the pup and she took him to a vet for a clinical examination. Vets concluded the pup had suffered as a consequence of physical abuse and the fractures he had suffered were consistent with non-accidental injuries. In addition to an indefinite ban on keeping all animals, which cannot be appealed for five years, the accused was sentenced to a 12-month Community Order requiring 300 hours of unpaid work in the community. He was also ordered to pay £300 costs and a victim surcharge of £90. The court placed a deprivation order on the pup meaning the RSPCA were able to find him a loving new home. The pup remained in RSPCA care during the investigation and has since made a full recovery from his injuries. An ex-family member confirmed her daughter had suffered from domestic violence from the defendant over a number of years. There were a number of animals that just seemed to disappear. The offender had also been violent to subsequent girlfriends (Image 5.3).

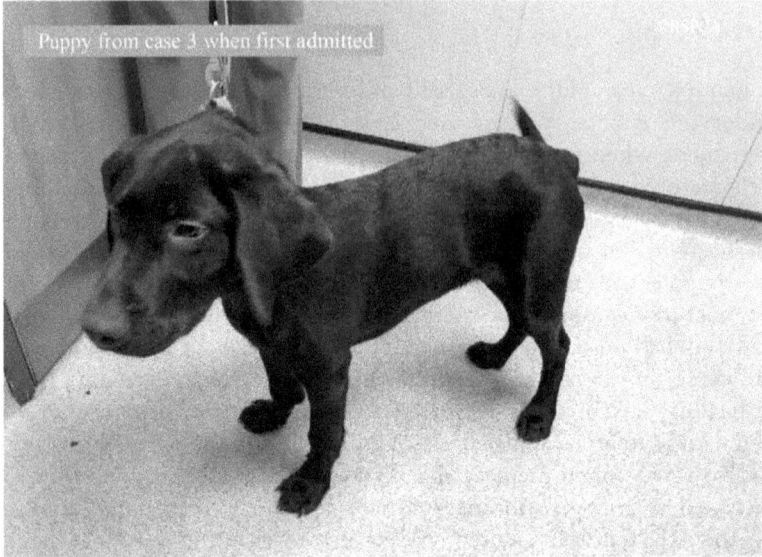

Image 5.3 Puppy from case 3 when first admitted.

Case 4

A couple was charged under the Animal Welfare Act 2006 for cruelty and neglect of a one-year-old Staffordshire bull terrier. Following reports of an injured dog the RSPCA and Police entered a property to find a young dog that had multiple cuts, dislocated femur, swelling, two large head wounds that were so severe vets were unable to examine his right eye, a fractured tooth, cheek, three fractured ribs, and a fracture to the right hock which was several weeks old and so severe the leg had to be amputated. Both accused claimed the dog had injured his leg more than a month earlier while trying to jump over a gate and denied mistreating him, although text messages between the two revealed what had happened after one of the accused admitted harming the dog with the second accused demanding to know why the dog had sustained injuries.

The male accused was given a suspended four-month jail sentence. He was told to do up to 10 days' anger management with probation and 60 hours of unpaid work. He was also banned from keeping animals for life and cannot appeal the ban for ten years and ordered to pay £300 costs and an £122 victim surcharge. The female accused who did not cause injuries to the dog, admitted a lesser charge under the Animal Welfare Act. She was ordered to carry out 10 Rehabilitation Activity

Image 5.4 Dog from a case before and after.

Requirement days and 240 hours unpaid work. She was also disqualified from owning any animal for 15 years, with no application to lift this for five years, and must pay £200 costs and an £85 victim surcharge. The male accused was known to have anger issues. The female accused had moved into refuge by the time the court case was heard (Image 5.4).

Do all investigations lead to prosecutions?

Prosecution is always deemed as a last resort and should only be pursued if it is deemed that the case is in the public interest. The preferred option is that animals are signed over into the care of an organisation such as an SPCA. Prosecution is deemed necessary when a ban is required to prevent that person from having ownership of an animal therefore avoiding future mistreatment, or in cases where there has been a clear disregard for animal welfare, intentionality, or where animal abuse may be linked with other serious crimes. It is important to note that a prosecution may also not be taken forward due to the age of the person involved or if there are mental health concerns for the perpetrator.

The debate around what age someone should be held criminally responsible has been pivotal in discussions in countries choosing to adopt the UNCRC approach (United Nations, 2022) which has 54 articles that cover all aspects of a child's life. Brown and Charles (2021) looked at the MACR (Minimum Age of Criminal Responsibility) globally. They highlight that as part of a consultation regarding the revision of the Committee on the Rights of a Child General Comment 10 in 2018 a proposal was made that the MACR globally should be set no lower than 14 years of age. They indicate that MACR varies considerably across the globe with some countries adopting a very low MACR. They go on to give the example that '*in the United States, many states do not employ a MACR, while a number of those that have adopted legislation have set their MACR as low as 7 years of age*'.

In England and Wales, the age of criminal responsibility remains at 10 years old (Brown & Charles, 2021 and Crown Prosecution Service, 2022). Children between the ages of 10 and 17 can be arrested and taken to the youth court if they do commit a crime. In Scotland, the Age of Criminal Responsibility (Scotland) Act 2019 (Legislation[2]) came fully into force in December 2021. In the act it states a child under the age of 12 cannot commit an offence. Prior to this new legislation the age was 8 years old.

Here is an example of a case that the Scottish SPCA investigated involving a child. Reference is made to the boy being referred on to the Scottish SPCA's Animal Guardians programme (details of this programme can be found in Chapter 8). Again, details have been changed to protect anonymity.

Case 5

A young boy (pre-school age) was reported to the Scottish SPCA for killing kittens. A Scottish SPCA inspector investigated and sought support from other agencies such as social work. The investigation concluded that two kittens had been killed and due to the complex nature of this case, and specifically the age of the boy involved, the offer was made for him to take part in the Scottish SPCA's Animal Guardians programme. Participation in this programme was voluntary. Consent was given for the boy to be included in evaluation research conducted by the University of Edinburgh on the Animal Guardians programme. When taking part in this research the young boy stated that "… sometimes I hurt animals, but I don't actually hurt them very … I don't hurt them in badness, I just, sometimes I just hurt them by trying to help them" (Wauthier and colleagues, 2022). Wauthier and colleagues (2022) go on to state that near the end of the interview the boy described an instance of where his brother ("I've got a very bad brother") was responsible for killing a fish and subsequently got kicked out of the house.

Having read about using the Scottish SPCA's **ANIMAL** approach in Chapter 1 as a potential tool to use when faced with an incident of animal abuse, if you were involved in Case 5 what would you do?

Case 5 is a good example of when a young person has been involved in serious animal abuse, but the vulnerability of that young person must be taken into account when deciding what course of action to take. Cases involving young people who on many occasions are younger than the age of criminal responsibility are explored further in Chapter 8. Recognition that early childhood experiences can influence childhood animal abuse can help identify intervention points in someone's life so that the cycle of abuse can be broken and preventative actions can be taken prior to that person reaching adulthood.

Motivations behind animal cruelty

As demonstrated in Case 5, investigations can be very complex and illustrate that motivations behind animal abuse are sometimes difficult to discern. Newberry (2018) investigated associations between different motivations for animal cruelty amongst 130 undergraduate students. Through looking at animal-related experiences and impulsive behaviour Newberry (2018) found that 55% of students had committed at least one act of animal abuse. Dogs were the most commonly abused animal. The most frequently reported motivations were prejudice, amusement, control (of an animal) and retaliation (against an animal). The most frequently reported methods used by adults in this study included beating/kicking, squashing, throwing an object at an animal, shooting, drowning and burning.

Whitfort and colleagues (2021) conducted a retrospective study of 254 suspected cruelty offences recorded by the Hong Kong SPCA over a six-year period (2013–2019). Again, they found that the most common species involved were dogs with the majority of prosecuted cases involving traumatic physical injury (30% causing death). The second most common type of harm was neglect resulting in 27% of cases causing the death of the animal.

This chapter has very much focussed on cases involving adults. Children, sadly, can also be involved in cases of cruelty as seen in Case 5. Interventions for tackling both intentional and unintentional animal abuse or cruelty are evolving and this is covered in depth in Chapter 8. It is here where we will look at intervention programmes that have predominantly been created for children however it highlights potential developmental work that could be undertaken to create a more targeted adult preventative programme.

Sharing intelligence – why is this so important?

Throughout this book, the link between violence towards animals and violence towards people has been established. Jegatheesan and colleagues (2020) state that violence towards animals can be a strong predictor that the abuser may inflict violence on people, however, it must not be assumed that this is always the case. The One Welfare framework was designed to recognise the interconnections between animal welfare, human well-being and environmental well-being

(Pinillos, 2018). As seen in the introduction (Figure 1.2) the Scottish SPCA has expanded the ideas behind this framework so that these interconnections also take into account human and animal developmental phases. For example, if a human or animal is experiencing the negative impact of living in an environment where alcoholism and drug addiction is the norm, the physical and emotional effects that experience will have on them will be dependent on the age and stage of development that they are at.

Jegatheesan and colleagues (2020) have stated that the use of Bronfenbrenner's bioecological systems model has the potential to better support animal and human health and welfare professionals in the identification of strategies for animals and humans caught up in abusive settings. Bronfenbrenner's bioecological systems enable the examination of human development within nested contexts of relationships with individuals within the family (e.g., parents, siblings, companion animals), schools, neighbourhoods, religious centres, health institutions, human health and safety services, animal welfare services among others. Socio-cultural beliefs and norms are also considered as influencing factors of human development. This model has been adopted by many professionals who are responding to family violence and relies on agencies working together, sharing intelligence and providing the best outcomes for all involved.

Another example of a multi-agency tool that is used is the Dash Risk Checklist. This checklist is used when supporting a potential victim of domestic abuse. The purpose of the Dash Risk Checklist is to give a consistent and simple tool for practitioners who work with adult victims of domestic abuse in order to help them identify those who are at high risk of harm and whose cases should be referred to a MARAC (Multi-Agency Risk Assessment Conference) meeting in order to manage their risk. If a practitioner is concerned about the risk to a child or children, they should also make a referral to ensure that a full assessment of their safety and welfare is made (Lives, 2014). Question 19 on the Dash checklist asks the following – Has [name of abuser(s)] ever mistreated an animal or the family pet? If the answer is 'yes' then the risk from the perpetrator towards the victim is scored higher, however at present it is rare that this answer is followed up further. For example, as part of the assessment if the answer has been yes, whoever is conducting the assessment should be then checking to see if animals are still within the household and if the perpetrator does have access to any animals out with the property. Likewise, if a child has witnessed abuse towards an animal this needs to be addressed.

Conclusion

In conclusion, taking that multi-agency approach when investigating any crime is vital and where both animals and humans are involved it is important that expertise is sought that represent both parties. What has been demonstrated in this chapter is that the environment that surrounds an animal, a child, or an adult can be pivotal in what happens in each of their lives. Communication needs to take place regularly between those practitioners who are working hard to prevent abuse towards animals and/or people. Having an understanding of 'The Link' and psychological risks for animal abuse regardless of what role you play in society can make a difference between the life and death of an animal and/or a human.

Questions to consider

1 Do you think the sentences applied to each of the cases highlighted in the chapter were adequate? If not, why?
2 Based on the definitions provided, would you be able to distinguish between what would be classed as unnecessary suffering, what would be classed as neglect and what would be classed as abuse?
3 What age do you think someone should be criminally responsible for their actions?

Key Messages

1 If you are involved in protecting human welfare or animal welfare you can play a vital role in tackling the link between animal abuse and human abuse.
2 **Partnerships are key** – identify who your local support team would be if you came across a case that involved both animal and human abuse. Do you know who your local SPCA inspector is? Do you know who your local police officer or social worker is? Have you attended a case conference meeting where you think an agency is missing?
3 **The evidence timeline** – keeping a record that shows the timeline of when various incidents that are relevant to a case have occurred is crucial.
4 **Communication** – When appropriate partners who can support a person or an animal have been identified it is important that regular communication takes place between those partners and details of that communication is recorded.
5 **Speak up** – Even if you are not sure whether what you have observed or heard needs looked into always speak up, speak to someone you trust and seek that advice. Sometimes an ongoing investigation just needs that extra bit of information in order to take action and protect the welfare of an animal or human or both.

References

ASPCA (2022, August 22). *About Us*. https://www.aspca.org/about-us/aspca-policy-and-position-statements

Crown Prosecution Service (2022, August 22). *Youth Crime*. https://www.cps.gov.uk/crime-info/youth-crime

Council, F. A. W. (2009). *Farm animal welfare in Great Britain: Past, present and future*. Farm Animal Welfare Council.

Gomes, L. B., Paiva, M. T., de Oliveira Lisboa, L., de Oliveira, C. S. F., Garcia, R. D. C. M., & de Magalhães Soares, D. F. (2021). Diagnosis of animal abuse: A Brazilian study. *Preventive Veterinary Medicine*, *194*, 105421.

Heimbürge, S., Kanitz, E., & Otten, W. (2019). The use of hair cortisol for the assessment of stress in animals. *General and Comparative Endocrinology*, *270*, 10–17.

Hong Kong (2022, August 22). *Who we are*. https://www.spca.org.hk/en/about-us/who-we-are#:~:text=Our%20Mission,may%20live%20together%20in%20harmony.%E2%80%9D

Jegatheesan, B., Enders-Slegers, M. J., Ormerod, E., & Boyden, P. (2020). Understanding the link between animal cruelty and family violence: The bioecological systems model. *International Journal of Environmental Research and Public Health*, *17*(9), 3116.

Legislation (2022, August 22)[1]. Animals and Wildlife (Penalties, Protections and Powers) (Scotland) Act 2020. https://www.legislation.gov.uk/asp/2020/14/contents/enacted

Legislation (2022, August 22)[2]. The Age of Criminal Responsibility (Scotland) Act 2019. https://www.legislation.gov.uk/asp/2019/7/contents/enacted

Lives, S. (2014). Safe Lives Dash risk checklist-Quick start guidance. https://safelives.org.uk/file/dash-risk-checklist-quick-start-guidance-finalpdf

Lockwood, R., Touroo, R., Olin, J., & Dolan, E. (2019). The influence of evidence on animal cruelty prosecution and case outcomes: Results of a survey. *Journal of Forensic Sciences*, *64*(6), 1687–1692.

Loraszko, G., Racz, B., Gerencser, F., & Ozsvari, L. (2021). The prosecutors experiences on court cases with animal cruelty in Hungary. *Magyar Allatorvosok Lapja*, *143*(3), 165–172.

Morton, R., Hebart, M. L., & Whittaker, A. L. (2020). Explaining the gap between the ambitious goals and practical reality of animal welfare law enforcement: A review of the enforcement gap in Australia. *Animals*, *10*(3), 482.

Mellor, D. J., Beausoleil, N. J., Littlewood, K. E., McLean, A. N., McGreevy, P. D., Jones, B., & Wilkins, C. (2020). The 2020 five domains model: Including human–animal interactions in assessments of animal welfare. *Animals*, 10, 1870. 10.3390/ani10101870

Newberry, M. (2018). Associations between different motivations for animal cruelty, methods of animal cruelty and facets of impulsivity. *Psychology, Crime & Law*, *24*(5), 500–526.

Pinillos, R. G. (Ed.). (2018). *One welfare: A framework to improve animal welfare and human well-being*. Cabi.

RSPCA Australia (2022, August 22) – https://kb.rspca.org.au/knowledge-base/rspca-australia-mission-statement-vision-and-objectives/

RSPCA (2022, August 22). *Together for Animal Welfare*. https://www.rspca.org.uk/whatwedo/strategy

Scottish Government (2006). *Animal Health and Welfare (Scotland) Act 2006*. https://www.gov.scot/publications/animal-health-and-welfare-scotland-act-2006-guidance/

Scottish Government. (2020). Animal welfare prosecutions reported by the Scottish SPCA (2011-2019). *Social Research Series*.

Scottish Government. (2021). *The Not Proven Verdict and Related Reforms*: Consultation.

Scottish Government. (2022). Restorative justice and empathy training for animal welfare and wildlife offences. *Social Research Series*.

Scottish SPCA. (2022, August 22). *For All Animals*. https://www.scottishspca.org/forallanimals

Solodov, D. (2021). Crimes of animal cruelty in Poland: Case studies. *Forensic Science International: Animals and Environments, 1*, 100010.

SPCA International (2022, August 22). *Mission, Vision and Values*. https://www.spcai.org/about/mission-vision-values

United Nations (2022, August 22). United Nations Human Rights Office of the High Commissioner. *Convention on the rights of the child*. https://www.ohchr.org/en/professionalinterest/pages/crc.aspx

Wauthier, L., Scottish Society for the Prevention of Cruelty to Animals (Scottish SPCA), & Williams, J. M. (2022). A qualitative study of children's accounts of cruelty to animals: Uncovering the roles of trauma, exposure to violence, and attachment. *Journal of Interpersonal Violence, 37*(9-10), NP6405–NP6438.

Whitfort, A., Woodhouse, F., Ho, S., & Chun, M. (2021). A retrospective analysis of typologies of animal abuse recorded by the SPCA, Hong Kong. *Animals, 11*(6), 1830.

World Animal Protection (2022, August 22). *Animal Protection Index*. https://api.worldanimalprotection.org/

6   What to do about animal cruelty from a veterinary perspective

Independent Vet and former Chair of The Links Group UK

Aims of this chapter

Throughout the book there have been many references to the critical role the veterinary profession needs to play in recognising and acting on the link between human and animal abuse. This chapter focuses on abuse in companion animals, including horses, rather than livestock in an agricultural setting, because there is more knowledge and better-developed frameworks for remedial action in the domestic setting. The aim is to provide members of the veterinary team with basic knowledge to recognise animal abuse and know what to do. It explores the challenges of recognising abuse to animals and beyond that, what to do if there is disclosure of wider abuse to the humans in a household. The implications for members of the veterinary team are discussed and protocol templates are provided for practice guidance. The first part of the chapter looks explicitly at deliberate harm to animals and then how to deal with disclosure of abuse to both animals and humans in the same household. Cases of deliberate, intentional abuse in livestock are either (quite) rare or few incidents make it to wider attention. Abuse, or more likely, misuse, of livestock more commonly relates to welfare issues arising from neglect, often by the keeper's negligence or animals may suffer neglect through farmer circumstances (e.g., a lack of financial resources to look after their animals or by the desertion of duty through circumstances, such as declining mental or physical health). The complex topic of abuse or exploitation of wildlife is well described in Chapter 4 and will be mentioned only briefly in this chapter, mainly in relation to seeking the help of specific expertise if dealing with a live case, or forensic pathologists, should a cadaver be presented.

DOI: 10.4324/9781003165552-6

Background

The concepts of 'One Health' and 'One Welfare' are widely understood and have done much to improve inter-disciplinary collaboration on an international level. Both recognise the interconnections between animal welfare and human wellbeing and the environment but while One Health aspires to achieve optimal health outcomes by disease control, One Welfare is the most appropriate term to encompass the topic of animal abuse, which in this chapter is intended for members of the veterinary team. Animal abuse occurs when the bonds of mutual respect are broken between man and animals and for multiple reasons, some of which have been discussed in other chapters in this book, animals become the target for abuse.

Abuse of animals is an abhorrent topic for all except those who perpetrate the acts of cruelty, but members of the veterinary team are in a unique situation and are often disproportionately affected by discovering that animals are the victims of abuse. Vets are highly trained individuals with expert knowledge of the animals that they treat and generally, members of the vet team have great respect, even affection for the animals' owners. However, despite treating cases of animal abuse being a reflectively common experience for vets (Williams and colleagues, 2022) there are 'difficulties of diagnosis' of animal abuse (Munro & Munro, 2008) and often small signs of repeated abuse may be missed. Vets can feel ineffectual once they recognise the abuse, but this chapter will endeavour to explain that no one should feel inadequate; professionals with years of experience are commonly unaware of a problem until all the signs are considered in the round and even then, there may be ambiguity.

If the question "Do you see much evidence of animal abuse in your practice?" was asked of a group of veterinary surgeons in the early 2000s, the collective answer was generally a shake of the head and 'no', or 'rarely'. In 2001, Helen Munro (veterinary pathologist) and Mike Thrusfield (veterinary epidemiologist) published a series of four papers (e.g., Munro & Thrusfield, 2001) in the Journal of Small Animal Practice, which coined the term 'the battered pet'. This was pioneering work and was the first time a large study had looked at the pathological findings from cases of 'non-accidental injury' (NAI) in the dog and cat. The term 'non-accidental injury' was poorly understood, and many vets did not read the papers, or possibly did not fully comprehend the implications of the pathological findings detailed in the Journal.

Over the next few years, even as a better understanding of the complexities of violence towards animals was developed by members of the veterinary team through collaboration with colleagues in human healthcare professions, many in the veterinary profession were still not recognising cases of abuse. The Links Group UK (www.thelinksgroup.org.uk) was formed in 2001 to ensure that the veterinary teams were better informed because the presentation or signalment of non-accidental injury is often subtle and confusing. Vets and human healthcare professionals collaborated in this multi-agency group with a common interest: to promote the safety and welfare of vulnerable children, animals and adults so that they are free from violence and abuse. Through this relationship, vets gained a better understanding of what could be done to successfully intervene in the cycle of violence. The Links Group also recognised the need for human healthcare professionals who visit violent homes with an animal in the house to understand the basic welfare needs of pets. A comprehensive online module for vets was prepared to describe when an animal's welfare needs are compromised so they can be removed to safety.

As Chapter 3 describes, animals can be deliberately harmed or used as a tool to control or manipulate behaviours of a vulnerable individual in the household and this would be a form of abuse. The language used for 'abuse' however is complex despite efforts to simplify guidelines (Arkow, 2003; Arkow, 2013). This chapter deals with deliberate cruelty, not neglect or ignorance, teasing or tormenting. Hoarding is not in the scope of this book. The age of the perpetrator may be surprisingly wide as other chapters (such as Chapters 3, 5 and 8) describe, children may do considerable damage to animals for multiple complex reasons and if not detected early, these young people can continue to harm animals into adulthood, with increasing severity of cruelty. However, first and foremost, the duty of the veterinary team is to provide immediate care to the injured animal before delving into the complex web of animal abuse or harm to family members.

Educational resources

Vets generally fall into three categories: those who don't recognise and/or claim never to see abuse; those who recognise non-accidental injury (NAI) but for multiple, complex reasons, choose to ignore it; and finally, a growing cadre of vets and veterinary nurses/technicians/receptionists (defined as 'members of the veterinary team' in this chapter) who recognise that they are seeing evidence of NAI and want to do something about it.

There is little excuse for claiming ignorance of the topic although it is recognised that older vets did not have the advantage of undergraduate training at vet school. Access to the current cadre of veterinary undergraduates has helped educate a new generation and almost all the UK veterinary schools welcome expert speakers, which contributes to a growing number of graduates with a better understanding of the topic. However, even now, this important subject is still presented to students in the UK only as an addendum to their main syllabus – a part day of lectures from an external speaker.

Members of the veterinary team now have regular access to a nationwide training programme – the Links Veterinary Training Initiative (LVTI), delivered in partnership with veterinary associations (e.g., the British Small Animal Veterinary Association (BSAVA) and the British Veterinary Association (BVA)). Many of the courses are now presented online, which means that vets from abroad can join in although many of the reporting or control measures are specific to the UK.

In the UK, the USA and Europe, there has been multiplication of corporate practices, which allows data gathering on a vast scale and a cross-border flow of information. Incidents of animal abuse are thus well recognised and to that end, one UK/Europe corporate (IVC Evidensia) has established a profession-wide support network, available 24/7 for any member of the veterinary team (not just IVC Evidensia staff members) to seek advice if they have concerns. A QR code directs people to a webpage where they fill in their details with a brief outline of their concern and they receive a response within four hours. There is also a number to call for immediate assistance in urgent cases. Not all countries will be fortunate enough to have access to this resource, but the ethos of this initiative is one of supporting vets to recognise animal abuse and to know what to do and the altruistic format could possibly be repeated in other countries.

Cultural differences, animal cruelty and domestic abuse

The world has developed a much better understanding of the human-companion-animal bond over the last 30 years, however, vets will understand that there are cultural differences in animal relationships across the world. In a wide range of cultures including South American, the USA and the UK, people can live with dogs that are pets, but also status animals used for protection and fighting (e.g., Harding, 2010 and Alonso-Recarte, 2020). In China and South-East Asia, traditional pet species (dogs and cats) are slaughtered for their meat, a practice that is abhorrent to people in Western cultures. Although there is a declining consumption of 'pet species' meat, and many Far Eastern families own much-loved pets, eating dog and cat meat is accepted as normal in many countries (e.g., Dugnoille, 2018; Poon, 2014). The inevitable welfare contraventions of this trade (especially the way animals are caged and slaughtered) are outside the scope of this chapter but the work of animal charities (e.g., Animals Asia Foundation, and SPCA's from around the world) is acknowledged. Across Africa, horses and donkeys may be poorly treated through overwork and deprivation of treatment for illnesses although should a charity hospital be available, then the owners will seek help (e.g., American Fondouk, Brooke and SPANA) because human lives and economic survival depend on the equids' health.

Those who work in agricultural practice will know that farmers care deeply for the welfare of their livestock, even though some may perform procedures that seem bizarre outside their own cultures (e.g., the ritual blood-letting in the cattle of the Maasai tribe to provide an important food source for tribe members). In India, Hindus worship cows (amongst a list of other sacred animals) but it is acknowledged that abuse still occurs in Indian pets, for all the reasons that are recognised in the UK. Other than specific cultural practices, farmers in developed countries may also treat animals harshly (e.g., twisting cows' tails to make them move or beating pigs with the same intention). These actions cannot be condoned, and vets should be able to influence behavioural changes to the benefit of the animals.

In Europe, the USA and the UK, vets are peculiarly aware of the strong emotional links that exist between companion animal owners and their animals. Thus, this chapter is written more for countries with owners who consider their pets to be valued members of their family and, in the agricultural context, farm animals who exist within a framework of the Five Freedoms (or Five Domains) and high welfare standards (see Chapters 1, 4 and 5).

We know that sometimes individuals choose to harm animals and humans and it is necessary to direct the reader towards the subject matter in Chapter 3. Animal abuse is not a stand-alone issue (Arkow, 2015) and the chapters in this book explore fully the reasons behind why hurting animals matters and some of the emerging research that leads us to a better understanding of why perpetrators of all ages perform despicable acts of cruelty.

Animals, women and children all have one thing in common – they are all easy to hurt and in cultures where these things matter and are recorded, there is ever-increasing evidence about individuals who perpetrate animal cruelty in association with other human abuse. Thus, frequently veterinary practices may see cases of suspected abuse, and the careful questioning that is necessary in these cases to elicit the truth may lead to concerns about family members, including children. This adds additional complexity to the consultation, but every practice should have a protocol to follow, and all members of the veterinary team should have practiced the procedures outlined therein.

Animal abuse: Difficulties of diagnosis

Most physical injuries have an innocent or understandable cause, for example, a road traffic accident or trauma due to genuine accidents. Sometimes the signs of animal abuse are obvious but often they are not, and an animal may be presented on numerous occasions with small, often 'insignificant' injuries, like a small cut on the head, or unexplained tenderness over the chest, tail or specific joints. It is only when someone has the time to look back through the history that the multiplicity of minor injuries over variable periods of time, and their implication, becomes apparent.

There is an additional barrier to the ability of the clinician to recognise the signs of abuse; veterinary surgeons are caring individuals and there is often a powerful emotional block that prevents acceptance of the possibility that a client could have deliberately harmed an animal. This impediment is also recognised in medical doctors and dentists. It is essential that clinicians and veterinary nurses force themselves to think about the possibility of non-accidental injury and place it on the list of differential diagnoses. It will not be at the top of the list but if it is part of the potential diagnosis list, then it will always be considered.

A further challenge to early diagnosis is observed in multi-vet or multi-centre practices. Animals may be presented with multiple small injuries at variable intervals. If several different clinicians or veterinary nurses see the animal on separate occasions, it takes time to read back through the history to join the diagnostic dots that finally give rise to suspicions of repeated injuries. In busy practices, this may not happen until someone begins to wonder why the animal (or other animals from the same household) is/are being presented repeatedly.

Diagnostic indicators: Joining the dots

Before reading further, look at Case Study 1 in relation to a three-month-old kitten.

Case Study 1 Subject: Three-month-old kitten

First appointment: kitten presented with swelling above one eye – reason given: 'cupboard door fell on the kitten'. Treated symptomatically and sent home.

Two weeks later: kitten presented with dyspnoea – diagnosis: 4 fractured ribs. Reason for injury: "2-year-old child sat on cat". Treated symptomatically, sent home but vet's concerns are now slightly raised (Salient fact: *there is a) an unsafe house and b) a child in the house*).

Two weeks later: kitten presented with severe ataxia and distress; and it deteriorated neurologically over next 24 hrs and was euthanised.

Vets reported case to Royal Society for the Prevention of Cruelty to Animals (RSPCA) for investigation. Post mortem (necropsy) confirmed:

- Skull fractures and severe contusions (from most recent injury)
- Rib fractures (from the previous injury)

The RSPCA Inspector interviewed the owners (on two occasions) and recorded some concerns about the attitude of the owners:

- Discrepant history (no consistency in the stories).
- Injuries to the kitten were trivialised ('injuries weren't very serious').
- Little concern expressed for the kitten.

The RSPCA Inspector consulted a vet experienced in non-accidental injury and was advised that the presentation, clinical signs and necropsy results indicated deliberate harm. The RSPCA Inspector contacted the police for a criminal record check and there were standing allegations of domestic abuse and child abuse (but with insufficient evidence to proceed) against the male in the house. By moving house and area, the family had fallen off the social services radar but because of the death of this kitten, they were investigated, and the male partner was sent to a Young Offenders Institution. Both partners were disqualified from keeping animals indefinitely. The child was placed into special safeguarding measures.

The most important step in diagnosing non-accidental injury is to think about it in the first place. No single feature of the physical signs or the history (signalment) is diagnostic – it is the combination of factors that raise suspicions in the mind of the clinician. Given the 'difficulties of diagnosis' outlined above, it can be daunting for young vets to be sure of recognising the tell-tale signs, so the Links Group recommend that you become familiar with the following list of indicators:

- The history is inconsistent, that is, the story does not 'fit' with the injury.
- The history is contradictory.
- The story changes between each telling.
- More than one explanation for the injury.
- The story varies from person to person.
- There is reluctance to give straight answers.
- There is no believable history of a road traffic accident (RTA).
- There may have been multiple injuries or deaths in one household.
- Multiple injuries in the same animal even when the animal is house-bound (e.g., cats).
- Repetitive injuries (e.g., wounds to the head, limb or tail, or bruises in multiple joints).
- Evidence (on radiographs) of old fractures (commonly rib fractures).
- Fractures (old and new) are frequent findings, multiple fractures in various bones.
- 'Greenstick' fractures in immature long bones are indicative of intense trauma.
- Behavioural changes: the animal appears happier when separated from the owner.
- Young animals appear to be disproportionally impacted by malicious actions.

There is an uncommon type of abuse described by the term 'fabricated or induced illness' (FII) – previously known as Munchausen syndrome by proxy or just Munchausen's. In the veterinary world, this means that animals are presented with false (fabricated) signs justifying the visit. The syndrome can take different forms:

- A normal patient is presented with a history of signs that are found not to exist.
- A normal patient is presented with a history of signs that exist but are not serious and yet the owner demands attention and treatment, out of proportion to the clinical findings.
- An animal is presented with signs that are found to be owner-induced, which is usually an attention-seeking act.

These are difficult cases to identify cause/effect and reality because of the discrepancies between reported history and recorded signs of illness/injury plus implausible descriptions of circumstances. If there are unusual signs in the course of the illness that are not clinically logical or the illness improves or ceases altogether when the pet is separated from the perpetrator, then FII should be considered. An additional consideration, is that symptoms are fabricated to acquire access to medicines, not for the pet but for the perpetrator. These are cases that deserve referral or at least, extensive consultation with experienced colleagues.

How to approach a clinical situation where non-accidental injury is suspected

Every practice, large and small, should have a protocol for members of the veterinary team to follow, should a clinical case give cause for concern. By following the practice protocol (see Practice Protocol I and Practice Protocol II), every member of the veterinary team – vets, veterinary nurses/technicians and receptionists should know exactly what to do and how to approach the case with confidence. Although it may be challenging in a busy practice to find time to collectively study the protocol and to practise the recommendations, your veterinary team will be grateful for the additional confidence when an animal is presented with non-accidental injuries.

Practice Protocol I (animal abuse)

The protocol for each practice will be different, dependant on factors such as the number of vets, or support staff, and your external contacts with welfare officers or community police officers. The points below are offered for each practice to consider while formulating a plan of action, should a case of abuse be suspected. Each point should be considered and discussed regularly with all members of the practice team.

- Recognise the possibility of animal abuse and place it on the differential diagnosis list.
- Arrange a simple code to alert staff members that there is a 'situation' causing concern (e.g., Dr Smith has a 'Code Blue', could you come and help?').
- In larger practices, appoint a safeguarding officer – a go-to person with some in-depth, specialist training. Smaller practices might choose to share one with neighbouring practices.
- Discuss the severity and range of possible injuries: abusive injuries cover the full spectrum from tiny scratches to major fractures, gunshot or knife wounds or death.
- Recognise that the injuries (minor or major) may be the first and only episode or, looking back in the history, there may be notes of previous minor or major injuries in this animal/other animals belonging to the same owner.
- Explain to all staff members what contemporaneous (at the time) notes are; understand their importance should a case need to be investigated further or go to court.
- Discuss how clinicians should record verbatim (precisely) what the client says, using their own language and words, no matter how colourful or profane. E.g., Write exactly what was said: "*He hit the dog on the head*" not your interpretation: "*The dog sustained blunt trauma to the cranium.*"
- In contrast, clinicians should use professional language when describing the case; this should be objective, honest (not embellished) and thorough with no abbreviations.
- If the story changes, then note the date/time of the conversation and record the new history.
- Emphasise that all members of staff should keep themselves safe; if a 'Code Blue' has been called, everyone should be alerted to the situation, remembering it could escalate to confrontation/aggression.
- Practise questions that are non-threatening; the animal may be accompanied by a perpetrator who may remove the animal before treatment or intimidate the clinician if they feel threatened.
- Discuss the chain of communication in the practice; (senior) colleagues, welfare officers, community police officers. Talking about the case is helpful before making any major decisions; share your concerns.
- Recognise that certain things (multiple injuries, discrepant history, family dynamics) will make you uncomfortable – the 'gut feeling' that something is wrong.
- Discuss what might work in your practice to progress the case slowly; taking the animal out of the consulting room; perhaps hospitalising the animal (with the permission of the owner).

- Maintain objectivity – re-examine initial concerns after discussion with colleagues (or a welfare officer or a local community police officer).
- Client/animal details should not be shared at this point, but the discussion will help clarify a way forward.
- Decide (with colleagues if possible) if you can hospitalise the animal – if the injuries justify it. Keeping the animal in removes the immediate urgency of decisions because the animal is safe.
- Seek permission from the owner for hospitalisation/radiographs/lab test/photographs (use the practice camera – do not use mobile phones; may be taken as evidence).

Practice Protocol II (disclosure of human abuse)

Remember that animal abuse may be part of a wider cycle of violence in that household; and your notes may, one day, make the difference to a victim's life. As a trusted individual, members of the veterinary team may receive confidence. All the points from the animal abuse practice protocol are relevant but there is added complexity as the vet steps outside their 'comfort zone' and area of expertise.

- If a staff member receives a disclosure of deliberate harm to the animal or a member of the family, or the vet has concerns, then they should request a colleague to join them in the consulting room to assist.
- If the animal has not been removed, this will allow the vet to concentrate on the history while the animal can be secured by the second person, or better removed, so that full attention can be given to the client.
- Choose a confidential space where the consultation can be continued. If the client is a single woman, then male vets should consider having a chaperone (if possible). Two people from the practice may be helpful if the victim is not overwhelmed or intimidated.

In addition, the Links Group (UK) recommends an approach termed A R D R (Ask, Reassure, Document, Refer/Report Figure 6.1 with a detailed pathway action highlighted in Figure 6.2.

In larger practices, it is helpful to perform some role play, using a case (such as Case Study 1) to familiarise practice staff with the protocol. Few vets enjoy role play but in hindsight, after tackling a difficult case, will appreciate the exposure to brief discomfort amongst colleagues when they are placed in a

ASK:

Survivors have confirmed that they would like to be asked about what is going on in their lives. Use non-threatening questions like: 'Sometimes when I see / hear about injuries like this, it means that you / your animal has been hurt by someone they know. Is this possible?' 'Is everything okay at home?'

REFER / REPORT:

This may not be an immediate action; take time for reflection with the client, senior members of staff, or external resources. If the client wants a safe space to phone for personal help, have a list of contact numbers and offer the chance to phone from the surgery. Your responsibility remains with the pet only.

The Links Group (UK) recommends an approach termed A R D R (Ask, Reassure, Document, Refer/Report).

Links Group

REASSURE:

the victim by showing compassion and understanding. Use validating statements like 'I am concerned for your safety' or 'It is not right for you (and your animal) to be hit or hurt.' This is an opportunity for the practice to offer help: for the animal – and for the victim – possibly giving them a safe space to phone a domestic violence helpline.

©The Links Group

DOCUMENT:

Contemporaneous, factual, and non-emotional. If two people are in the room, then one might ask and listen, the other can scribe.

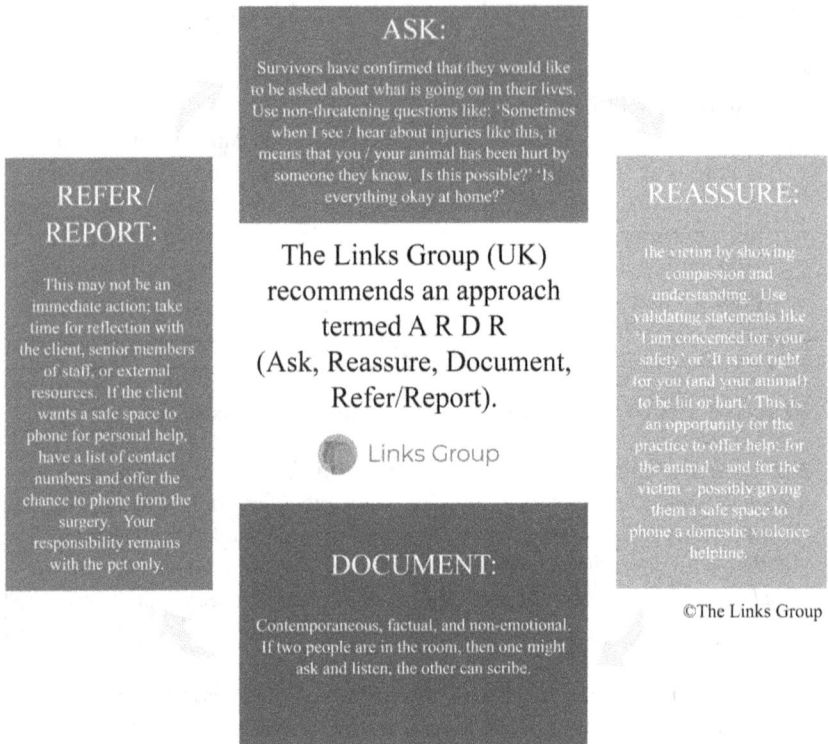

An approach called A R D R (Ask, Reassure, Document, Refer/Report)

Figure 6.1 The Links Group A R D R for recognising and reporting abuse.

real-life situation coping with multiple, less familiar considerations. Even the skill of asking 'non-threatening' questions does not come naturally without a little practice.

Again, study the case history in Case Study 1. The case has been anonymised and simplified but demonstrates clearly how challenging these cases can be to be sure that there is deliberate harm to an animal. Often animals are presented with a series of small injuries, which in themselves do not alert the vet or veterinary nurse to look for malicious actions. These consultations may be interspersed with routine visits for vaccination and worming or neutering, which may prevent the trail of injuries being immediately picked up.

The presentation of these cases can be confusing (e.g., multiple small injuries over a period or a major life-threatening injury that only becomes suspicious after radiology, or further examination of the history). Few vets in the UK or Europe would instantly recognise gunshot or stab wounds but cigarette burns, once seen, are never forgotten. There is much to bear in mind when realisation dawns that there might possibly be deliberate harm to the

The ARDR process if any animal abuse is suspected: Ask, Reassure, Document, Report

Review clinical history for any previous NAI;look for:
• Inconsistent • Repetitive • Discrepancies • Other animal involved • Previous vet practices attended

Initial examination

Suspect non-accidental injury

See page 14 for diagnostic indicator of NAI

Confidentially flag potential NAI to colleagues and consult with them

Take further history: be aware of indicators relating to the **presentation, history, clinical findings, and both client and animal behaviour.**
USE ARDR

Questions may lead to a disclosure of domestic abuse. If this happens, follow the process on page 29

"How are things at home?"
"Sometimes when I see injuries like this. it means the animal has been hurt by someone, could this have happened?"

A = ASK

| Story plausible and concerns relieved-provide treatment then document original concern and reason for discounting | Client denies abuse, but story not plausible - explore further and consult with colleagues, consider contacting SPCA Inspectorfor advice | PERPETRATOR? Client discloses abuse, but they may be the perpetrator. Take care; ask non-judgemental questions | VICTIM-SURVIVOR? Client discloses that there has been abuse ofthe pet; may also disclose domestic abuse (follow process on page 29) |

No further action

R = REASSURE
"Your animal doesn't deserve to be hurt, no matter what happened; how can we help?"

Further clinical investigation and/or appropriate treatment

Allow time to review the case / seek advice while keeping them safe

Consider admitting the animal for investigation
(getting permission for any procedures, including photos,if possible)

Client will leave animal
Admit as usual, getting permissions

Client won't leave animal
Is the animal suffering?

YES
If the animal is suffering and requires urgent treatment, the law allows for a vet to intervene with police support. If the owner still won't leave the animal despite being advised of this, contact the RSPCA / SSPCA and the police to take the animal into their possession

See page 19

NO
If the animal is not suffering, owner to sign form; 'Animal removed against veterinary advice'

D = DOCUMENT
Clear,precise, contemporaneous notes. See guidance on evidence collection on page 25

R = REPORT
Report the case to relevent animal welfare agency: RSPCA in England and wales' SSPCA in Scotland or local council Animal Welfare Officer in Northern Ireland

If there are any immediate danger, follow your practice safeguarding policy and phone 999

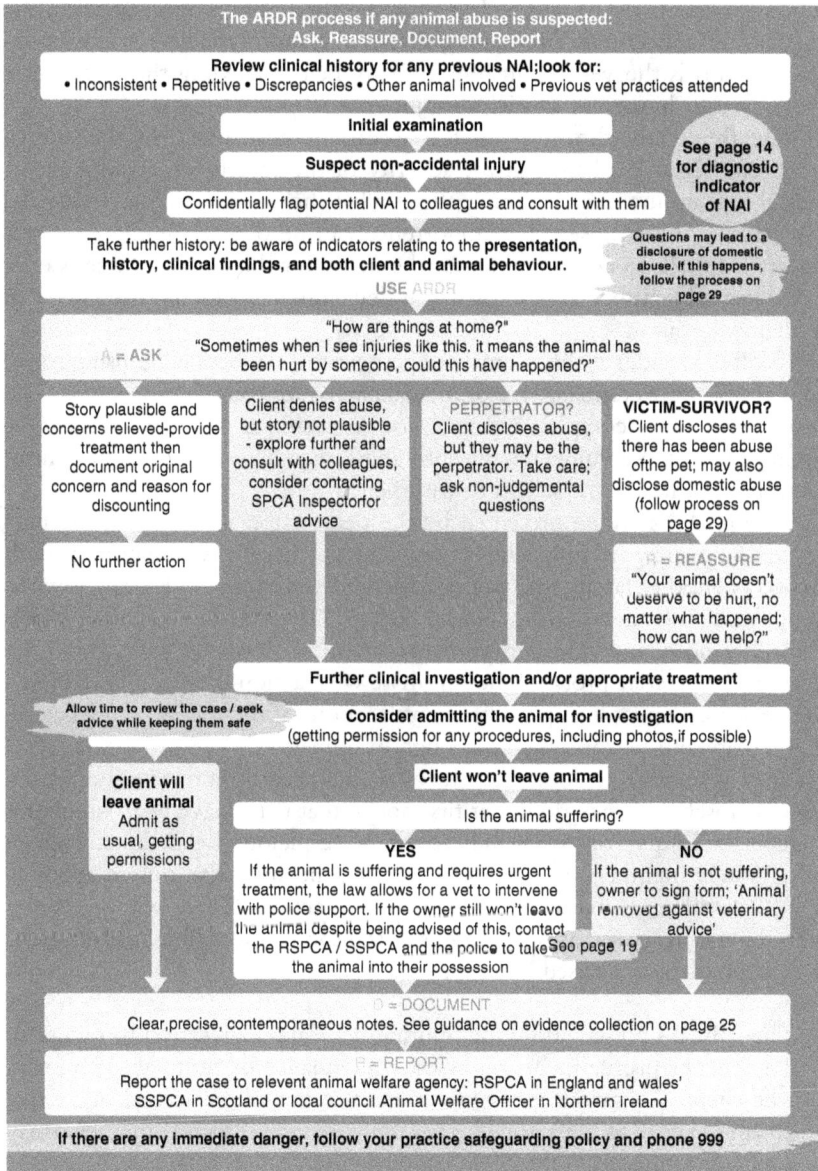

Figure 6.2 A detailed overview of the Links Group ARDR pathway for reporting animal abuse and domestic abuse.

animal, not least considering who has presented the animal (perpetrator or an innocent owner). By having a clear protocol that staff are familiar with, the clinician can concentrate on treating the animal appropriately – it is emphasised that this is the vet's main responsibility before tackling the wider issue of a discrepant history or suspicious injuries.

Quite frequently the end point is death, or euthanasia, of the animal victim due to an escalation in the severity of the injuries. It is difficult for veterinary team members to think about what the animal may have suffered at the hands of an abuser. The abhorrence can be overwhelming, and it is important to talk to colleagues about the case after the clinical phase is over to preserve objectivity and allow some detachment from the intricacies of the deliberate harm.

Vets often wonder at the anomaly of perpetrators deliberately causing harm, and then seeking veterinary care or indeed paying for routine procedures. The reasons for this are complex and may not be dissimilar to what doctors specialising in child (or vulnerable person) abuse recognise as a form of control (controlling suffering and access to treatment).

The animal(s) may be presented by the perpetrator, a partner of the perpetrator (who may be innocent of, or complicit in, any wrongdoing), both partners or another family member or a friend. Even more challenging is when young family members are brought in, perhaps intentionally to create a group of possibly noisy individuals that divert attention from the animal and the injuries. The practice protocol should advise what action should be taken (e.g., remove as many people as possible from the room) if there is difficulty getting a full history and performing a thorough examination.

It may take time to look back through the records and vets should not blame themselves if they do not at first notice that there have been numerous incidents of injury, or other indications of suspicious behaviours, such as several family members, or friends, presenting the animal(s), missed appointments, or evidence of attendance at multiple practices. There will be a point when the vet decides that that abuse is at the top of the differential diagnosis list because there is a raised index of suspicion around:

- The animal's presentation: the injuries, demeanour, reaction to owner(s).
- The client's profile including practice attendance or turnover of animals.
- The client's behaviour is suspicious; indifference to the animal, aggressive or intimidating to the animal, or to family members. Family members may appear intimidated.
- The history may be factual, embellished, fabricated or flexible.

It is the combination of factors that leads the vet to consider non-accidental injury and then the clinician must decide on what to do. Sometimes, there is clear evidence that a child has perpetrated the damage to the animal and the parents may be distraught. It is important to reassure them that you understand, and that there may be help at hand (such as through programmes like

Animal Guardians which is discussed in detail in Chapter 8). The actions of a child may indicate problems in the home and thus the vet, after careful consideration and further consultation, may decide to share this knowledge with human healthcare professionals.

At the very least, the practice member, including receptionists, dealing with the owner and animal(s) should always take contemporaneous (at the time) notes and keep themselves safe. Note that the animal may be accompanied by a perpetrator and thus questions should be kept as neutral as possible.

In the consulting room, non-threatening questions can be formulated around a sentence starting: *Sometimes when I see injuries like this, they may have been caused by someone close to the family; Could this have happened to Sooty/Tiddles?* This opens a new line of questioning but to avoid direct questions that may attribute blame, ask about all the people in the household or indeed, friends or family who may have visited. If radiology has been performed, and previous bony injuries are visible, the same oblique technique can be followed; *I can see some older, healing injuries in this x-ray; do you know how these might have happened?*

It can be difficult for vets not to immediately level accusations (because it appears obvious that the injuries have been deliberately perpetrated). However, there is an advantage to remaining unbiased to maintain the flow of information, even if you appear (to the perpetrator) to be naïve or gullible. Perpetrators may become over-confident if they feel superior to a professional, and they may begin to impart more information. Record everything assiduously because often errors and contradictions in the history will creep in and this all helps to build a case. If the client and the animal(s) leave the practice, a staff member should ensure that all members of the practice, including in other branch surgeries, are aware of the circumstances to ensure that relevant further clinical notes can be made. Perpetrators can be clever at hopping between practices and branches to divert suspicion. Every time a clinician sees a potential case of abuse, the comprehensive and focussed notes will aid future definitive decisions.

Conflicts within codes of professional conduct: Doing the right thing

The Royal College of Veterinary Surgeons (RCVS) in Great Britain (GB) is responsible for, among other things, the fitness to practise of veterinary surgeons and veterinary nurses and to that end provides extensive guidance in the Codes of Professional Conduct (www.rcvs.org.uk). A vet's rights and responsibilities are encapsulated in the solemn declaration that all vets swear to follow on admission to the RCVS:

> *"I PROMISE AND SOLEMNLY DECLARE that I will pursue the work of my profession with integrity and accept my responsibilities to the public, my clients, the profession and the Royal College of Veterinary Surgeons, and that, ABOVE ALL, my constant endeavour will be to ensure the health and welfare of animals committed to my care."*

The five principles of practice are:

1 Professional competence
2 Honesty and integrity
3 Independence and impartiality
4 Client confidentiality and trust
5 Professional accountability

As in all walks of life but particularly when animal abuse is suspected, there may be conflicts that mean vets and veterinary nurses face dilemmas between their care for the animal, concerns to 'do the right thing' while maintaining client trust. Despite the comprehensive guidance in the Code, it can place vets in a lonely place when they contemplate breaching client confidentiality in difficult circumstances.

The standards of professional conduct are set out in the Code but there is broader advice in the Supporting Guidance. Few countries have the advantage of clearly defined veterinary guidance but there is no reason why non-GB practices should not read and choose to adopt some of the principles contained in the RCVS Code of Professional Conduct for Veterinary Surgeons Supporting Guidance as highlighted in below.

RCVS Code of Professional Conduct Supporting Guidance

Section 14: Client Confidentiality: disclosing to the authorities

14.6 In circumstances where the client has not given permission for disclosure and the veterinary surgeon or veterinary nurse considers that animal welfare or the public interest is compromised, client confidentiality may be breached, and appropriate information reported to the relevant authorities. Some examples may include situations where:

a an animal shows signs of abuse
b a dangerous dog poses a risk to safety
c child or domestic abuse is suspected
d where a breeder in England has presented litters without possessing a licence to breed, or has breached the licence conditions (where applicable)
e where the information is likely to help in the prevention, detection or prosecution of a crime
f there is some other significant threat to public health or safety or to the health or safety of an individual.

The main concern for veterinary surgeons in the UK is breaching client confidentiality by reporting suspected abuse. Client confidentiality is a strongly held commitment for both veterinary surgeons and veterinary nurses and thus clear country-specific guidance on what to do is essential. The mandate for reporting animal abuse varies widely across the world (as seen in the box below) and most advice will direct a vet to report abuse to an animal welfare organisation, the police or a humane society.

Reporting Animal Abuse

Currently (2022), there is no mandatory reporting of animal abuse in the UK, Australia or New Zealand. Vets in New Zealand are advised not to ignore circumstances where there are reasonable grounds to suggest transgressions against the animal welfare act and they should act immediately. In Australia, advice from the Australian Veterinary Association (2022) written in 2013 states: '*Veterinarians should report suspected animal abuse to the relevant authorities. Veterinarians should not be required by law to report instances of suspected animal abuse as this may discourage owners from seeking essential treatment for their injured animals.*'

The USA has variable reporting status: 20 states now have mandatory reporting, and 20 states have voluntary reporting. Thirty-three (out of these 40 states) have immunity from civil and/or criminal liability for making a report in good faith. Ten states have no law.

In Canada the regulations in each province or territory determine what agencies have the authority to investigate suspected cases of animal abuse and to lay charges. The 10 provinces require veterinarians to report, however the three territories – Yukon, Northwest Territory and Nunavut – have no requirements. In almost all cases, the local or provincial SPCA or humane society is involved in the investigation, and any charges laid are usually laid either by the police or in conjunction with the police (CVMA, 2022).

The way animal welfare legislation transgressions are dealt with in Europe vary across borders but most place a moral responsibility on the professional to share their concerns. In Finland, animal welfare transgressions are dealt with by official veterinarians and although historically have concentrated on production animals, maltreatment of companion animals commonly leads to action involving the police.

In India, there is advice to contact the Animal Welfare Board of India (2022) or District Societies for Prevention of Cruelty to Animals although many online sources emphasise that reporting is only the first step and the animal(s) may be returned to the owner after the first hearing unless the case is vigorously pursued by the complainant.

Vets in Great Britain/UK can refer to Section 14.6 in the RCVS Supporting Guidance 'Disclosing to the authorities' to reassure vets that there are specific circumstances when the vet can be confident about reporting a situation.

The guidance helpfully states:

> "*The duty of confidentiality is important but it is not absolute and information can be disclosed in certain circumstances, for example where the client's consent has been given, where disclosure can be justified by animal welfare concerns or the wider public interest, or where disclosure is required by law.*" and

> "*The more animal welfare or the public interest is compromised, the more prepared a veterinary surgeon or veterinary nurse should be to release information to the relevant authority.*"

A survey of UK vets (Alleyne and colleagues, 2019) looked at their reporting behaviour and their 'perceived self-efficacy', which drives decision-making (for example, to break client confidentiality and report suspected abuse). The study concluded that specialised training could help develop self-efficacy, which in this study was positively correlated with years in practice and familiarity with abuse cases.

Less experienced clinicians and veterinary nurses are encouraged to discuss cases with senior colleagues, or welfare officers. It is important that all discussions, with the client and with colleagues, are documented so that actions that may contravene professional advice may be justified in the face of a challenge to professional conduct.

Disclosure of non-accidental injury against family members: "Everything is (not) fine"

The complexities of extended abuse beyond animals to humans in a violent household are discussed in detail in Chapter 3, which should be read in conjunction with this section. Veterinary staff should understand that they can intervene and improve these heart-breaking situations. Practicing the animal abuse protocol will have prepared vets and veterinary nurses for the 'simpler' situation of abuse in an animal only. However, having recognised that an animal has been deliberately harmed, practices should know that when animals are abused, people are at risk and when people are abused, animals are at risk (Arkow, 2003).

Veterinary surgeons, veterinary nurses and receptionists are trusted individuals, and their gentle (non-threatening) questions may release a flood of confidences that can cause conflicting emotions in the veterinary staff member. There may initially be some pride at the faith placed by the client in the staff member, but this is often quickly followed by dismay and a feeling of inadequacy and uncertainty about what to do. Guidance in the second part of the practice protocol offers a clear way forward to offer support to the client when abuse to human members of the family is divulged.

Veterinary surgeons may question why we should get involved in family matters beyond the care of an abused animal. However, members of the veterinary team can play an important role in breaking the cycle of violence. The concept of 'safeguarding' vulnerable adults or children does not come naturally to vets but human healthcare professionals welcome our active participation to establish cross-reporting procedures. Informed human healthcare professionals recognise that asking patients about their pets facilitates easier history-taking and allows a deeper insight into a household situation (Hodgson and colleagues, 2017). Animals may be the index case from a violent household and could provide a reason for social services or the police to seek access behind closed doors, where there may be vulnerable humans unable to escape an abusive relationship. Veterinary intervention in cases of abuse, whether to animal, adult or child, may be reported to the relevant authority and at that point, the vet may step back and allow the human professionals to take over.

Vets do not need to be experts in animal or human abuse; they just need to be prepared to extend a compassionate 'paw' to comfort a potential victim even though they are outside their comfort zone. The Links Group (UK) talks about grasping the 'golden moment' - that point where a client admits to deliberate harm (to the animal or themselves) and may even consider asking for help. By using the A R D R (Ask, Reassure, Document, Refer/Report) method (Figures 6.1 and 6.2) more information may be gained about the case:

Ask: A simple method to gain more information. Survivors of abuse have confirmed that they would like to be asked by healthcare professionals (Nelms and colleagues, 2009 and Femi-Ajao, 2021), it may be the first time that anyone has shown any interest in, or sympathy towards them. Use non-threatening questions like: *Sometimes when I see/hear about injuries like this, it means that you/your animal has been hurt by someone they know. Is this possible?* Or perhaps explore a little by saying: *Is everything okay at home?* Survivors confirm that they will nearly always reply *'fine'* to this question because they cannot admit or explain the reality that everything is not fine but they are terrified of the consequences of admitting their circumstances. If there is disclosure of abuse (to the animal or a human victim), then move gently on to the next step.

Reassure: Reassurance provides support to the victim, whose self-esteem may have been destroyed. Use statements like *I am concerned for your safety,* or *it is not right for you (and your animal) to be hit or hurt.* This provides great comfort to victims and studies have shown that this might be the point that the victim actively considers seeking help. The next question might be *Is there anything you would like to talk about or that I can help you with?* Remind them that they are not to blame for a perpetrator's behaviour and that they are not alone. Explain that the practice can get help for the animal(s) if that's what they would like. And if they want a safe space to phone for personal help, then the practice can assist.

Document: Continue to document your conversation without allowing the scribing to become a barrier. If there are two veterinary staff members in the room, then one person can scribe while the other listens. Notes should be accurate, contemporaneous, factual and non-emotional. Photos are invaluable but ensure they are taken on a practice camera with a removable SD card. Ask permission for all that you do. Continue to show compassion despite being 'professional'.

Refer/Report: This does not need to be immediate. Your responsibility is to the animal(s), and you should ensure they are safe. If the client insists on taking the animal home (because of what will happen if she does not) then record in your notes that this was with your agreement / against your advice. A period of consultation with colleagues or welfare officers should follow and then the decision to seek external help, with or without releasing client details, can be made.

Animal abuse investigations: Forensic examination

"The diagnosis of non-accidental injury is not an exact science either in children or in the family dog or cat."

(Munro & Thrusfield, 2001)

Members of the veterinary team often feel they are not competent to handle cases of abuse, especially in species that they are unfamiliar with (e.g., wildlife), however, they have knowledge that makes their opinion vitally important when bringing animal abusers to account. This book should help vets understand how they can make an important contribution, even if abuse cases occur infrequently. One of the common misconceptions is that the vet must be one hundred percent certain that an animal has been a victim of abuse before reporting, however, all that is needed is to have a reasonable, objective belief (Merck, 2012) before passing the case to the authorities. Dr Merck says there are compelling reasons to report because a vet's intervention in an abuse case may disrupt a cycle of violence and prevent further harm to an animal or human.

Veterinary records

If the case is reported to the authorities - the police, animal welfare officers or finally the courts, everything that the vet does, writes, or says will be disclosed (Merck, 2012). Thus, the language used should be professional, and yet understandable (e.g., if acronyms or technical terms are used provide a key/ glossary to explain them).

Veterinary records may include written notes (handwritten or electronic), photographs, radiographs, laboratory tests and treatment records. It is important to get the owner's permission (if possible) for any photos or radiographs/scans. Do not use your own mobile phone to take photos; the phone will probably be removed as evidence, to your great inconvenience.

Vets in practice are the point of first opinion advice, usually dealing with a live animal, but sometimes cadavers are presented by the owner, or a third party, or a welfare officer. At this point, it is stressed that if there is any hint of abuse, or deliberate harm, then, *if possible,* the cadaver should be immediately passed on to a forensic pathologist. However, this will not always be possible in remote areas.

Before taking on the case, it is essential to follow the advice from experienced forensic veterinarians. It is outside the scope of this book to describe necropsy procedures in detail but extensive guidance may be found in Veterinary forensics: investigation, evidence collection and expert testimony (Rogers & Stern, 2018). Excellent, concise advice can be found in Animal Abuse and Unlawful Killing – Forensic Veterinary Pathology (Munro & Munro, 2008), a book that should sit on every practice bookshelf, especially if there is no access to a forensic pathologist. This list (adopted from Munro & Munro, 2008) will help:

- Ensure that you have all records of the case to hand: species, owner (if known), address/contact.
- Keep collars or identity discs, scan for microchips.
- Record what you are examining: cadaver, or individual specimens, or blood etc.
- Record how the specimen has been presented: e.g., in a blanket, with rope around the neck, presence of maggots etc.
- Give each specimen a unique reference number and label them clearly, using freezer-proof tape and an indelible pen.
- Maintain a chain of evidence: record all examinations with the definition of each specimen and how they have been received and examined and stored.
- Try to ensure you have suitable storage facilities: fridges, cold storage boxes or freezers.
- Avoid cross-contamination and store specimens separately; each bag/box clearly labelled.
- Establish a routine of labelling radiographs or photographs or videos, linking them to the case.
- Use diagrams to identify wounds or trauma, like the extent of burns or location of cigarette burns.
- At the end of the necropsy, restore the cadaver to a presentable state in case further examination is requested or the owner wishes to take it away.

Munro and Munro (2008) emphasise that '... *the better the notes taken at the time of the post-mortem examination, the better will be the report and any evidence given in Court months or years later.*'

Report writing

When you write a report, use ordinary language – your report is meant for lay people and they will appreciate simple terminology, like 'lower jawbone' rather than 'horizontal ramus of the mandible'. Since fractures may feature in these cases, instead of talking about 'comminuted' fractures explain the bone was broken into small pieces. Get someone to sense-check it when you have finished, to ensure you've said exactly what you mean. Sign it and date it. If you need to make changes or additions, delete nothing, but write more paragraphs, explain why you've added the addendum – again signed and dated.

Consider having a practice template with the following headings:

- Title: name of animal (if known), owner (if known) and reference number (if applicable)
- Index of contents
- Qualifications and experience: of all those involved in the case
- Description of circumstances: who presented the animal, full history and clinical signs
- Detailed history with dates
- Comments and conclusions
- Signature and date
- Appendices: abbreviations or glossary of terms
- Amendments

Limit your opinions to statements of fact, particularly when body weight is an issue (e.g., state that the animal was underweight (quoting the body weight range of the species)). Do not elaborate by commentating that, for example, 'it cannot have eaten for weeks', because you cannot know or prove this. You will almost certainly be asked if the animal (live or cadaver) was in pain or suffering. Do not speculate but use your professional opinion to state that, given the circumstances (that you find), it is your opinion that the animal would have experienced pain or suffering. A clear concise veterinary report will contribute much to help the welfare agencies and the courts to bring perpetrators to justice; this will be your contribution to a better world.

Role-play exercise: There's something about Cleo the cat (and her owner) that isn't right …

Here is a role-play exercise that helps put everything discussed in this chapter into practice. Have a go!

Background

You are a recent graduate. One hot Friday afternoon, a woman walks in without an appointment. The receptionist asks you to look at the case quickly since the cat seems to have a broken leg. You examine the 2-year-old cat, Cleo, and confirm that the femur is fractured. You ask the client how it happened, and she says she thinks it fell down the stairs. The lady seems subdued, and you are puzzled by the fact that she is still wearing her sunglasses inside the surgery. You note that Mr and Mrs Mason have another cat, Petra, who also came in with a fracture (of the humerus) one year before. The notes state that Mr Mason brought the cat in and was unpleasant and rude to the VN who carried out the initial examination. He could not say how the injury happened: "it's my wife's cat; can't stand the thing myself but she seems to like it". You try to get more information about Cleo from Mrs Mason but she's difficult to talk to and in fact, begins to give you conflicting information: her husband actually found the cat and he thinks it might have fallen off the garage roof; yes, it could have been hit by a car; yes, it's unfortunate that it's the second time that one of their cats has received an injury; no, she didn't know how that happened either. She loves her cats dearly...there's something about this lady that's not quite right.

Examination

The radiographs confirm a fractured femur and evidence of older fractures in several parts of Cleo's body: the ribs and toes. You are horrified by what you see and realise that Cleo has been injured on several occasions. Suddenly you realise that these injuries may have been deliberate; but by whom? Mrs Mason? Unlikely – she seems genuinely fond of her cats. Mr Mason? He 'found' the injured Cleo and last year he brought in his wife's other cat and stated that he didn't like it.

Considerations

Background

- a young cat with a fractured leg and an unclear history
- another cat presented with a fracture one year ago

This could be a case of non-accidental injury (NAI).

Examination

- radiographs confirm there are older fractures in several parts of Cleo's body: the ribs and toes
- suspicions of NAI are nearly confirmed
- has Mrs Mason also suffered domestic violence; perhaps the sunglasses are hiding bruises?

What happens now?

There is a high index of suspicion that this is a case of NAI. The young vet approaches the practice principal. There are two possible scenarios:

A   The practice principal

- listens sympathetically, examines the cat and looks at the x-rays
- agrees that this could be NAI and advises the young vet that he (as a senior experienced clinician) will take over the case
- shows the young vet the practice policy that relates to cases of suspected NAI, and the Guide to Professional Conduct
- the young vet writes up the consultation clearly and accurately

Conclusion: the practice principal refers the case to the SPCA and mentions the concerns for the well-being of Mrs Mason. The SPCA inspector is familiar with the local multi-agency cross-reporting and will contact the relevant agency.

B   The practice principal

- listens impatiently
- says that "it's nothing to do with us; just treat the cat and make sure that we get paid."

Conclusion: the practice principal refuses to discuss the matter further.

What happens next?

Your concerns should be taken to a more senior member of the practice, but this may not help. However, you are qualified to act independently. Discuss with your colleagues as you work through the scenario what you can/should do in the different circumstances, following the practice protocols. In the UK and Canada, there is an anonymous reporting mechanism through Crimestoppers.

The immediate concern is for Cleo, to assess if she is in shock, administer appropriate emergency therapy and get consent for anaesthesia and surgery. Remain calm and objective. Consider the situation carefully before coming to any conclusions. Be courteous and polite with the client. If the client is still in the surgery, reassure her that Cleo will be well looked after and ask if there is anything else she'd like to say or tell you? If nothing is forth-coming, there is little more to do beyond giving out the normal in-formation about when to phone etc. Your kindness and sympathy will not be forgotten, and the client may feel able to tell you more on her next visit. If the client discloses deliberate harm to Cleo, or to herself, follow the practice protocol.

Conclusion

In conclusion, everyone who works in a veterinary practice has a role to play when it comes to recognising non-accidental injury and reporting incidents of both animal abuse and domestic abuse. What has been outlined in this chapter are key tools such as The Links Group A R D R (Ask, Reassure, Document, Refer/Report) method that can assist with this recognition and reporting process. Using tools such as this is something that every veterinary practice should adopt as part of their standard protocols so that all of the team are equipped with the skills and knowledge they need to respond confidently to a suspected case of animal abuse and/or human abuse that enters through their practice doors.

Questions to consider

1 Considering the guidance outlined above do you feel more better equipped to deal with cases on animal abuse?
2 Does your practice have practice protocols for animal abuse and human abuse?
3 What advice would you give other pets about treating cases of animal abuse?

Key Messages

1 Diagnosis of abuse is challenging on an **intellectual** and **emotional** level and needs **time, experience** and **emotional energy.**
2 Often there is an **emotional block** in the mind of the clinician.
3 The most important step in diagnosing non-accidental injury is to think of it in the first place.
4 Follow the practice protocol; don't forget to breathe and slow the consultation down.
5 Remain objective, calm, polite and avoid confrontation.
6 Sometimes it is not possible to be sure what is going on – just remember your commitment is to the animal and it needs your care and attention.
7 Re-examine your initial concerns and discuss with colleagues/welfare agencies.
8 Communications vs confidentiality - explore the cost to you as a professional against the benefit to the animal (or vulnerable humans) if you report.
9 If possible, use a forensic pathologist to perform post-mortems.
10 Develop your contact networks: animal welfare officers, community police, social services and victim support.

References

Alleyne, E., Sienauskaite, O., & Ford, J. (2019). To report, or not to report, animal abuse: The role of perceived self-efficacy in veterinarians' decision-making. *Veterinary Record*, *185*(17), 538–538.

Alonso-Recarte, C. (2020). Pit bulls and dogfighting as symbols of masculinity in hip hop culture. *Men and Masculinities*, *23*(5), 852–871.

Animal Welfare Board of India (2022, February 2). *Ministry of Fisheries, Animal Husbandry and Dairying (Department of Animal Husbandry and Dairying)*. http://www.awbi.in/

Arkow, P. (2003). *Breaking the cycles of violence: A guide to multi-disciplinary interventions. A handbook for child protection, domestic violence and animal protection agencies.* Alameda, CA: Latham Foundation.

Arkow, P. (2013). The impact of companion animals on social capital and community violence: Setting research, policy and program agendas. *Journal of Sociology & Social Welfare*, *40*(4), 33–56.

Arkow, P. (2015). Recognizing and responding to cases of suspected animal cruelty, abuse, and neglect: What the veterinarian needs to know. *Veterinary Medicine: Research and Reports*, *6*, 349.

Australian Veterinary Association (2022, August 22). Australian Veterinary Association 2013. www.ava.com.au

CVMA (2022, August 22) *Canadian Veterinary Medical Association.* https://www.canadianveterinarians.net/

Dugnoille, J. (2018). To eat or not to eat companion dogs: Symbolic value of dog meat and human–dog companionship in contemporary South Korea. *Food, Culture & Society*, *21*(2), 214–232.

Femi-Ajao, O. (2021). Perception of women with lived experience of domestic violence and abuse on the involvement of the dental team in supporting adult patients with lived experience of domestic abuse in England: A pilot study. *International Journal of Environmental Research and Public Health*, *18*(4), 2024.

Harding, S. (2010). 'Status dogs' and gangs. *Safer Communities*, *9*(1), 30–35.

Hodgson, K., Darling, M., Freeman, D., & Monavvari, A. (2017). Asking about pets enhances patient communication and care: A pilot study. *INQUIRY: The Journal of Health Care Organization, Provision, and Financing*, *54*, 0046958017734030.

Merck, M. (Ed.). (2012). *Veterinary forensics: Animal cruelty investigations.* John Wiley & Sons.

Munro, H. M. C., & Thrusfield, M. V. (2001). Battered pets': non-accidental physical injuries found in dogs and cats. *Journal of Small Animal Practice*, *42*(6), 279–290.

Munro, H.M.C., & Munro, R. (2008). *Animal abuse and unlawful killing: Forensic veterinary pathology.* Elsevier Ltd.

Nelms, A. P., Gutmann, M. E., Solomon, E. S., DeWald, J. P., & Campbell, P. R. (2009). What victims of domestic violence need from the dental profession. *Journal of Dental Education*, *73*(4), 490–498.

Rogers, E., & Stern, A. W. (Eds.). (2017). *Veterinary forensics: Investigation, evidence collection, and expert testimony.* CRC Press.

Rogers, E.R., & Stern, A.W. (2018). *Veterinary forensics: Investigation, evidence collection and expert testimony.* Boca Raton, FL: CRC Press.

Poon, S. W. (2014). Dogs and British colonialism: The contested ban on eating dogs in colonial Hong Kong. *The Journal of Imperial and Commonwealth History*, *42*(2), 308–328.

Williams, J.M., Wauthier, L., Scottish SPCA, & Knoll, M. (2022). Veterinarians' experiences of treating cases of animal abuse: An online questionnaire study. *Vet Record Open*, e1975.

7 What parents and professionals working with children and young people can do about animal abuse

Joanne M. Williams

Clinical and Health Psychology, University of Edinburgh

Aims of this chapter

This chapter considers what parents and professionals working with children and young people can do to prevent and intervene in cases of animal abuse. We start in the home with a focus on parents and carers and what we can do in our everyday lives with children to promote positive behaviour towards animals and to prevent and intervene when incidents of animal abuse occur. The chapter then focuses on teachers and how in our teaching practice we can incorporate animal welfare and compassionate behaviour towards animals. Focusing on animals and animal welfare can be a vehicle to attain other learning objectives (e.g., literacy and numeracy). Teachers also have a role in supporting children's wellbeing and intervening in cases of animal abuse as this can be an indicator of other issues the child is facing. Social workers have a key role in supporting children's and families' welfare and often have a role in supporting families in crisis or experiencing domestic abuse. We outline why social workers should be concerned about animal abuse and things you can do in social work practice to support the children and animals involved. Finally, we turn attention to health and mental health professionals, and highlight the important roles that mental health professionals have in identifying and intervening in animal abuse.

The aims of the chapter are: 1) to highlight the importance of paying attention to childhood animal abuse, 2) to suggest ways you can incorporate animal abuse prevention into your practice and 3) to suggest approaches for intervening in cases of childhood animal abuse and highlight the benefits of inter-agency working.

DOI: 10.4324/9781003165552-7

Introduction

Those most closely working with or caring for children and young people are in an ideal position to intervene to promote positive behaviour towards animals among children and young people. However, from our experience, intervention opportunities are sometimes missed as animal abuse can be difficult to recognise and there are rarely guidelines for how we intervene. Moreover, animal abuse is often not recognised as being within the remit of professions working with children and young people. In this chapter we start with the adults closest to the child and then work through a range of professional groups (see Figure 7.1) who regularly have contact with children and young people and consider approaches to preventing and intervening in animal abuse in ways that support the animals and young people involved.

Parents and carers

As the majority of families with children in many Western contexts have pets (Marsa-Sambola, Williams, Muldoon and colleagues, 2016), parents and carers

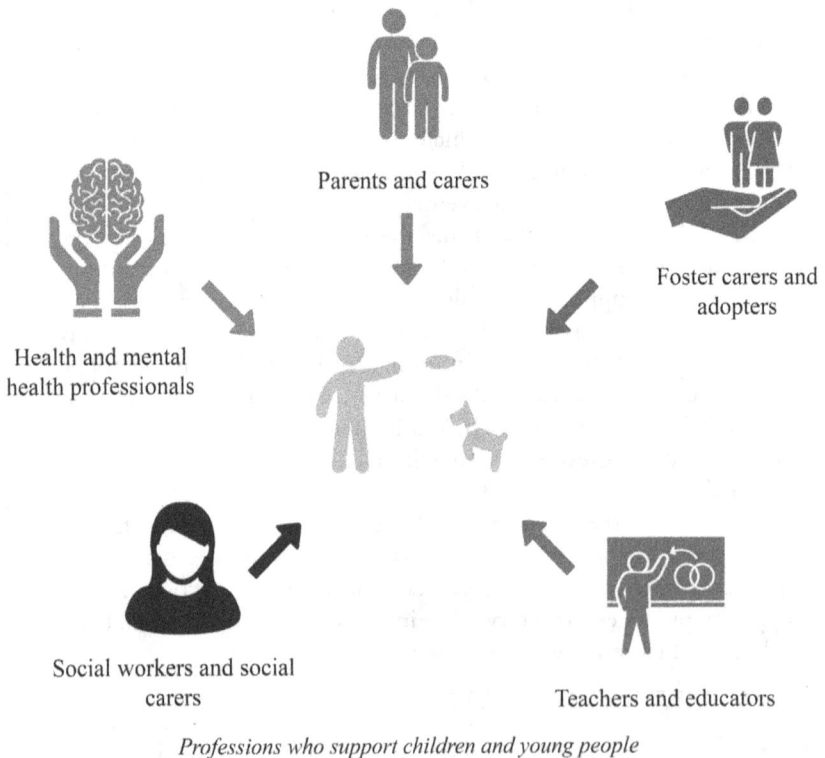

Parents and carers

Foster carers and adopters

Health and mental health professionals

Social workers and social carers

Teachers and educators

Professions who support children and young people

Figure 7.1 Professions who support children and young people.

have a legal responsibility to care for the health and welfare of the children and pets in their family (see Chapter 4). Aside from this legal obligation, parents and children see pets as part of their families, and pets can have an important effect on family functioning. For example, research has shown that a pet can be preferred as a source of comfort and support over siblings by some young people (Cassels and colleagues, 2017). Furthermore, adolescents who are strongly attached to a pet have greater wellbeing (Marsa-Sambola, Muldoon, Williams and colleagues, 2016) and better communication with parents and close friends (Marsa-Sambola and colleagues, 2017), with the pet forming a shared interest and safe topic of conversation. Children can be a key motivator for buying pets, and many children have active roles in pet care within the family (Muldoon and colleagues, 2015).

A key role for parents is modelling positive behaviour to animals, and scaffolding their children's interactions with pets to ensure that both the child and the pet are safe and interactions are positive. Careful monitoring and supervision will ensure that parents can guide their child's behaviour and explain why particular behaviours (e.g., waking a sleeping dog, approaching a growling dog) are not safe or may cause harm to the animal (e.g., falling on or dropping a pet during play). Parents can explain to a child how an animal might be feeling and help the child to interpret the pet's behaviour (e.g., cat hissing, dog growling or rabbit avoiding contact).

As dogs are the most common companion animal in most Western countries it is worth focusing on them a little to provide some examples of parental roles. Children are more at risk of being bitten by dogs than other age groups and often these incidents occur in the home (Jakeman and colleagues, 2020; Kaye and colleagues, 2009; Mathews & Lattal, 1994). These can be extremely traumatic and distressing for children, sometimes leading to the need for surgery, and sometimes having long-term psychological effects, including dog phobias (Boat and colleagues, 2012). In severe cases, it may lead to the pet dog being euthanised too (Schalke, 2017). When the potential outcomes of dangerous interactions between children and pets are so high, it is important to prevent them from happening. Intervention programmes to support children's behaviour with dogs and prevent dog bites highlight some simple steps to keeping children's interactions with dogs safe (Schwebel and colleagues, 2012; Meints & De Keuster, 2009). Parents can play an important role in spotting potentially dangerous situations (child removing dog food bowl from dog), and in guiding children's interactions to keep everyone safe (Náhlík and colleagues, 2022).

Supporting children's positive interactions with pets requires ongoing parental monitoring and support to encourage caring behaviour and manage any risks involved in interactions. Through this ongoing support, children will learn about which behaviours are appropriate and safe, and also why they are appropriate. In this way parents will support children in developing knowledge of animal welfare needs, how to recognise pets' emotions (cognitive empathy) and guide their behaviour (see Chapter 2). This will prevent un-intentional animal abuse in the home.

Parents sometimes see behaviours in their children that are concerning and require intervention. If a child is displaying harmful behaviour to a pet or other animals (e.g., wild animals such as birds or hedgehogs), it is important that this behaviour is addressed and discussed. As we have seen in Chapter 2 a range of factors can influence children's behaviour to animals and animal abuse can be an indicator of an issue the child needs some support with. In order to support a child, parents need to discuss the situation and listen to their child. Sometimes children find it very difficult to talk about abusive behaviour, so parents need to be patient and understanding. Firm boundaries also need to be put in place to guide a child's behaviour (e.g., permitted and unacceptable behaviour with pets).

In some cases, parents may need additional support in intervening if their child is engaging in animal abuse. Reaching out to professionals such as teachers or social workers who also have a role in the child's life can be really helpful. In some areas, animal welfare charities may be able to offer support too. In Scotland the Scottish SPCA offers Animal Guardians (see Chapter 8), an education programme, run mainly in schools, for children who are at high risk of harming, or who have already harmed an animal. As a parent or carer, you can refer your child to Animal Guardians. An example of a parent referral case is presented in Figure 7.2.

Foster care and adoption

Care-experienced children and young people often have histories of Adverse Childhood Experiences, complex trauma and challenging relationships with the people in their lives, with psychological impacts on their attachment relationships and mental health. They experience changes in homes

Referral 1	Case details	Intervention response
Parent Referral to Animal Guardians	A boy aged 7 was referred to the programme by his parents for rough handling the family dogs and cats.	Whilst participating in the programme it was discovered that he was able to display empathy towards animals.
	He had a diagnosis of ASD and was referred to the intervention programme to learn more about animal emotions and behaviour.	He had a great ability to learn new information about animal welfare needs and how to care for the family pets.
	An older sibling had previously completed Animal Guardians and had benefitted from the programme.	Feedback from school was excellent and both support staff and his class teacher said he really enjoyed the programme and greatly benefited from it.

Figure 7.2 Parental referral of a child to the Scottish SPCA's Animal Guardians programme.

and family contexts that have a huge impact on their mental health and wellbeing, with placement instability a key factor in mental health outcomes (Barth & Jonson-Reid, 2000; Jonson-Reid & Barth, 2000; McGuire and colleagues, 2018). A recent meta-analysis of 25 studies on the mental health outcomes of foster children who had experienced abuse and/or neglect found a prevalence rate of 40% for developmental difficulties, mental health problems and insecure attachment (Vasileva & Petermann, 2018). Care-experienced children and young people are among the most vulnerable in society yet their views on what is important to them and their wellbeing has so far rarely considered pets. There are two sides to this issue: 1) the importance and benefits of pets to vulnerable children; 2) the challenge of managing the risks of harm to animals and children.

Research with children on their mental health (Hicks and colleagues, 2011) and specifically with care experienced children, highlights pets as important for wellbeing (Wood & Selwyn, 2017). There is evidence that the emotional bond or attachment formed with pets can support children's emotional development especially among highly vulnerable children or where human relationships have been compromised (Cassels and colleagues, 2017; Hawkins and colleagues, 2017, see Chapter 2). However, surprisingly little research has been conducted on the role of pets for care-experienced children and young people, who may have a history of home and housing changes with consequent challenges for the human-animal bonds, pet ownership and pet care. Care-experienced children and young people may experience the loss of pets as they change home/housing contexts. They may have to leave pets behind, may become attached to pets in foster care and then experience the loss of the pet and further attachment disruptions, if the foster placement breaks down. This lived experience has not been fully captured in research and has resulted in a mixed pattern of evidence, where cared-for children are identified as at heightened risk of animal abuse due to their exposure to trauma and violence (Wauthier, Scottish SPCA & Williams, 2022) but also as strongly attached to pets, which may to some extent compensate for challenging human relationships (Carr & Rockett, 2017). Furthermore, homeless youth, who are disproportionately care experienced, report strong emotional attachments to pets and are willing to forgo sheltered accommodation precluding pets (Cleary and colleagues, 2020; Schmitz and colleagues, 2021). Pets may compensate for a lack of trust in human relationships, and even form a bridge to creating stronger human relationships, as capitalised upon in animal-assisted therapies.

It is really important that carers understand the important role pets can play for children who have experienced family trauma. The Scottish Care Inspectorate report, 'Animal Magic' (2022), advocates the inclusion of pets and animal care in all care establishments, including residential care facilities for children and young people, to enhance the quality of life and wellbeing of residents. Furthermore, many foster carers have pets and highlight the instances where a child's relationship with the pet has been a crucial factor in a positive foster placement experience. As outlined above it is really important that interactions between children and pets are monitored and scaffolded, and that the risks involved are carefully managed.

Teachers and educators

Teachers have a huge positive impact on children's lives in terms of their cognitive, social and emotional development, and a large percentage of children's waking hours are spent in schools (e.g., Bardach & Klassen, 2020). There are numerous ways in which teachers can bring animal abuse prevention into their classrooms without adding to pedagogical and administrative tasks, compounding excessive workloads and burnout that many teachers already face (Garcia-Carmona and colleagues, 2019; Yin and colleagues, 2019). Two simple things can make a big difference:

1 Firstly, you can demonstrate compassionate behaviour to animals in your own behaviour, and in managing classroom behaviour, consider encouraging children and young people to treat all living things with respect and compassion.
2 Secondly, consider how animal abuse and compassionate behaviour links to school curricula, and to your teaching specialism (i.e., in secondary school). While efforts are ongoing to bring animal welfare into school curriculums in the UK, there is still scope for teachers to bring it into their classrooms within their own teaching.

Teachers could, for example, use animal abuse prevention and compassion towards animals thematically across curriculum areas in primary school. Below are some examples of activities where the primary learning objectives are achieved while also promoting learning of animal welfare.

Literacy

Selecting age-appropriate books that touch on human treatment of animals by well-respected children's authors (e.g., Michael Morpurgo) and using comprehension tasks to focus on animal and human characters can support cognitive empathy development. Engaging children in creative writing about positive behaviour towards animals (Krueger & Krueger, 2014) can also achieve literacy goals while encouraging children to think about animals' welfare needs and emotions. Children's literature can be a way of engaging children in ecological thinking and encouraging them to take inter-species perspectives (Goga, 2018).

Numeracy

Numeracy tasks could be brought to life by calculating the costs of caring for pets or measuring the size of enclosures needed for different animals (e.g., rabbits,

Williams and colleagues, 2021). As maths anxiety can prevent children and young people from engaging in numeracy tasks (Petronzi and colleagues, 2019), focusing on animals' needs might be a way to build confidence in maths.

Science education

Knowledge of animal welfare needs and domains (Mellor and colleagues, 2020) has it's evidence-base rooted in animal welfare science and biological sciences, so there are plenty of opportunities in science education to focus on topics relevant to increasing children's understanding of animal welfare and appropriate interactions between people and animals. Applied sciences such as environmental science also provide opportunities for examining human impact on ecological systems and the consequences for animals: from litter harming wildlife; to species extinction due to habitat loss (e.g., Born, 2018).

Personal and social education

In personal and social education animals can be used to open conversations about difficult topics through analogy. Sometimes talking about the experiences of an animal provides a safe context for children and young people to discuss their own feelings and difficulties. Promoting compassion, for self and others, can be an important element of learning about self-care, and care for others could include animals. An emerging mental health issue for young people is eco-anxiety or eco-distress (Coffey and colleagues, 2021). This concerns psychological distress and anxiety about the climate crisis and associated ecological crises (e.g., species extinctions). We need to consider how we can provide pastoral support for young people experiencing this new form of anxiety and distress (Pihkala, 2022) and how we can build it into education (Pihkala, 2020). This will support young people experiencing psychological difficulties associated with eco-anxiety while promoting behaviours that support animals and the natural environment.

These teaching and learning activities are ones many school teachers routinely engage in, so the suggestion is to adapt teaching content and delivery rather than trying to squeeze in animal welfare and animal abuse prevention into the curriculum as a new separate topic. If you do not have the time to create new learning materials, you can use materials developed by animal welfare charities. Many animal welfare charities such as the Scottish SPCA, RSPCA, Blue Cross, Cats Protection, Dogs Trust offer education programmes with either school visits or curriculum-matched materials that be can used in that classrooms. For further information on animal welfare education programmes see Chapter 8.

In terms of intervention in cases of animal abuse, the key message is to assess and intervene rather than to ignore animal abuse when it comes to your attention in school. Intervention is important for the child who may be experiencing a range of psychological issues (Wauthier, Farnfield, Scottish SPCA

Referral 2	Case details	Intervention response
Teacher Referral to Animal Guardians	A young girl aged 8 was referred for rough and physical handling of the family dog and other animals. She had a diagnosis of ASD. Key learning objectives were around appropriate animal handling and boundaries in connection with interactions with animals.	Through the programme it was discovered that the girl showed empathy towards animals. She learned to recognise animal emotions and welfare needs and how to handle her dog and what it needed to be happy and healthy. She reacted positively to guidelines and boundaries about what she could and couldn't do with the family pet. From discussions with her family and feedback from school the girl enjoyed the programme and was able to talk about animal emotions and how to care for them correctly.She talked about wanting to work with animals in the future.

Figure 7.3 Deputy Head Teacher referral of a child to the Scottish SPCA's Animal Guardians programme.

& Williams, 2022) and also to prevent further animal abuse. Within school, educational psychologists, school counsellors, mental health leads or guidance staff might all have roles in supporting the young person and linking with the family and other professionals (social work) where appropriate.

In Scotland, teachers can also refer children to the Scottish SPCA Animal Guardians programme. Figure 7.3 is a case that relates to a child who was referred to Animal Guardians by a Deputy Head Teacher of a primary school. In referring the child to Animal Guardians, the teacher ensured that the child received the support they required in order to prevent future animal harm.

Animal-assisted learning in schools

A growing trend has been to engage animals in learning through bringing them into the school classroom. In addition to the intended learning outcomes for children, for example literacy (Hall and colleagues, 2016), animal-assisted learning offers opportunities for engaging children in learning about animal welfare and compassionate behaviour towards animals. Bringing animals into the classroom, especially dogs, has grown recently in the UK and USA, and the research has grown too (Kropp & Shupp, 2017; Brelsford and colleagues, 2017). However, practice has out-paced research evidence and there is currently a drive to provide practice guidelines to support this activity and maintain the welfare of the children and animals involved (Meints and colleagues, 2017). A recent survey of primary school teachers found that teachers were overwhelmingly positive about the impact dogs in the classroom had on children's reading and also their mental wellbeing (Steel and colleagues, 2021). Reviews of the evidence have shown that interventions involving reading to dogs have measurable positive impacts on reading and literacy (Hall and colleagues, 2016).

However, there have been concerns about the welfare of animals engaged in animal-assisted learning interventions in schools, which has led to the development of risk assessment tools for children and animals used in this type of learning intervention (Brelsford and colleagues, 2020). For example, it is important that dogs enjoy the experience, that they do not become over-tired, that they can remove themselves from interactions and that their welfare needs are met. These guidelines encourage everyone in the class, including children, to be aware of the dog's welfare, to be able to assess basic behavioural indicators of stress in the animal and to ensure the animal's welfare is as important as the benefits children may enjoy from interacting with the animal/s. Recently the authors have engaged in developing an online guide to support teachers in engaging animals in their classrooms: from non-intrusive approaches (such as encouraging wildlife into the school grounds and monitoring it); to bringing an animal into the classroom for specific learning activities. To ensure that animal welfare is safeguarded as well as learning objectives are achieved for children, we encourage teachers to become involved in co-designing animal-assisted interventions with others (including NGOs working in animal-assisted interventions), so that the learning activities fit safely within the classroom (Steel and colleagues, 2022).

Social workers and social care

There are many ways in which human-animal relations are of relevance to social work (Arkow, 2020). As we have reviewed in Chapter 3, animal abuse is linked to other forms of abuse, in particular: child abuse, domestic abuse and elder abuse. Social work has a key role to play in breaking cycles of abuse and supporting young people involved. Faver and Strand (2008) highlight that although historically social work has focused on human welfare there are five reasons why social workers should care about animal abuse:

1   Animals are part of the natural environment and part of people's families.
2   People are highly attached to their pets, pets provide comfort and non-judgemental support, and people grieve when they experience pet loss.
3   Animal abuse is linked to other forms of abuse.

4   Animal abuse has been part of social works' history and social work research has contributed much to our understanding of animal abuse.
5   Ignoring an animals' suffering diminishes a social worker's empathy and compassion for the human client.

There are a range of ways in which social workers can prevent and intervene in cases of animal abuse (see also Chapter 3).

1   Promote animal welfare education and compassionate treatment of animals with all families that are engaged with social work services.
2   Include questions about animals and animal abuse in assessment interviews to gauge if animal abuse is a feature of the challenges a child and their family are facing. This will also allow you to identify other potential issues (e.g., other forms of abuse; psychological difficulties).
3   Educate other professionals about 'The Link', so that they are aware of the importance of animal abuse in relation to other forms of abuse and childhood trauma.
4   Engage in inter-agency working with animal welfare charities, vets, psychologists and schools to support children and their families.

Inter-agency working can include sharing information about a case with other professionals involved and also working together to provide a range of support for children and young people. In some cases, supporting a child who has engaged in animal abuse might involve referring the child to specialist interventions offered by other organisations. The case outlined in Figure 7.4 is of a child who was referred to the (e.g. Scottish SPCA) Animal Guardians programme by a community worker.

Health and mental health professionals

Child health and mental health professionals also have a role in intervening in animal abuse. In relation to physical health, animal bite injuries might be an indicator of rough handling, and are most commonly experienced by children (e.g., Boat and colleagues, 2012; Jakeman and colleagues, 2020). Also, pets have been found to increase childhood asthma (Luo and colleagues, 2018) and pet allergies (Pyrhönen and colleagues, 2015) and guidance on animal handling might support the management of these conditions in families with pets. When an animal is implicated in a child's health condition, it raises opportunities for discussion about safe handling of pets. On a more positive note, positive interactions with animals and animal-assisted interventions can be extremely supportive for children who have physical health conditions or when they are undergoing medical procedures. For example, a range of studies has found that animal-assisted therapies can be helpful for children undergoing treatment for cancer (e.g., Silva & Osório, 2018; Cotoc and colleagues, 2019) and other health conditions and medical procedures.

Referral 3	Case details	Intervention response
Social/Community Worker Referral to Animal Guardians	A girl aged 7 was reported as being quite rough towards the family dogs and not understanding what was appropriate behaviour when interacting with them. There were concerns around both the welfare of the dog and possible harm to the child. The girl had a significant learning disability and communication challenges. Learning objectives focused around her boundaries when interacting with animals and understanding their emotions and needs.	Through the programme it was discovered that she would use negative behaviours towards the animals to attract a reaction from her family. By the end of the programme the girl had a good understanding of animal emotions and how her behaviour had an impact on them. From discussions with the family support worker the girl's behaviour around the family dogs had greatly improved and she was able to share the knowledge she had learned on the programme.

Figure 7.4 Community worker referral of a child to the Scottish SPCA's Animal Guardians programme.

The health professionals most likely to come across cases of childhood animal abuse are psychiatrics, clinical psychologists, mental health nurses and allied health professionals working in child and adolescent mental health services. Animal abuse is included as a diagnostic feature of Conduct Disorder in DSM-V (APA, 2013), so children and adolescents presenting with conduct problems will be asked about this explicitly as part of the process of diagnosis and treatment planning. However, Signal and colleagues (2013) highlight that childhood animal abuse may be overlooked by psychologists in cases where conduct disorder is not indicated. Thus, potential opportunities to intervene in animal abuse, or identify other emotional/behaviour problems or child abuse and trauma, are missed. Signal and colleagues (2013) also found that even where animal abuse was acknowledged as a significant indicator of conduct disorder, very few of the psychologists they surveyed indicated that it would be a primary area for intervention. So even where animal abuse is identified specialist intervention for animal abuse is not carried out.

Children who have experienced Adverse Childhood Experiences such as abuse or exposure to domestic violence may also have engaged in animal abuse (e.g., Wauthier and colleagues, 2022; see Chapter 3) but this may not be revealed during consultations or therapy, so opportunities to prevent further animal abuse may be missed. There is only one psychological therapeutic programme for childhood animal cruelty, the AniCare Child Approach (Shapiro and colleagues, 2013). This US psychological therapy is based on a conceptual framework where attachment is a foundation, building up to emotional intelligence (empathy), self-management skills (self-regulation) and considering the influence of family and sub-culture (see Chapter 2 for a full review of these factors). Although the therapy has not been evaluated, recent research on children at high risk of animal abuse has shown support for it's conceptual framework (Wauthier and colleagues, 2022). More information on AniCare Child can be found in Chapter 8.

A key message to mental health professionals is to take animal abuse seriously in clinical practice, especially where there are indicators of intentional animal abuse or animal abuse is severe or repeated (see Chapter 2). There are three main reasons why health care professionals should pay more attention to animal abuse in clinical practice:

1   Animal abuse is not only relevant to Conduct Disorder, but may be linked to other psychiatric conditions, personality disorders and trauma associated with abuse or witnessing abuse. If animal abuse is overlooked, or minimised in importance when disclosed, intervention opportunities are missed to support the child and prevent further animal abuse.
2   Animal abuse should also be a primary area for intervention and therapy. Considering animal abuse as an important mental health indicator should follow through into considering it to be an important element of therapy. As this is a gap in current provision internationally, it is imperative that psychological therapies for childhood animal abuse are developed and evaluated.
3   Animal abuse is a concern for all professionals working with children, so paying attention to it in clinical practice will enable multi-agency working to support the children and animals involved.

Conclusions

Animal abuse should be a concern for parents and all professionals working with children and young people. However, currently, only social workers would readily recognise it as within their professional remit. In this chapter we have made a case for why parents, teachers and educators, and health and mental health professionals should also see childhood animal abuse as within their roles. When a child or young person abuses an animal, especially if the pattern of abuse appears to be intentional and repeated or leads to significant harm and suffering, then intervention is necessary to prevent recurrence of abuse, and also to provide support to the child who may be experiencing psychological difficulties or trauma. Parents and teachers can do simple things to bring animal welfare into their care and work with children to promote positive behaviour to animals and reduce the risks of animal abuse. Social work and health professionals can ensure that animal abuse is identified and considered when children present with challenges, and that animal abuse is actively targeted in therapeutic interventions.

Key questions to consider

1 Do you think recognition of animal abuse as an indicator of other issues should be included as part of the formal training for professionals working with children and young people?
2 Having read this chapter has it made you think about specific children or young people that you have supported in the past? If so, was there a history of animal abuse and are you seeing connections with other behaviours/actions that they displayed?
3 Knowing what you know now, would you approach things differently if a child or young person has been reported to you as abusing an animal? This includes if you are the parent and they are your child. Do you know who you would seek support from?

Key Messages

1 Parents have a key role in modelling positive behaviour to animals, scaffolding positive and safe interactions between children and pets. Through their parenting they can enhance children's empathy to animals, understanding of animals' welfare needs and pet care. Parents can prevent animal abuse and also intervene when they see abuse incidents.
2 Teachers can incorporate animal welfare into many parts of the curriculum to prevent animal abuse and also have an important role in supporting children's mental health and wellbeing. If childhood animal abuse incidents are disclosed these may indicate other difficulties a child is facing and where education/wellbeing support is required.
3 Social work and community work is core to breaking the Link between different forms of abuse and preventing cycles of abuse. Promoting positive animal care in families, asking about animals and animal abuse in assessments, educating other professionals about the Link and inter-agency working are all key to tackling animal abuse in children and young people.
4 Health and mental health professionals may not see animal welfare as within their remit, however, as childhood animal abuse is connected with psychological issues and child abuse it is essential that opportunities to identify and intervene in childhood animal abuse are taken. There is a need for psychological interventions to consider childhood animal abuse and a need for new therapies to be developed and evaluated.
5 By working together, professionals can support children and adolescents, their families and the animals in their lives.

References

American Psychiatric Association. (2013). *Diagnostic and statistical manual of mental disorders* (5th ed.).Washington, DC: APA.

Arkow, P. (2020). Human–animal relationships and social work: Opportunities beyond the veterinary environment. *Child and Adolescent Social Work Journal, 37*(6), 573–588.

Bardach, L., & Klassen, R. M. (2020). Smart teachers, successful students? A systematic review of the literature on teachers' cognitive abilities and teacher effectiveness. *Educational Research Review, 30*, 100312.

Barth, R. P., & Jonson-Reid, M. (2000). Outcomes after child welfare services: Implications for the design of performance measures. *Children and Youth Services Review, 22*(9–10), 763–787.

Boat, B. W., Dixon, C. A., Pearl, E., et al. (2012). Pediatric dog bite victims: A need for a continuum of care. *Clinical Pediatrics, 51*, 473–477.

Born, P. (2018). Regarding animals: A perspective on the importance of animals in early childhood environmental education. *International Journal of Early Childhood Environmental Education, 5*(2), 46–57.

Brelsford, V. L., Meints, K., Gee, N. R., & Pfeffer, K. (2017). Animal-assisted interventions in the classroom—A systematic review. *International Journal of Environmental Research and Public Health, 14*(7), 669.

Brelsford, V. L., Dimolareva, M., Gee, N. R., & Meints, K. (2020). Best practice standards in animal-assisted interventions: How the LEAD risk assessment tool can help. *Animals, 10*(6), 974.

Care Inspectorate (2022, August 22). *Animal Magic: The benefits of being around and caring for animals across care settings.* https://hub.careinspectorate.com/media/1451/animal-magic.pdf

Carr, S., & Rockett, B. (2017). Fostering secure attachment: Experiences of animal companions in the foster home. *Attachment & Human Development, 19*(3), 259–277.

Cassels, M. T., White, N., Gee, N., & Hughes, C. (2017). One of the family? Measuring young adolescents' relationships with pets and siblings. *Journal of Applied Developmental Psychology, 49*, 12–20.

Cleary, M., Visentin, D., Thapa, D. K., West, S., Raeburn, T., & Kornhaber, R. (2020). The homeless and their animal companions: An integrative review. *Administration and Policy in Mental Health and Mental Health Services Research, 47*(1), 47–59.

Cotoc, C., An, R., & Klonoff-Cohen, H. (2019). Pediatric oncology and animal-assisted interventions: A systematic review. *Holistic Nursing Practice, 33*(2), 101–110.

Coffey, Y., Bhullar, N., Durkin, J., Islam, M. S., & Usher, K. (2021). Understanding eco-anxiety: A systematic scoping review of current literature and identified knowledge gaps. *The Journal of Climate Change and Health, 3*, 100047.

Faver, C. A., & Strand, E. B. (2008). Unleashing compassion: Social work and animal abuse. In F. R. Ascione, *The international handbook of animal abuse and cruelty: Theory, research, and application*, 175–199.

García-Carmona, M., Marín, M. D., & Aguayo, R. (2019). Burnout syndrome in secondary school teachers: A systematic review and meta-analysis. *Social Psychology of Education, 22*(1), 189–208.

Goga, N. (2018). Children's literature as an exercise in ecological thinking. In *Ecocritical Perspectives on Children's Texts and Cultures* (pp. 57–71). Cham: Palgrave Macmillan.

Hall, S. S., Gee, N. R., & Mills, D. S. (2016). Children reading to dogs: A systematic review of the literature. *PloS One, 11*(2), e0149759.

Hawkins, R. D., Williams, J. M., & Scottish Society for the Prevention of Cruelty to Animals (Scottish SPCA). (2017). Childhood attachment to pets: Associations between pet attachment, attitudes to animals, compassion, and humane behaviour. *International Journal of Environmental Research and Public Health, 14*(5), 490.

Hicks, S., Newton, J., Haynes, J., & Evans, J. (2011). *Measuring children's wellbeing.* London: ONS and BRASS, Cardiff University.

Jakeman, M., Oxley, J. A., Owczarczak-Garstecka, S. C., & Westgarth, C. (2020). Pet dog bites in children: Management and prevention. *BMJ Paediatrics Open, 4*(1).

Jonson-Reid, M., & Barth, R. P. (2000). From maltreatment report to juvenile incarceration: The role of child welfare services. *Child Abuse & Neglect, 24*(4), 505–520.

Kaye, A. E., Belz, J. M., & Kirschner, R. E. (2009). Pediatric dog bite injuries: a 5-year review of the experience at the Children's Hospital of Philadelphia. *Plastic and Reconstructive Surgery, 124*(2), 551–558.

Kropp, J. J., & Shupp, M. M. (2017). Review of the research: Are therapy dogs in classrooms beneficial? In *Forum on public policy online* (Vol. 2017, No. 2). Oxford Round Table. 406 West Florida Avenue, Urbana, IL 61801.

Krueger, D. W., & Krueger, L. N. (2014). Animals in children's stories. In S. Akhtar & V. D. Volkan, *Cultural Zoo: Animals in the human mind and it's sublimation* (pp. 127–143). Abingdon Oxon: Routledge.

Lovibond, S. H., & Lovibond, P. F. (1995). *Manual for the depression anxiety & stress scales.* (2nd ed.) Sydney: Psychology Foundation.

Luo, S., Sun, Y., Hou, J., Kong, X., Wang, P., Zhang, Q., & Sundell, J. (2018). Pet keeping in childhood and asthma and allergy among children in Tianjin area, China. *PloS One, 13*(5), e0197274.

McGuire, A., Cho, B., Huffhines, L., Gusler, S., Brown, S., & Jackson, Y. (2018). The relation between dimensions of maltreatment, placement instability, and mental health among youth in foster care. *Child Abuse & Neglect, 86*, 10–21.

Marsa-Sambola, F., Williams, J., Muldoon, J., Lawrence, A., Connor, M., Roberts, C., … & Currie, C. (2016). Sociodemographics of pet ownership among adolescents in Great Britain: Findings from the HBSC study in England, Scotland, and Wales. *Anthrozoös, 29*(4), 559–580.

Marsa Sambola, F., Muldoon, J., Williams, J., Lawrence, A., Connor, M., & Currie, C. (2016). The short attachment to pets scale (SAPS) for children and young people: Development, psychometric qualities and demographic and health associations. *Child Indicators Research, 9*(1), 111–131.

Marsa-Sambola, F., Williams, J., Muldoon, J., Lawrence, A., Connor, M., & Currie, C. (2017). Quality of life and adolescents' communication with their significant others (mother, father, and best friend): The mediating effect of attachment to pets. *Attachment & Human Development, 19*(3), 278–297.

Mathews, J. R., & Lattal, K. A. (1994). A behavioral analysis of dog bites to children. *Journal of Developmental and Behavioral Paediatrics, 15*(1), 44–52.

Meints, K., & De Keuster, T. (2009). Brief report: Don't kiss a sleeping dog: The first assessment of "the blue dog" bite prevention program. *Journal of Pediatric Psychology, 34*(10), 1084–1090.

Meints, K., Brelsford, V., Gee, N. R., & Fine, A. H. (2017). Animals in education settings: Safety for all. In N. R. Gee, A. H. Fine, & P. McCardle, *How Animals Help Students Learn: Research and Practice for Educators and Mental-Health Professionals* (pp. 12–26). New York: Routledge.

Mellor, D. J., Beausoleil, N. J., Littlewood, K. E., McLean, A. N., McGreevy, P. D., Jones, B., & Wilkins, C. (2020). The 2020 five domains model: Including human–animal interactions in assessments of animal welfare. *Animals, 10*(10), 1870.

Muldoon, J. C., Williams, J. M., & Lawrence, A. (2015). 'Mum cleaned it and I just played with it': Children's perceptions of their roles and responsibilities in the care of family pets. *Childhood, 22*(2), 201–216.

Náhlík, J., Eretová, P., Chaloupková, H., Vostrá-Vydrová, H., Fiala Šebková, N., & Trávníček, J. (2022). How parents perceive the potential risk of a child-dog interaction. *International Journal of Environmental Research and Public Health, 19*(1), 564.

Petronzi, D., Staples, P., Sheffield, D., & Hunt, T. (2019). Acquisition, development and maintenance of maths anxiety in young children. In I. C. Mammarella, *Mathematics Anxiety: What is Known and What is still to be Understood* (pp. 77–102). Abbingdon Oxon: Routledge.

Pihkala, P. (2020). Eco-anxiety and environmental education. *Sustainability, 12*(23), 10149.

Pihkala, P. (2022). Eco-anxiety and pastoral care: Theoretical considerations and practical suggestions. *Religions, 13*(3), 192.

Pyrhönen, K., Näyhä, S., & Läärä, E. (2015). Dog and cat exposure and respective pet allergy in early childhood. *Pediatric Allergy and Immunology, 26*(3), 247–255.

Schalke E. (2017). Best advice to a dog owner whose dog has bitten someone. In D. S. Mills & C. Westgarth (Eds.), *Dog bites: A multidisciplinary perspective* (pp. 343–349). Sheffield, U.K.: 5m Publishing.

Schmitz, R. M., Carlisle, Z. T., & Tabler, J. (2021). "Companion, friend, four-legged fluff ball": The power of pets in the lives of LGBTQ+ young people experiencing homelessness. *Sexualities*, 1363460720986908.

Schwebel, D. C., Morrongiello, B. A., Davis, A. L., Stewart, J., & Bell, M. (2012). The Blue Dog: Evaluation of an interactive software program to teach young children how to interact safely with dogs. *Journal of Pediatric Psychology, 37*(3), 272–281.

Shapiro, K., Randour, M. L., Krinsk, S., & Wolf, J. L. (2013). *The assessment and treatment of children who abuse animals: The AniCare child approach.* Springer Science & Business Media.

Signal, T., Ghea, V., Taylor, N., & Acutt, D. (2013). When do psychologists pay attention to children harming animals. *Human-Animal Interaction Bulletin, 1*(2), 82–97.

Silva, N. B., & Osório, F. L. (2018). Impact of an animal-assisted therapy programme on physiological and psychosocial variables of paediatric oncology patients. *PLoS One, 13*(4), e0194731.

Steel, J., Williams, J. M., & McGeown, S. (2021). Reading to dogs in schools: an exploratory study of teacher perspectives. *Educational Research, 63*, 279–301. 10.1080/00131881.2021.1956989.

Steel, J., Williams, J. M., & McGeown, S. (2022). Teacher-researcher collaboration in animal-assisted education: Co-designing a reading to dogs intervention. *Educational Research, 64*, 113–131. 10.1080/00131881.2021.2016061

Vasileva, M., & Petermann, F. (2018). Attachment, development, and mental health in abused and neglected preschool children in foster care: A meta-analysis. *Trauma, Violence, & Abuse, 19*(4), 443–458.

Wauthier, L., Scottish SPCA, & Williams, J. M. (2022). A qualitative study of children's accounts of cruelty to animals: Uncovering the roles of trauma, exposure to violence, and attachment. *Journal of Interpersonal Violence, 37*(9–10), NP6405–NP6438.

Wauthier, L., Farnfield, S., Scottish SPCA, & Williams, J. M. (2022). A Preliminary Exploration of the Psychological Risk Factors for Childhood Animal Cruelty: The Roles of Attachment, Self-Regulation, and Empathy. *Anthrozoos*, 1–23.

Williams, J. M., Cardoso, M. P., Zumaglini, S., Finney, A. L., & Knoll, M. A. (2021). "Rabbit Rescuers": A school-based animal welfare education intervention for young children. *Anthrozoös*, *35*, 55–73. 10.1080/08927936.2021.1944561

Wood, M., & Selwyn, J. (2017). Looked after children and young people's views on what matters to their subjective well-being. *Adoption & Fostering*, *41*(1), 20–34.

Yin, H., Huang, S., & Chen, G. (2019). The relationships between teachers' emotional labor and their burnout and satisfaction: A meta-analytic review. *Educational Research Review*, *28*, 100283.

8 Interventions for intentional and unintentional abuse towards animals

Gilly Mendes Ferreira
Scottish SPCA

Aims of this chapter

When animal abuse occurs it creates anger, hurt and often disbelief that such an incident has happened. Many animals recover but sadly some do not. These incidents understandably have a significant impact on the person who committed the act or indeed someone who witnessed that act when it happened. There are many reasons why someone may abuse an animal as highlighted in previous chapters and the importance of distinguishing between intentional and unintentional animal abuse is explored further in this chapter. Various intervention tools have been created to support those who have been involved in an animal abuse incident. They often focus on that person's empathetic and compassionate behaviours. When developing any type of intervention, evaluation is key to ensure that the desired impact is being achieved. This chapter highlights a number of programmes that are being utilised, particularly with children and the associated referral pathways that anyone working with young people should be aware of. It also highlights the gaps, including provision of non-custodial interventions for adults convicted of animal offences. The chapter also provides recommendations on how to prevent abuse from occurring in the first place and ultimately break that cycle between animal abuse and human abuse.

What is the difference between unintentional and intentional abuse?

People's relationships with animals can involve both positive and negative interactions. This is true regardless of whether you are a child or an adult (see also Chapter 2). As seen in Chapter 1 the Scottish SPCA's Animal WISE® footprint framework shows that in order to promote positive human-animal interactions and protect that human-animal bond you need

DOI: 10.4324/9781003165552-8

to tackle the negative environmental and societal influencing factors throughout a child or animal's development. Human-animal interactions, particularly when involving a child, may be influenced by that child's belief in animal minds if they are sentient and whether they believe animals experience thoughts and feelings as well as their knowledge of welfare needs (e.g., Hawkins & Williams, 2016).

Within this chapter both intentional and unintentional animal abuse is referred to. Many definitions exist for intentional and unintentional animal abuse. The Scottish SPCA views intentional abuse as actions by someone towards an animal where there is the motivation and intent to physically and/or emotionally harm that animal. It could be that the act is premediated, it is planned and there will be awareness of the outcomes for the animal involved. Unintentional abuse, however, is often as a result of a lack of knowledge and understanding of animal welfare needs and can include unintentional neglect of an animal (depriving it of basic needs such as food, water – the five domains). Unintentional abuse can often be addressed through participation in animal welfare education programmes whereas intentional abuse needs more targeted intervention and would involve a mix of educational and psychological/psychotherapy techniques.

Many interventions have been created over the years to address both intentional and unintentional abuse towards animals although many have not been evaluated in detail and do not measure the direct impact on participants particularly longitudinally. This chapter highlights various examples of intervention programmes and provides recommendations for potential pathways for those who have committed acts of animal abuse either intentionally or unintentionally.

Reasons for intentional or unintentional abuse towards animals

As already covered in detail in previous chapters there are many reasons why someone abuses an animal. This could be due to:

- Lack of knowledge
- Attachment issues
- Lack of empathy/compassion
- Inability to recognise and regulate emotions
- Inability to regulate behaviour
- Trauma – linked to Adverse Childhood Experiences (ACEs) such as abuse (physical, sexual, verbal), neglect (emotional and/or physical) or growing up in a household where there are a variety of issues (adults with poor mental health, domestic violence, alcohol issues, drug issues, divorce, separation, adult has been incarcerated [in prison]).

Examples of intentional and unintentional abuse towards animals

Figure 8.1 provides some examples of both intentional and unintentional animal abuse. It is important to note that these scenarios have been changed to preserve anonymity but the core themes remain. Often when referrals are made to an intervention programme you are not provided with much background information. When looking at the scenarios detailed in figure 8.1 below do you think they have been categorised correctly? Are there any you feel that have been listed as unintentional but should in fact be in the intentional abuse column or vice versa? Does the additional information column which has details that were provided following when that scenario first occurred change your view on how that scenario has been categorised?

Scenario	Intentional abuse (IA)	Unintentional abuse (UA)	Intervention response
1. A woman has a severely overweight black Labrador dog called Bruce who has been living with her for the past 8 years. Bruce is not being excercised and is allowed to eat anything he likes.	NO	YES	The woman became a widow two years ago. Bruce was usually walked by her husband. Bruce is now her only companion and is the only one that gives her the incentive to get up each day.
2. A man often likes to engage in badger baiting, that is the process of setting a dog on a badger and placing bets (and often filming) who will win the fight between the two animals. The man often takes his teenage son with him and his friends when pursuing this type of activity.	YES	NO	The man has been involved in badger baiting for many years. He has seen generations in his family take part in this 'recreational activity' and is keen his son grows up to be just like him.
3. A couple live in a two-bedroom flat with a number of cats. They are not sure how many cats they have but love them dearly. The cats do not go outside, they are provided with food and water but do not have access to litter trays.	NO	YES	When visiting the house inspectors struggled to walk between the rooms due to the amount of possessions the couple had which included a historical collection of newspapers and magazines. The couple were known to the local authority as struggling with hoarding disorder.

Figure 8.1 Examples of intentional and unintentional animal abuse.

The scenarios in Figure 8.1 highlight the complexities around human-animal relationships, and how it is easy to potentially make the wrong judgement prior to knowing all the facts. What would you do if faced with these situations? Not sure? This chapter encourages anyone who spots a case of animal abuse whether intentional or unintentional to take the Scottish SPCA's ANIMAL approach to that situation as highlighted in Chapter 1.

When animal abuse has been detected what do you do?

As a reminder when animal abuse has been detected, you could take the Scottish SPCA's **ANIMAL** approach to the situation.

Assess – What is the situation, is the person vulnerable, are they in immediate danger? Where is the animal concerned?

Need – What does the person need? What does the animal need?

Insight – What information do you have that will help you make a decision – is the person a minor? Do you know if other agencies are already involved?

Make a decision – Make a decision on what you are going to do, do you take action? Do you wait and monitor the situation? Do you wait but seek further advice? If so who from?

Action – Put the Safeguarding four R's into Action – Recognise, Respond, Refer, Record (NSPCC, 2021). The Respond and Refer part may be reporting it to an SPCA or police or referring individuals/groups to engage with a general animal welfare education programme or indeed a targeted intervention programme.

Listen and Learn – What is the impact of your decision? What have you learnt from the experience? Would you do anything differently next time?

By applying the Scottish SPCA's **ANIMAL** approach to the scenarios in Figure 8.1 has that changed your perception of those scenarios? What about some more challenging situations which you may see in the line of your work?

Animal Welfare Education for unintentional abuse

Interventions that tackle unintentional abuse towards animals often focus around increasing animal welfare knowledge and often feature as part of formal education. In the UK, animal welfare education is seen as an optional element to the curriculum (Muldoon & Williams, 2021) although there are many calls to make it mandatory. It is known that participating in animal welfare education can indeed have a significant impact on animal welfare knowledge and the belief in animal minds (that animals have feelings) whilst also influencing attachment to pets and attitudes towards animal cruelty (Hawkins and colleagues, 2017a). Attachment to pets does have an important role in children's social, emotional and cognitive development, mental health, well-being and quality of life and can significantly predict positive attitudes towards animals (Hawkins and colleagues, 2017b). Exposing young people to positive interactions with animals, rewarding positive behaviours towards animals and correcting negative behaviours in a calm and encouraging manner can have a significant effect on how that person interacts with an animal as they develop into adulthood.

The methods used to teach animal welfare education have expanded over the years, can differ between countries and can vary from using videos and board games (Hawkins and colleagues, 2017a), to computer games (Hawkins and colleagues, 2019a; Hawkins and colleagues, 2019b), to being part of vocational courses such as veterinary education (Main, 2010; Rayner and colleagues, 2020) or as part of training for those working with animals (for example those working in the food production chain) (Gallo and colleagues, 2010). More recently animal welfare educational programmes have evolved to use tools such as mechanical animals (Williams, and colleagues, 2022) and also real animals as part of animal-assisted interventions (Olmert, 2021; Scandurra and colleagues, 2021; Ngai and colleagues, 2021). Dogs in particular are being used not as part of traditional animal welfare education but more as a tool to support people, in particular children with tasks such as reading and general support for wellbeing (Uccheddu and colleagues, 2019; Lenihan and colleagues, 2016; Henderson and colleagues, 2020; Steel and colleagues, 2021).

The Scottish SPCA has been delivering animal welfare education for a number of years and it's current Animal WISE® initiative has four key principles:

- **WATCH** interactions between humans, animals and their shared environment making sure everyone is kept safe and through research learn more on what positive interactions are and mean.
- **INFORM** people that animals matter, be a key influencer when it matters and instil the belief that animals experience emotions and they deserve to be shown compassion and empathy.
- **SUPPORT** those who need it, particularly those who suffer from mental health, poverty, isolation and loneliness, and use our expertise when it comes to tackling the link between animal cruelty and violent crime.
- **ENCOURAGE** people to report concerns to the Scottish SPCA's animal helpline, test their knowledge and test ours.

The Scottish SPCA's targeted educational programmes aim to tackle both unintentional and intentional abuse towards animal's and centre around three core themes: emotions, needs and responsibilities.

a   Theme 1 – Animals (and us) are sentient and can experience emotions.
b   Theme 2 – Animals (and us) have needs that need to be met in order to survive which includes experiencing positive emotions (which links to the recognised model called the 'Five Domains') (Mellor and colleagues, 2020).
c   Theme 3 – We have a responsibility to safeguard the welfare of animals we encounter regardless of species (which links to our actions, the environment we share and one welfare).

People need to be able to recognise both human and animal emotions, that both have needs and that we as a society have a responsibility to the animals we encounter in our environment. Activities are often game based, will include video footage, includes the use of robotics and encourages scenario-based decision-making tasks.

The Scottish SPCA has seen an increase in interactions between humans and animals since Covid-19 not just in relation to companion animals such as dogs and cats but also wildlife (Scottish SPCA, 2021). This is echoed by the fact that as a result of the Covid-19 pandemic and restrictions being linked to an increase in mental health conditions, a considerable body of evidence shows that spending time in and engaging with nature can improve human health and wellbeing (Robinson and colleagues, 2021). Vimal (2022) found that the impact of the lockdown in France was stronger on people's relationship with their pets, farm animals, home plants and with birds than with other plants and animals. Therefore, animal welfare education should not only focus on companion animals (e.g., dogs and cats) but should also include farm and wildlife taking into account geographical and cultural differences.

As seen in previous chapters, humans can affect the welfare of animals both positively and negatively and these interactions not only relate to companion animals but also in relation to farm animals and wildlife. Humans often have a hierarchical view of animals that they look to engage with. A recent study by Wilks and colleagues (2021) revealed that children had a weaker tendency than adults to prioritise humans over animals. They often chose to save multiple dogs over one human and many valued the life of the dog as much as the life of a human. Interestingly although children in this study valued pigs less, the majority still prioritised 10 pigs over one human. By contrast, Wilks and colleagues (2021) found that almost all adults chose to save one human over even 100 dogs or pigs. They concluded that the common view that humans are far more morally important than animals develops late in adulthood, and is likely socially acquired. This should be taken into account when considering developing or modifying animal welfare education programmes that were originally created for children and utilising these with an adult audience. This should also be considered when choosing the type of educational programme you are looking to engage with.

Key decisions to make when considering participating in animal welfare education are as follows:

- Why do you or the people you work with want to participate in animal welfare education? Is it in response to an animal abuse incident? Is it to encourage empathetic and compassionate behaviours? Is it to support general health and wellbeing? Is it a way to connect with other STEM (Science, technology, Engineering and Mathematics) related activities?
- Are you looking at running a programme yourself or inviting an external organisation to deliver a session?
- Do you want participation to be in person or via virtual means?
- Do you want participation to involve physical interactions with animals?

Importantly if the reason why you are considering engaging in animal welfare education is part of a response to an incident that has occurred involving an animal, you need to consider whether that incident was intentional and whether a more targeted intervention is required. Sometimes both approaches are taken where maybe a class or group takes part in a broad general animal welfare education programme (particularly if some have witnessed or heard about a specific incident) and individuals involved in the incident itself, in addition, take part in a targeted intervention. Already in this chapter and also in Chapter 9 methods have been highlighted on how to identify if an act has been intentional or not, how to conduct an assessment around that act and examples of animal welfare educational tools commonly used for unintentional acts of animal abuse. What about interventions for intentional acts of animal abuse?

Examples of interventions for intentional abuse towards animals

The Scottish SPCA's Animal Guardians programme was launched in Scotland in 2018. To date, it has received over 270 referrals and has supported young people aged 3 years old and upwards. A young person would usually take part in weekly one-to-one sessions, running from 15 minutes to 1 hour, over a 8–10 week period. The programme encourages a young person to first take part in game-based learning activities that help them recognise both human and animal emotions. They then go on to complete tasks that help them identify the welfare needs of a variety of species, and they are asked to apply the knowledge gained on emotions and needs to a variety of situations that they may face. This last section encourages participants to take responsibility and make the right decision when faced with different situations. What has been identified through the research conducted by the University of Edinburgh is that negative incidents involving animals can occur due to that young person having trouble regulating their emotions and behaviours (Wauthier and colleagues, 2022). Therefore, at the time of writing the responsibility section of the programme is being revised to support the research findings keeping in mind that Animal Guardians is an 'educational' programme and not a psychological therapy intervention. The programme is also being expanded so that a service can be offered to those who are attending secondary schools and therefore increasing the age-range that Animal Guardians supports from 3 years old to 16 years old.

Figure 8.2 are just some examples of cases that have been referred to the Scottish SPCA's Animal Guardians programme. Again, details in these cases have been changed to preserve anonymity but the core themes remain.

Try and apply the Scottish SPCA's **ANIMAL** approach to some of the cases in Figure 8.2.

	Case details	Intervention response
Case 1	A young boy aged 4 was reported to have harmed two kittens resulting in their death. The referral came from a social worker. The two kittens were killed on two separate occasions and there were immediate concerns around the safety of the other kittens in the house, which in turn were removed to a safe location. The boy had no diagnosis but social work, CAMHS and health visitors were working with the family. He did have multiple ACEs including parental separation and domestic violance and on-going trauma within the family environment.	The boy was referred to an intervention programme where attention was particularly focused around empathy, animal emotions and his behaviour around all animals. Through the programme it was discovered that the boy was very interested in animals and how to look after them. By the end of the programme the boy had a good understanding of the emotions animals feel and the right way to behave around them. From discussions with the social worker and family the boy's behaviour around animals improved and he could talk about animals having feelings.
Case 2	A girl aged 11 was reported as hurting the family dog when angry. The referral came from a children's charity worker, the dog involved was quite small and although the young person loved the dog there were concerns for it's welfare when she was in a heightened state. The girl had suffered trauma in her life, had severe attachment challenges and was working with social work, CAMHS and a national children's charity. She was referred to an intervention programme where attention was particularly focused around animal's feelings and the impact of her behaviour when around animals.	Through the programme it was discovered that the young girl had a great love and knowledge of animals, especially her dog, and wanted to work with animals in the future. By the end of the programme the girl had a good understanding of how to behave around her dog and the positive and negative behaviours that would have an impact on how the dog felt when with her. From discussions with her parent the programme had taught her about responsibilities with regard to her pets, how to understand them more and in turn how to have a healthy relationship with them.
Case 3	A young boy aged 8 was reported as being aggressive towards animals. The referral came from a CAMHS nurse. The boy was assessed for ADHD and had three ACEs which included parental separation and domestic violence. The boy was referred to an intervention programme where attention was particularly focused around animal emotions and the importance of giving animals the space they need when they need it and avoid disturbing them when they don't want to be disturbed (such as the when his cat was sleeping).	Through the programme it was discovered that he had attachment challanges and had quite low self-esteem. He felt that it was him and his cat against mum and her cat and described himself as being evil if talking about any negative incident involving his cat. The boy clearly loved animals as any time spent speaking about animals getting hurt, or being hurt by someone he would heavily defend the animal and said he would want to attack the human doing it. By the end of the programme the boy had a good understanding of how to recognise an animal's emotions in particular with regards to cats and know what to do when faced with different challanges in particular at home where a decision needs to be made with regards to the animal's welfare. From discussions with the class teacher and parent the boy's behaviour with the cat improved and he chose to do less 'challenges' between his and his mum's cat. He was able to quote a lot of knowledge on what he had learnt regarding other species of animals too.

Figure 8.2 Example cases referred to the Scottish SPCA's Animal Guardians Programme.

- What information would you seek to gain that insight required to make the right decision on what you would do?
- Think about some of the experiences you have had in your role particularly if they have involved a relationship between a young person and an animal. How did you deal with that situation at the time?
- Given what has been highlighted in this chapter and indeed other chapters in this book, is there anything that you would do differently if faced with the same situation again?

An example of a psychological intervention programme that supports children who abuse animals is AniCare, offered in some parts of the USA. Attachment theory forms the basis of the AniCare approach and this theory is applied to both the assessment and treatment stages of the programme (Shapiro and colleagues, 2014). The assessment stage includes asking the child about their relationships with animals and possible motivations if they are the perpetrators (not witnesses) of animal abuse. When it comes to treatment Shapiro and colleagues (2014) AniCare Approach uses a variety of methods once that connection has been made between the client (the child) and the therapist. Methods used could include Animal Assisted Therapy (AAT) providing safeguards are in place to ensure contact with animals is highly supervised. Therapists may also use puppet role-play activities, and emotion-based exercises that explore feelings, and finally they will encourage discussions around a variety of events using drawings of scenes that involve children, companion animals and sometimes an adult. Ultimately the therapist will directly address the client's behaviour towards animals in an explicit and direct way. Shapiro and Henderson (2016) have also published an AniCare Approach for Adults, which follows a similar treatment pathway but focuses much more on accountability and the development of empathy.

Importance of measuring impact

It is important that any educational or targeted animal abuse prevention intervention programmes delivered to either young people or adults are properly evaluated so that impact can be assessed at both individual and group levels and improvements made accordingly. A variety of measures have been developed to support these evaluation toolkits as already highlighted in Chapter 2. Indeed, evaluation pre- and post-intervention questionnaires have now been built into the process of the Scottish SPCA's Animal Guardians programme to help the organisations Youth Engagement Officers to properly support young people going through the programme and assess what has been learnt and the impact of the activities that have taken place.

Muldoon and Williams (2021a) have identified that many animal welfare organisations do indeed deliver education programmes for children and young people, or design materials for school teachers to use but few of these are scientifically evaluated. This makes it difficult to track impact. Muldoon and

Williams (2021b) conducted a Delphi study and as a result created a toolkit that will enable practitioners to follow evidence-based guidance and allow organisations to assess the effectiveness of the interventions for children and young people. This toolkit is provided in Chapter 9 of this book.

Conclusions

In the USA those adults that have been convicted of animal abuse crimes may be required to attend an intervention programme such as AniCare as part of their court mandate. In the UK and in particular in Scotland it has been stated that there are a number of barriers which would hinder using restorative justice and empathy-based approaches for animal-related crimes. These include who would speak for the animal, who would be involved in the approach and identifying when to use such interventions depending on the nature of the offence (Scottish Government, 2022).

In most cases participation in intervention programmes for those (child or adult) who have been involved in either intentional or unintentional abuse towards animals is very much on voluntary terms. It's important that anyone who is in a role that supports a young person or adult knows what services are available in their area that can help safeguard the welfare of both humans and animals.

There is also a lack of longitudinal studies where the impact of participating in an animal welfare intervention programme is measured over a long period of time particularly if that intervention has taken place during the early developmental years of a young person's life. There is a growing call for animal welfare education to be included in the curriculum in the UK with 84% of the population supporting this call (RSPCA & Scottish SPCA, 2022). Engaging in animal welfare education at an early age can help nurture those relationships between young people and animals. Participation in such programmes can act as an early indicator that a young person may need support from others therefore becomes a preventative tool for challenges later on in that person's life and potentially breaking that cycle between animal harm and human harm.

Key questions to consider

1 Do you think animal welfare should be included as a mandatory component of core curriculums across the world?
2 Should anyone convicted of abusing animals be court mandated to attend a suitable animal abuse intervention programme?
3 Are you confident you know who you would seek advice from if a child or young person you were supporting showed behaviours towards animals that were concerning?

Key Messages

- **Spot the early warning signs**, are there behaviours between a person (in particular a young person) and an animal that are a cause of concern? Are they quite rough with animals? If an animal is hurt, do they show compassion? If they have hurt an animal, do they show remorse?
- **Seek advice** – know who your local network of support would be. Would it be police, local animal welfare organisation that offer animal welfare education programmes, local CAMHS (Child and Adolescent Mental Health Services) team, School Educational Psychologist or a play therapist?
- **Always ensure the welfare of any animal involved**. This may be limiting contact with that animal and seeking support from a local SPCA.
- **Try applying** the Scottish SPCA's ANIMAL approach to a situation.
- **Remember the importance of the Safeguarding four Rs** – Recognise, Respond, Refer and Report.
- If the reason why you are considering engaging in animal welfare education is part of a response to an incident that has occurred involving an animal, you need to consider whether that incident was intentional or not and whether a more targeted intervention is required.

References

Gallo, C., Tadich, N., Huertas, S., César, D., Da Costa, M. P., & Broom, D. M. (2010, October). Animal welfare education in Latin América. In *Proceedings of the International Conference on Animal Welfare Education: Everyone Is Responsible*, Brussels, Belgium (pp. 1–2).

Hawkins, R. D., & Williams, J. M. (2016). Children's beliefs about animal minds (Child-BAM): Associations with positive and negative child–animal interactions. *Anthrozoös*, *29*(3), 503–519.

Hawkins, R. D., Williams, J. M., & Scottish Society for the Prevention of Cruelty to Animals. (2017a). Assessing effectiveness of a nonhuman animal welfare education program for primary school children. *Journal of Applied Animal Welfare Science*, *20*(3), 240–256.

Hawkins, R. D., Williams, J. M., & Scottish Society for the Prevention of Cruelty to Animals (Scottish SPCA). (2017b). Childhood attachment to pets: Associations between pet attachment, attitudes to animals, compassion, and humane behaviour. *International Journal of Environmental Research and Public Health*, *14*(5), 490.

Hawkins, R. D., Ferreira, G. A. M., & Williams, J. M. (2019a). The development and evaluation of 'Farm Animal Welfare': An educational computer game for children. *Animals*, *9*(3), 91.

Hawkins, R., & Williams, J. (2019b). The development and pilot evaluation of a 'serious game' to promote positive child-animal interactions. *Human-Animal Interaction Bulletin, 8*(2), 68–92.

Henderson, L., Grové, C., Lee, F., Trainer, L., Schena, H., & Prentice, M. (2020). An evaluation of a dog-assisted reading program to support student wellbeing in primary school. *Children and Youth Services Review, 118*, 105449.

Lenihan, D., McCobb, E., Diurba, A., Linder, D., & Freeman, L. (2016). Measuring the effects of reading assistance dogs on reading ability and attitudes in elementary school-children. *Journal of Research in Childhood Education, 30*(2), 252–259.

Main, D. C. (2010). Evolution of animal-welfare education for veterinary students. *Journal of Veterinary Medical Education, 37*(1), 30–35.

Mellor, D. J., Beausoleil, N. J., Littlewood, K. E., McLean, A. N., McGreevy, P. D., Jones, B., & Wilkins, C. (2020). The 2020 five domains model: Including human–animal interactions in assessments of animal welfare. *Animals, 10*(10), 1870.

Muldoon, J. C., & Williams, J. M. (2021a). Establishing consensus on the best ways to educate children about animal welfare and prevent harm: An online Delphi study. *Animal Welfare, 30*(2), 179–195.

Muldoon, J. C., & Williams, J. M. (2021b). The challenges and future development of animal welfare education in the UK. *Animal Welfare, 30*(2), 197–209.

Ngai, J. T., Yu, R. W., Chau, K. K., & Wong, P. W. (2021). Effectiveness of a school-based programme of animal-assisted humane education in Hong Kong for the promotion of social and emotional learning: A quasi-experimental pilot study. *PloS One, 16*(3), e0249033.

NSPCC (2021) *Child protection officer scotland training course book.* NSPCC.

Olmert, M. D. (2021). The comfort dog project of Northern Uganda: An innovative canine-assisted psychosocial trauma recovery programme. *Intervention, 19*(1), 21–25.

Rayner, E. L., Airikkala-Otter, I., Bacon, H. J., Walters, H. M., Gamble, L., & Langford, F. M. (2020). Assessment of an educational intervention on the knowledge and attitudes of Indian national veterinarians to animal welfare and euthanasia. *Journal of Veterinary Medical Education, 47*(2), 202–217.

Robinson, J. M., Brindley, P., Cameron, R., MacCarthy, D., & Jorgensen, A. (2021). Nature's role in supporting health during the COVID-19 pandemic: A geospatial and socioecological study. *International Journal of Environmental Research and Public Health, 18*(5), 2227.

RSPCA & Scottish SPCA (2022, June 22). *The Animal Kindness Index Report.* https://www.rspca.org.uk/whatwedo/latest/kindnessindex

Scandurra, C., Santaniello, A., Cristiano, S., Mezza, F., Garzillo, S., Pizzo, R., ... & Bochicchio, V. (2021). An animal-assisted education intervention with dogs to promote emotion comprehension in primary school children—The Federico II model of healthcare zooanthropology. *Animals, 11*(6), 1504.

Scottish Government Social Research. (2022). Restorative justice and empathy training for animal welfare and wildlife offences. *Social Research Series*, 1–16.

Scottish SPCA. (2021). One Welfare World Conference, 2021. Burgos, Spain (Virtual). September 15–16. ISBN-13 9780853583479

Shapiro, K. & Henderson A. J. Z. (2016). *The identification, assessment, and treatment of adults who abuse animals.* New York, NY: Springer Science & Business Media, 2nd Edition.

Shapiro, K., Randour, M. L., Krinsk, S., & Wolf, J. L. (2014). *The assessment and treatment of children who abuse animals: The AniCare child approach.* Springer Science & Business Media.

Steel, J., Williams, J. M., & McGeown, S. (2021). Reading to dogs in schools: An exploratory study of teacher perspectives. *Educational Research*, *63*(3), 279–301.

Uccheddu, S., Albertini, M., Pierantoni, L., Fantino, S., & Pirrone, F. (2019). The impacts of a Reading-to-Dog Programme on attending and reading of nine children with Autism Spectrum Disorders. *Animals*, *9*(8), 491.

Vimal, R. (2022). The impact of the Covid-19 lockdown on the human experience of nature. *Science of the Total Environment*, *803*, 149571.

Wauthier, L., Scottish Society for the Prevention of Cruelty to Animals (Scottish SPCA), & Williams, J. M. (2022). A qualitative study of children's accounts of cruelty to animals: Uncovering the roles of trauma, exposure to violence, and attachment. *Journal of Interpersonal Violence*, *37*(9-10), NP6405–NP6438.

Wilks, M., Caviola, L., Kahane, G., & Bloom, P. (2021). Children prioritize humans over animals less than adults do. *Psychological Science*, *32*(1), 27–38.

Williams, J. M., Cardoso, M. P., Zumaglini, S., Finney, A. L., Scottish SPCA, & Knoll, M. A. (2022). "Rabbit Rescuers": A school-based animal welfare education intervention for young children. *Anthrozoös*, *35*(1), 55–73.

9   A toolkit for evaluating animal welfare education interventions

Janine C. Muldoon and Joanne M. Williams
Clinical and Health Psychology, University of Edinburgh

Aims of this chapter

Until recently there was no guidance for those seeking to design, develop and evaluate animal welfare education (AWE) and animal abuse prevention programmes for children. This chapter provides a toolkit developed on the basis of in-depth research with experts in animal welfare education in the UK.

The toolkit provides a framework for understanding the purpose of evaluation and how it might be approached step-by-step, from the intervention/programmes planning stage right through to reporting and sharing the findings. Beginning with a definition of 'intervention' and 'evaluation', an overview of the evaluation process is subsequently provided. A helpful breakdown of seven key facets is described under two headings. The first, 'What should I do?', outlines three steps to work through when developing an *outcome* or *impact* evaluation. The second, 'How should I do it', focuses more on *process*, describing four areas (using the acronym CoRES) that require attention throughout in order to produce a high-quality intervention and evaluation.

Of most use to those new to evaluation, the toolkit is also highly relevant for practitioners working within the broader field of humane education, and other psychological interventions for animal abuse, and those wishing to gather more comprehensive data or stronger evidence of impact.

Introduction

[Animal welfare education or animal abuse prevention] is often delivered and designed without the necessary strategic planning and outcome mapping. It's also a highly under evaluated field with evaluation on the impact of an intervention on human behaviour change virtually non-existent.

(Emma, animal welfare educator)

DOI: 10.4324/9781003165552-9

Until now there has been no guidance for those seeking to design, develop and evaluate interventions that aim to educate children and young people about animals and their welfare, prevent animal abuse and promote positive relationships and interactions with animals. This chapter describes a toolkit that was developed as a result of the findings from a Delphi study that explored the views of professionals working in animal welfare education and animal abuse prevention.

This toolkit provides a framework for understanding the purpose of evaluation and how it might be approached step-by-step, from the intervention planning stage right through to reporting and sharing the findings. Of most use to those new to evaluation, the toolkit is also highly relevant for those wishing to gather more comprehensive data and stronger evidence of impact, and for practitioners working within the broader field of humane education.

A Delphi study provided the impetus for the development of this evaluation toolkit. This study, involving 31 animal welfare education (AWE) professionals, 27 of whom were UK-based, identified areas of practitioner consensus with respect to the goals and important components of successful AWE/animal abuse prevention interventions for young people (Muldoon & Williams, 2021a; 2021b). The study identified differing views with respect to structuring an intervention so that it can be evaluated effectively, and also recognition that measuring impact is a significant challenge for most animal welfare organisations. As the toolkit is described below, illustrative quotations from participants are used to highlight their perspectives. All names are pseudonyms.

The core aim of this toolkit is to support practitioners to develop strong evidence-based practice. It provides some simple guidance on the steps organisations can take to plan, evaluate, adapt and report on, their intervention work. It also provides a range of resources and developed evaluation templates specifically for those working in AWE. Importantly, it highlights the processes involved to ensure high-quality evaluation and, consequently, a comprehensive understanding of an intervention's impact.

Chapter 8 provided a rich review of the wide range of animal abuse prevention and AWE programmes currently offered. Here we examine what an AWE intervention is and what is meant by evaluation, including why it is necessary and the different types of approaches. An overview of the evaluation process is then provided before each step/facet is considered in detail.

What is an 'animal welfare education (AWE) intervention'?

Animal welfare education/abuse prevention teams in animal welfare charities carry out a range of activities with the ultimate aim of enhancing people's treatment of animals. They may choose to focus on helping others develop their animal welfare knowledge, understanding, behavioural skills with animals, attitudes about animals, empathy and perspective-taking or to reflect more fully on their own behaviour and/or moral and ethical values.

From our perspective, an 'intervention' is a structured, planned and integrated set of activities designed to have specific types of impact on recipients. Ideally, those developing an intervention will describe it in detail, identify the goals and intended impact of each activity and illustrate how their input will effect change in recipients.

Why is it important to evaluate interventions?

If interventions are carried out without due attention to what is working well and what is not, it is impossible to establish with any certainty if the work being undertaken is successful and, if not, what needs to be done to ensure success in the future. The practitioners in our Delphi study described the enormous potential of AWE, moving beyond just improving life for animals. To ensure this potential is achieved and to persuade others of it's significance, it is essential that organisations clearly demonstrate the value and effectiveness of their work. This is particularly critical as we enter an era where priorities are changing, competition for funding is likely to be stronger than ever and sources of financial support more limited. There are a range of benefits associated with systematically evaluating an AWE/animal abuse prevention intervention. These include·

a   Providing evidence of impact, demonstrating if, how and when (under what circumstances) an intervention has been successful; highlighting the specific changes that children/young people experience as a result of participating;
b   Pinpointing where improvements need to be made, ensuring an intervention is the best it can possibly be;
c   Helping to show others what has been achieved, stimulating support for the cause; and
d   Allowing others to replicate successful intervention and evaluation work, leading to wider reach and impact.

Evaluation is most effective when it involves a continuous reflective process and not a one-off assessment. There should be opportunities built in for all those involved to self-evaluate; systematically documenting and reflecting on what they are doing, what is working well and why, and what problems are being encountered along the way. It also involves refining or making changes to elements that are not working smoothly or achieving intended outcomes. Piloting an intervention and evaluation on a small scale is therefore extremely useful prior to rolling out the full programme. The reflective process can be informal, focusing on everyday experiences of working with children and young people, or more formal and comprehensive. However, it is important to produce robust evidence of effectiveness. Children/young people may engage well, but this does not necessarily lead to improvements (e.g., in perceptions of animals, animal welfare knowledge, understanding, behavioural skills, attitudes about animals, empathy or animal abuse behaviour).

Different types of evaluation

Outcome or impact evaluation

This type of evaluation assesses the results of the intervention; changes brought about by the programme, activity or series of sessions. It entails the collection and analysis of data relating to the outcomes that are expected; the areas the intervention is targeting and trying to improve. The findings will demonstrate if the intervention is successful in achieving those outcomes (i.e., changes in children and young people's knowledge, attitudes, behaviour). It is also useful to examine if the intervention only has an impact on certain people. This makes the decision about **what** to measure and **how** to measure it very important, and is an area that AWE professionals identify as a key challenge in the field. The evaluation measures chosen need to strongly reflect the content of the intervention. If there is an expectation that the intervention is likely to have a greater/less impact on some children/young people than others, it is useful to include measures that will capture this differential impact (e.g., age, gender, ethnicity, locality). However, organisations will not be able to collect UK data that could lead to individuals being identified, and any data collected needs to be GDPR compliant (Information Commissioner's Office, 2022); an issue that must be addressed when tracking children. If there is an aim to publish findings in academic journals ethical approval for evaluation studies will also need to be sought and partnership with academic teams is encouraged.

Outcome/impact evaluations can vary from a single group pre-/post-test design to a more comprehensive approach that compares what happens for those participating in the intervention with a group who have not taken part, and examines if any resulting changes have longevity. To enable effective comparison, a 'control' group needs to closely represent the group who have participated. This is called a 'matched control'. A 'waiting list control' may be used; a group that is due to take part in the intervention at a later date. An examination of change over time (i.e., collection of data at different points following the intervention) requires careful data management to ensure each participant's data are linked. The more comprehensive the evaluation design, the more likely it will be that observed changes can be attributed to the intervention itself, rather than other things that are happening simultaneously to participants (e.g., as a result of general schooling). A range of other methods can be used to assess impact, from brief questionnaires/interviews with participants about the experience of taking part, through to comprehensive case studies that gather evidence from those directly involved and the people connected to them. Teachers (in school-based interventions) or parents/caregivers in more tailored individualised interventions, are good examples.

Process evaluation

A process evaluation is quite different to an outcome evaluation, but under-taken at the same time. It is vital for making improvements to interventions and determining future priorities. It is concerned with how an intervention is working in practice, if it is being delivered as planned, and identifying strengths and weaknesses in content and delivery. If a standardised approach has not been followed in certain circumstances, it is important to document and reflect on the reasons for this and any adaptations that have been made (you may sometimes see this referred to as intervention/treatment fidelity). Process evaluation seeks to capture the experiences of those implementing and delivering the intervention to identify what is working well, and aspects that are, or may prove to be, problematic. A range of methods is typically used to assess ways in which an intervention is working and why it might work better in certain settings or with particular groups. This is helpful in enabling optimal targeting of particular interventions, and highlighting which aspects need to be changed for other groups. A key component of a process evaluation is the construction of a logic model that explains how the intervention is thought to generate outcomes (Public Health England, 2022).

An overview of the evaluation process

Ideally, an intervention and accompanying evaluation should be planned to-gether from the outset, with formal opportunities to reflect on, assess and document progress built-in throughout. Figure 9.1 highlights different facets of the evaluation process. There is an obvious chronology to the first three steps that show **what** needs to be done in order to develop an outcome or impact evaluation. Facets 4 to 7 reflect a series of steps too, but these really show **how** to produce high-quality interventions and evaluations and are crucial to carrying out Steps 1 to 3 well. Facet 6 will form a process evaluation that is essential to the future development of AWE and should feed into Facet 7.

The steps in the evaluation process – what should I do?

This section outlines three key steps in the evaluation process

1 Describing the intervention, aims and expected outcomes.
2 Creating a logic model of change processes.
3 Deciding on the type of evaluation.

Step 1: Describe intervention, aims and expected outcomes

I would say MOST interventions are rather superficial or else cognitive in nature. They try to change attitudes but not teach actual behaviours. The most effective I've seen teach actual skills, practice, and provide environmental supports that are ongoing (parents, teachers).

(Amanda)

What should I do?

1   2   3

3.1
Monitor reach & engagement

3.2
Capture experiences

Describe
intervention,
aims & expected
outcomes

Create a
logic model
of change
processes

Decide on
type of
evaluation

3.3
Gather robust evidence of
change & impact

How should I do it? (CoRES)

4   Collaborate/identify expertise & decide on shared values, outcomes & approaches

5   Research, adapt & develop appropriate resources, delivery methods & assessment tools

6   Establish what is/is not working well; make necessary adaptations/refinements and re-assess

7   share findings and issues regarding future implementation

The evaluation process 'the what' and 'the how'

Figure 9.1 The evaluation process: the 'what' and the 'how'.

An essential first step when developing an evaluation is to describe exactly what the AWE intervention entails. Who does it target and why? What activities are involved? Who delivers it, how and where? What are it's key features and specific goals (both short and long-term)? What exactly are you teaching or promoting (e.g., what kind of knowledge, attitudes, skills)? What changes are anticipated in children/young people as a result of participating? This may well be a straightforward process if the intervention has been developed to improve one aspect of children's interactions with animals (e.g., build knowledge of welfare needs). However, if it is more complex, has multiple facets and goals, or is adapted to the specific needs of different recipients (e.g., to give behavioural guides for appropriate pet care), it may be more difficult to describe them in a way that fully captures what you are doing. This can be a barrier when trying to communicate with others (e.g., funders, stakeholders) about the animal abuse prevention work that is being carried out. The description should be detailed but not overly complex. It may help to separate out different elements and highlight how these are designed to produce specific outcomes. This will form the basis of a logic model, described in the next section.

It is useful to adopt a structured approach to document the whole process of evaluation. Using templates often helps to save time (e.g., Hoffmann and colleagues, 2014). The following information should be included:

- The intervention or programme name.
- The rationale or theory underpinning the intervention (e.g., knowledge and or behaviour change models).
- Physical materials provided to participants (e.g., videos, images, animal toys/robots).
- Procedures or activities involved in the intervention (e.g., group discussion, skills training).
- Details of who delivers each aspect of the intervention.
- The mode of delivery (e.g., face to face, in groups or individually, online, in school classes).
- Where the intervention takes place (e.g., schools, community, animal welfare shelters).
- How often the intervention is delivered and over what period (e.g., weekly, daily one-off).
- Whether any aspect of the intervention is tailored to certain participants (e.g., targeted versus universal approach).

We have also designed a template specifically for describing animal welfare education interventions (see Figure 9.2).

Describing an intervention in detail is not only important for evaluation, but it also allows organisations to communicate more effectively with schools and other settings, giving them a clear idea about what is being offered and how it might fit with other areas of the curriculum or other training. It is important to acknowledge that in the process of reflecting on and refining an intervention, this description will need to be revised. It is useful to document changes and show the evolution of a programme, highlighting for internal *and* external use, the knowledge that has been gained about (a) how to intervene most successfully and (b) how to overcome any obstacles that are typically encountered.

1   BRIEF NAME
    Provide a name and/or phrase that describes the intervention
2   RATIONALE FOR THE INTERVENTION
    Describe the reasons why the intervention is required and any theory underpinning its development
3   TARGET RECIPIENTS
    Describe who the intervention is for and why, and any rationale for targeting specific groups
4   SPECIFIC GOALS OF THE INTERVENTION
    Describe the anticipated outcomes, the changes the intervention should lead to in children/young
    people
5   COLLABORATION AND LINKAGES
    Describe if and how the intervention has been developed in collaboration with key stakeholders, and
    whether it links with other work (e.g., in schools, have teachers been involved and does it link to
    specific parts of the existing curriculum/current priorities?)
6   CONTENT OF THE INTERVENTION
    Describe the materials or resources that will be used in the intervention, including information that
    will be given to schools, parents/caregivers and children/young people, as well as the activities that
    will be involved
7   WHO WILL DELIVER THE INTERVENTION
    Describe the roles of all those involved in delivering each aspect of the intervention
8   DELIVERY PROCEDURES
    Describe how the intervention will be delivered and the mode/s of delivery, including whether it will
    be delivered to groups or individually
9   LOCATION
    Describe where the intervention will be delivered, including any constraints the location presents
10 TIMING
    Describe the number of times the intervention is to be delivered and over what period of time
    (number and sequence of sessions, their duration or intensity)
11 TAILORING
    Describe any plans to tailor any aspects of the intervention for specific groups or individuals (provide
    details of what, why, when and how it will be adapted)
12 MONITORING PROCEDURES
    Describe and provide a link to documentation of the extent to which the intervention has been
    delivered in the ways intended (adherence or fidelity to the original plans)
13 RISK ASSESSMENT
    Describe any potential issues that might arise and how these will be dealt with

Provide details of where information relating to each part of the intervention is documented

A template for describing an animal welfare intervention

Figure 9.2 Template for providing a detailed description of an intervention.

Step 2: Create a logic model of change processes

> *There is no point developing programmes and engaging materials that get great
> initial feedback from participants, and self-reported intention to make better choices,
> that then do not translate to a change in their behaviour when they get back into
> their 'real lives'.*

(Suzanne)

Having described the intervention and established who it is targeting, what it
involves, and the specific aims and anticipated outcomes, the next step is to
identify how and why the intervention works, through examining:

a the mechanisms of change – how each aspect of the intervention leads to specific outcomes and

b the factors that might influence how well the intervention works (e.g., does the context or style of delivery matter?)

A logic model is a simple way of mapping out everything that will take place in an intervention and the specific improvements that it has been designed to achieve (Wolpert and colleagues, 2016). Animal abuse prevention or AWE intervention may have been developed based on a theory of behavioural change where the mechanisms are specified. The list below shows the main changes the animal welfare education professionals in our study would like to see in children and young people as a result of participating in one of their interventions. There may also be other outcomes that would need to be included in the logic model.

1 Improved knowledge and understanding of animal welfare needs and specific welfare issues.
2 Greater recognition of animal sentience.
3 Improved skills in relation to interpreting animal behavioural signals and responding appropriately, handling animals correctly (fewer intrusive/forceful/rough handling behaviours), recognising poor welfare and cruelty, and knowing how to behave safely around animals.
4 Improved empathy and compassion towards animals.
5 Improved empathy towards others generally (improvement in pro-social behaviours).
6 Greater recognition of responsibility and an appreciation of their own impact on animals: increased self-awareness and self-reflection, and feeling more empowered to take action.
7 Being more respectful of, and improved attitudes towards, animals (including enhanced attitude that animal abuse is not acceptable).
8 Sustained behavioural change and reduced incidence of children harming animals or being harmed by animals.

An example of a logic model used for an animal welfare education intervention is provided in Figure 9.3.

Step 3: Decide on the type of evaluation

To be able to 'compete' with other subjects and gain credibility for the subject in it's own right, interventions need to be structured in line with other academic subjects ... Effective monitoring and evaluation of the course is dependent on structure.

(Anne)

Evaluation is often viewed as a one-off activity that happens at the end of an intervention. However, the best quality assessments of an intervention's

Target group/s

- Children age 7-12 years
- General population (not targeted at specific groups)
- For use in Scottish SPCA education programme

Intervention design

- Educational iPad game
- One 15 minute session in class
- 3 play levels targeting different aspects of child-animal interactions

Aim/s

To promote positive child-animal interactions, focusing on:
(1) Animal sentience
(2) Animal welfare needs
(3) Impact of behaviour on animals

Change mechanisms

- Understanding of animal sentience & ability to recognise pets' emotional signals
- Understand what animals need to be happy & healthy
- Understand impact of human behaviour on animals

Outcomes

- Increased belief in animal minds
- Improved knowledge of:
  - the five freedoms
  - appropriate & safe behaviour
- Increased compassion
- Lower acceptance of cruelty to animals

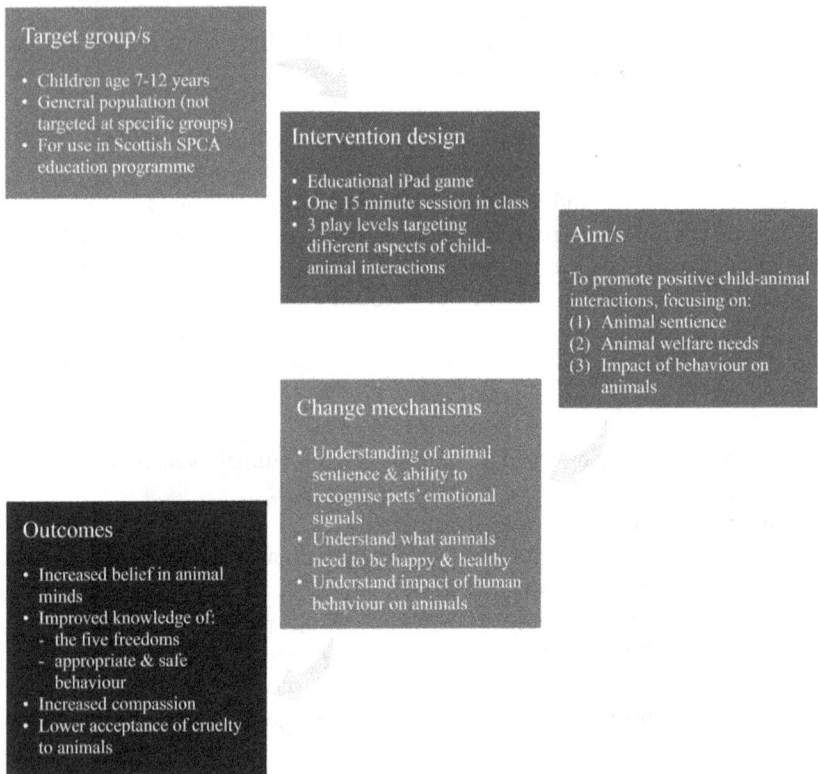

A logic model for a pet welfare intervention (adapted from Hawkins et al., 2019).

Figure 9.3 A logic model for a pet welfare intervention.

success have self-evaluation built in from the outset and continue as long as the intervention or service is being delivered. If the intervention forms part of a rolling programme, then between each phase, the findings from this process should lead to improvements in the next. It is important to continue using the resources or methods that have been found to work effectively and only adjust/refine areas that have not worked well.

As Figure 9.4 highlights, there are different ways of evaluating interventions; the decision as to which type is used often depends on the availability of time, resources, the skills of the team and the number of dedicated staff.

We have drawn a broad distinction between 'outcome/impact' and 'process' evaluation. The latter is the specific focus of Facet 6 in Figure 9.1 where we look to establish what is/is not working well; make necessary adaptations/refinements and re-assess. Here, we focus on the former, which can involve:

1) Monitoring reach and engagement

- Attendance
- Retention
- Intervention type/inclusivity/variation in delivery
- Community involvement

2) Capturing experiences

- Feedback forms
- Interviews
- Case studies
- Testimonials
- Images/objects

3) Gathering robust evidence of change and impact

- Standardised measures
- Routinely collected data
- Community level data
- National statistics

Different ways of carrying out an impact/outcome evaluation

Figure 9.4 Different ways of carrying out an impact/outcome evaluation.

a   A monitoring process, maintaining an accurate record of who is involved in the intervention, and the degree to which it is engaging participants,

b   Finding out how participants feel the intervention has helped them, perhaps carrying out some case studies to gain an in-depth understanding of the intervention's impact and how it resulted in change and/or

c   Assessing changes that have occurred in participants' knowledge, thoughts, feelings or behaviours using robust reliable measurement tools.

A comprehensive evaluation will include all of the above. However, no matter which type is used, information needs to be collected and documented systematically. Templates can help to capture everything that happens throughout the process. It is also important to recognise limitations, focusing first on establishing good quality systems for reliable monitoring and reflection. Once those are working well, evaluation can be extended to include the gathering of data that sheds more light on impact.

a   Monitoring reach and engagement

I believe the children need to complete activities and not just be talked to for them to engage properly with the subject. We've had very positive feedback from schools who have taken part in our school award as they've seen a difference in the children's attitudes towards animals in their class.

(Jenny)

Monitoring is an essential and basic form of evaluation. It is important to document all the work that is carried out as part of an intervention and how many people have taken part. All organisations should have some data of this kind available, so it is really just about putting in place a system to capture this information accurately so it is easy to report.

The following are types of information you might collect as part of a monitoring process:

- Attendance rates – the number of children and young people taking part in an intervention.
- Retention rates – the length of time children and young people are involved in the programme, and the extent to which they remain engaged.
- The type of intervention – whether it is 'universal' where everyone receives the same input, or 'targeted', including the distinct characteristics designed for particular individuals or groups. If there are elements of both, this should also be documented.
- Inclusivity – if this information is available to you, the backgrounds of the children and young people taking part in the intervention and the extent to which particular groups are involved (e.g., those who are more vulnerable, are at high risk of causing harm to animals, have special educational needs, live in a disadvantaged area or are in local authority care).
- Variation in delivery – the degree to which it is tailored to particular groups or individuals.
- Community involvement – who else in the local community is linked with the intervention either directly or indirectly (e.g., families, schools, youth offending teams, colleges, veterinarians, therapy animal organisations).

The degree to which participants are engaged should also be monitored and documented. This may be based on observations of those delivering the programme, or more formal assessments of engagement via interview or a written questionnaire about the experience of participating. A way to record all information collected should be decided at the outset so that everyone involved is clear on how and what to document.

b   Capturing experiences

I feel standard measures can end up driving the education so that on paper it looks great but the heart of the work is lost ... This burden of uniform evaluation can be one imposed by funders too though thankfully some are now coming to value 'stories' over statistics.

(Louise)

Finding out how people feel about an intervention, and the impact they feel it has had on them is extremely useful. This 'qualitative' evidence helps to bring the intervention to life when describing it to those unfamiliar with the programme. Depending on how comprehensive this process is, it can also shed light on change mechanisms, thus allowing re-evaluation of the initial logic model and assessment as to whether the intervention has worked in the ways anticipated or in a different manner. Participants can be asked open-ended or close-ended questions relating to how they think the intervention has changed their thoughts, feelings or intended behaviours. However, questions should not lead participants into responding in particular ways. Instead, they should allow those responding to express a view that the intervention did not result in change for them personally. This is also useful information that needs to be incorporated into any evaluation – when things do not work, as well as when they do.

Most animal welfare organisations offering animal welfare education, humane education or animal abuse prevention collect data like this already, but if not, it is relatively easy to implement procedures to do so. The following represent different ways in which participants' perceptions and experiences can be accessed:

- Feedback forms – given to participants at the end of the intervention, capturing how much they enjoyed taking part, if and how they feel the intervention has had an impact on them and any recommendations they have for changes. This can include rating scales as well as open-ended questions for participants to provide written comments.
- Case studies – personal stories about ways in which the intervention has impacted a child's or young person's life can be captured through interviews, participants' writing, drawing or photographs or through videos. Case studies are stronger if they include a range of perspectives (i.e., the child, their teacher, a parent/caregiver, etc.)
- Testimonials – accounts from other stakeholders (such as parents, carers, peers, teachers, youth leaders or other organisations) about the impact of the intervention; how it has made a difference, and to whom. These could be gathered in person or drawn from social media, such as tweets about the success of a project in different settings.
- Images/objects – drawings or photographs of young people taking part in the intervention, objects, posters or other outputs that have been created throughout the intervention process.

It is vitally important that organisations provide detailed information for participants and stakeholders about the type of data they will be collecting and what they will ask those involved to do; obtaining consent where necessary (especially if images of participants are to be used). This type of evidence provides compelling cases and clear examples of children's and young people's experiences. However, it is not possible to generalise the findings to the population as a whole.

c   Gathering robust evidence of change and impact

Having recently measured our own education pet care talks we were able to measure knowledge, attitudes and empathy and can show a significant increase in all areas. Knowledge was the highest and we are working on improving the other two.

(Maria)

Capturing the wider *impact* of an intervention requires robust evidence of change, and this was considered to be one of the most significant challenges facing animal welfare education specialists. This type of evaluation focuses on objectively assessing the outcomes and mechanisms of change that have been identified in the logic model. This is the most intensive type of evaluation, requiring the most planning, resources and skills, which perhaps explains why many organisations do not carry out evaluation of this kind on a regular basis. Some practitioners working with children and young people are not familiar with the assessment tools and the process of collecting and analysing data of this kind. However, it is the most powerful demonstration that an intervention is making a difference; enhancing welfare knowledge, improving attitudes towards animals, enhancing skills and reducing animal abuse behaviours of those participating. Some funders also require this type of evidence in order to invest in an intervention or service. It should be noted that some outcomes are easier or quicker to achieve than others (e.g., evidence of reduction in animal abuse behaviour is longer-term and difficult to measure, see Chapter 2).

Types of information that might be included:

- Standardised measures – usually questionnaires designed to measure the outcomes or change mechanisms you are interested in, but may also include other tools like observations or interviews.
- Routinely collected data – often relevant information is already being collected by other people (in the local community and nationally). Accessing this information can provide valuable evidence of impact. This may include records of animal cruelty cases/offences, the number and type of phone calls to rescue charities from children and the extent of positive behaviour examples, such as charitable work by children or schools.

Depending on the goals of the intervention, a pre-test, post-test and delayed post-test can be used to demonstrate immediate and longer-term impact on participants. However, it is important to note that collecting evidence before and after an intervention cannot tell you with confidence that it is the intervention that has caused a change. Something else may be responsible. To establish this, as we indicated earlier, it is very helpful to compare the children who are participating with another group who are not (a control group). Ideally, this would be a group who are on a waiting list to start the intervention, but if not, the control and intervention groups need to include participants with similar characteristics in order to make them comparable.

The process of evaluation: How should I do it?

This section outlines how to ensure high-quality animal welfare education and evaluation through four facets easily remembered using the acronym CoRES (also refer to Figure 9.1):

- **Co**llaboration/shared understanding and approaches
- **R**esearching thoroughly appropriate resources, methods and tools
- **E**stablishing what is/is not working through continual reflection, adaptation and refinement
- **S**haring learning (positives and negatives) beyond the organisation

Collaborate, identify expertise and decide on shared values, outcomes and approaches

> *Understanding and agreement on what we should be measuring. Agreement on meaningful criteria. How to report and illustrate the findings in a helpful and accessible way.*
>
> (Richard)

For an intervention and evaluation to be implemented successfully, it is important that everyone involved has an opportunity to contribute to the decision-making process. This way, as decisions are made, the whole team will develop a shared understanding of all aspects we have discussed thus far, resolving the issue highlighted by Richard in response to a question concerning problems associated with evaluation. Given the varied backgrounds of animal welfare education professionals, there is a wealth of experience and skills to draw on. Therefore, at the outset, it is good to draw a team together and identify expertise. At this point, it is also helpful to identify where extra support is needed.

Where there are identified gaps in skills, experience or knowledge within the team, a strategy needs to be developed to secure help at the appropriate time. It is good to establish those connections at the outset so that those providing support are advised well in advance and have the opportunity to contribute their thoughts early on. It is also valuable to discuss approaches to self-evaluation and what tools, techniques and templates the team will use to reflect on and document how things are progressing.

It is important that everyone in the team has an understanding of roles and responsibilities and who to contact for support. One area that may be worth careful consideration, as there was a lack of consensus in our study, is the language used to both describe and deliver the intervention (terminology and definitions). 'Harm' may be more appropriate to use than 'cruelty' for example. This issue would benefit from attention in the wider community of animal welfare educators (Muldoon & Williams, 2021a; 2021b).

Research, adapt and develop appropriate resources, delivery methods and assessment tools

> The nature of what is covered in workshops or interventions is aiming for long term behaviour change, which may not be evident for several years. It would be easy enough to measure the recall of information related to animal welfare, but the true measure of effectiveness wouldn't come until this either is or is not put into practice.
>
> (Martin)

It is essential that intervention and evaluation resources, delivery methods and assessment tools are age-appropriate, child/adolescent-friendly, engaging, non-discriminatory, unambiguous and closely related to the specific goals and anticipated outcomes of the intervention. Many AWE teams develop their own materials, multi-media resources, computer games and robotics, to support delivery, continually updating them to ensure they are still relevant and appealing. While this is critical, it is also valuable to identify which materials have worked well. These should be retained and the same process applied to examining how different delivery methods have been received. There is much emphasis now on interactive and peer learning, and many professionals felt it was important not to just talk to (at) children, but to ensure that sessions equip them with skills and a sense of responsibility, not just knowledge. Motivating children to learn about animals and inspiring them to find out more, were also viewed as key to promoting change in behaviours.

Key areas that concerned professionals in our study were how to gather robust evidence of change (particularly through the use of survey methods), how to assess if the change is sustained in the longer term and how to measure behavioural outcomes. The first step towards determining what to measure is the identification of clear outcomes. Then specific 'indicators' can be identified.

One of the problems facing animal welfare education/animal abuse prevention practitioners is finding appropriate measures that align with the work they are carrying out. The published standardised measures (see also Chapter 2) that can be used include the following dimensions of child-animal interactions:

1 Pet ownership and attachment
2 Knowledge, attitudes and beliefs about animals
3 Empathy and socio-emotional measures
4 Human-animal interaction behaviours (e.g., children's treatment of animals)

It is possible to design new measures for inclusion (particularly useful if the aim is to enhance specific areas of knowledge or assess if children know what to do in certain situations). These should be piloted to ensure they are easy to respond to. With survey items, it may be possible for individual items to be grouped to form a 'scale' that can aid analysis.

Establish what is working well and what is not; make necessary adaptations/refinements and re-assess

> *We can assume with programmes not utilising monitoring and evaluation processes, that required strengthening adjustments to output are not frequently applied.*

> (Emma)

Close attention is required throughout the whole evaluation process to the aspects that are working well and those that need improving or removing altogether. This is the goal of a process evaluation and is vital for making decisions about how to move forward to ensure interventions are high quality and as successful as they can be. It is essentially a process of analysing different elements of the intervention, and being able to reflect honestly on the skills, knowledge, materials and methods used. The outcome evaluation contributes to this by demonstrating exactly what has changed and what has not as a result of the intervention, but cannot tell you why or how it led (or failed to lead) to change. The logic model and the theory of change underpinning the intervention need to be examined and perhaps refined. Practitioners will undoubtedly find that things do not always go according to plan and it is important to capture this and consider how easy the intervention would be to replicate another time.

Many of the professionals in our study felt it was extremely important to be flexible and adapt to the different groups they work with. This is understandable and easy to evaluate if the flexibility and adaptations are planned in, but not so easy if changes are made in the process of delivering. For evaluation to be useful, it is important that any changes made in practice (that may be necessary) that deviate from planned activities/approaches are documented, including reasons for change, and taken back for discussion with the team and/or the wider community of AWE professionals. It is important that no one feels like they have failed if they had to deviate from the plan. It might be useful to identify core aspects of content and delivery that must be implemented in the same way, allowing for flexibility in other areas.

There are various ways of ascertaining what is working well and what is not. Below are some questions that may prove useful when examining data and reflections on each element of the intervention: delivery, content/resources, monitoring data, qualitative data, quantitative data.

1   To what extent were the aims achieved?
2   What problems were encountered or can be identified?
3   Is it possible to identify what led to success or lack of it?
4   Does it work better for certain groups than others?
5   What are the next steps? What is missing?

Any subsequent changes to the intervention should be based on the accumulation of evidence. If something is working well, this should continue and decisions will need to be made regarding lack of success.

Share findings and issues regarding future implementation

> *The sector could do more to work together in targeting a broader audience and ensuring messages are consistent and constant. The sector will not see the benefits of their interventions for 5–10 years, and then it will be hard to attribute to any one programme (if we all work independently).*

(Siobhan)

Work undertaken in a process and outcome/impact evaluation should lead to a sound understanding of the intervention; the effects it has had and not had, what has worked well (ideally knowing why and how) and what elements have not proved successful in achieving specified goals. While it is wonderful to find that your intervention has been successful, it is rare for one, particularly in the early stages, to be wholly successful. A great deal of time, energy, resources, funds and passion are invested in developing an intervention. Therefore, it is difficult to find out, and also admit, that it is not working well, especially when external funding has been secured, or is required for further work. However, we only ever learn through things not working as planned, and it is important that within this field, there is recognition of the challenges and openness about failures as well as successes. This is the only way that AWE can prosper in the future. This is an issue for academic research too, where papers are only submitted for publication when they find positive results. We need to learn from the negative and null results too.

It is important that the findings/results are presented clearly. To help share elements of work that have been successful and challenging, with a view to making significant differences to children, animals, the environment and society, that professionals feel is possible through AWE, it is useful to draw together all the learning from the process of designing, delivering and evaluating:

- What we expected to do.
- What we actually did.
- What difference we actually made.
- Challenges and changes.
- Learning for the future.

Opportunities to share these findings and reflections with the broader community should be sought. This will help others to focus on the key issues and evaluate their own practices in a similar manner. It is also useful to situate any discussion about moving forward in the context of new developments in scientific understanding of animal cognition, behaviour and sentience, that should feed into intervention programmes. There may also be developments within education that future interventions could link with successfully.

Conclusions

This chapter is written for those involved in designing and delivering programmes to prevent and intervene in cases of animal abuse. Based on evidence from animal welfare educators, it provides a step-by-step guide to designing an evaluation strategy for animal welfare education, humane education and animal abuse prevention programmes. Evaluation can sometimes feel daunting and the aim of this guide is to support animal welfare educators in evaluating the effectiveness of their interventions, sharing their findings and ultimately preventing or reducing animal abuse.

Key questions to consider

1   How important do you think evaluation is when developing a new animal welfare education/animal abuse prevention programme?
2   From your experience, what are the main challenges in conducting an evaluation of programmes?
3   Based on what you have learned in this chapter would you be confident conducting an evaluation of an animal abuse prevention or intervention programme yourself?

Key Messages

1   Being able to demonstrate evidence of impact is becoming increasingly important. The toolkit described in this chapter provides an evidence-based framework specifically designed for those wishing to develop and evaluate AWE interventions.

2　The framework provided is not only useful for understanding how to evaluate but also helps practitioners to think through and develop a high-quality intervention from the very beginning. Careful attention to implementing the four CoRES facets will enhance the impact potential of AWE interventions.

3　To make the process easier and less time-consuming, the toolkit provides easy-to-use guidelines and templates.

4　It is essential that AWE practitioners are open and honest when interventions do not achieve their aims. Effective process evaluation helps to identify why things have not gone to plan and this is extremely valuable information for all those working to help improve the lives of children and animals.

References

Hawkins, R., & Williams, J. (2019). The development and pilot evaluation of a 'serious game' to promote positive child-animal interactions. *Human-Animal Interaction Bulletin*, 8(2). 10.1079/hai.2020.0008.

Hoffmann, T., Glasziou, P., Boutron, I., Milne, R., Perera, R., Moher, D., Altman, D., Barbour, V., Macdonald, H., Johnston, M., Lamb, S., Dixon-Woods, M., McCulloch, P., Wyatt, J., Chan, A., & Michie, S. (2014). Better reporting of interventions: Template for intervention description and replication (TIDieR) checklist and guide. *BMJ*, 348, g1687.

Information Commissioner's Office (2022, August 23). *Guide to the General Data Protection Regulation (GDPR)*. https://ico.org.uk/for-organisations/guide-to-data-protection/guide-to-the-general-data-protection-regulation-gdpr/

Muldoon, J. C., & Williams, J. M. (2021a). Establishing consensus on the best ways to educate children about animal welfare and prevent harm: An online Delphi study. *Animal Welfare*, 30(2), 179–195.

Muldoon, J. C., & Williams, J. M. (2021b). The challenges and future development of animal welfare education in the UK. *Animal Welfare*, 30(2), 197–209.

Public Health England (2022, August 23) *Evaluation in Health and Wellbeing: Guidance Summaries*. https://www.gov.uk/government/publications/evaluation-in-health-and-wellbeing-guidance-summaries/evaluation-in-health-and-well-being-guidance-summaries

Wolpert M., Sharpe H., Humphrey N., Patalay P., & Deighton, J. (2016). *EBPU Logic Model*. London: CAMHS Press. https://www.annafreud.org/media/5593/logic-model-310517.pdf

10 Animal abuse: What we know, what we can do and what we need to know

Joanne M. Williams[1] *and Gilly Mendes Ferreira*[2]

[1] *Clinical and Health Psychology, University of Edinburgh*
[2] *Scottish SPCA*

Aims of this chapter

In this chapter we synthesise key points from across the chapters and highlight what the evidence tells us about psychological risk factors for animal abuse and 'The Link' between animal abuse and other forms of abuse. We highlight emerging trends in animal abuse and prevention interventions for animal abuse cases. We also consider research gaps and future directions for research and practice. In a final case study, we invite you to use your knowledge of animal abuse to consider who is at risk and how you might intervene from different professional perspectives. The case is complex, as real-life cases of animal abuse often are, and we encourage you to see the necessity of partnership work to ensure that all involved are protected and supported, and to recognise the actions that you can take to protect the people and animals involved.

What do we know about animal abuse?

Although definitions of animal abuse vary by discipline and over time, as is evident across the preceding chapters, there is growing consensus about the nature of animal abuse, risk factors for abuse and how to intervene. There are clear interconnections between humans, animals and the environment we all share. We know that just like humans, animals are sentient beings, they can experience positive and negative emotions and the surrounding environment can impact their quality of life. This book demonstrates that there is a link between animal abuse and human abuse. Children who have been exposed to domestic violence were three times more likely to be cruel to animals than children who have not (Currie, 2006). Children who were exposed to animal abuse were five times more likely to have "severe problems" and three times more likely to be "struggling" compared to their more resilient peers. Children were more than twice as likely to harm an animal when the mother's

DOI: 10.4324/9781003165552-10

partner had harmed an animal (McDonald and colleagues, 2015). We have also seen that many professions struggle to recognise cases of animal abuse and the links with other forms of abuse, with vets in particular being asked to play a pivotal role. Legislation continues to be compartmentalised into human and animal law (see Chapter 4), but as interconnections between human wellbeing and animal welfare are identified this gap in legislation will close and animals will begin to be regarded as more than just someone's 'property'.

How important is inter-agency working?

Many cases of animal abuse involve complex social situations, including vulnerable people and crisis situations, and therefore inter-agency working is essential. We have learned that different professions have distinct but complementary roles to play in the recognition and handling of animal abuse or human abuse (or both). Parents and carers have a key role in modelling positive behaviour to animals for their children, and scaffolding positive and safe interactions between children and pets. Through their parenting they can enhance children's empathy to animals, understanding of animals' welfare needs and pet care skills. Parents can prevent animal abuse and also intervene when they see abuse incidents. Teachers can incorporate animal welfare into many parts of the curriculum to prevent animal abuse and also have an important role in supporting children's mental health and wellbeing. If childhood animal abuse incidents are disclosed in school these may indicate other difficulties a child is facing where educational/wellbeing support is required. Social work and community work are core to breaking The Link between different forms of abuse and preventing cycles of abuse. Promoting positive animal care in families, asking about animals and animal abuse in assessments, educating other professionals about The Link and inter-agency working are all key to tackling animal abuse in the community. Health and mental health professionals may not see animal welfare and animal abuse prevention and intervention as within their professional remits, however, as animal abuse is connected with psychological issues and other forms of abuse, it is essential that opportunities to identify and intervene in animal abuse are taken. There is a need for psychological interventions to consider animal abuse and a need for new therapies for animal abuse (for children and adults) to be developed and evaluated. Animal welfare educators, many based in animal welfare charities, play a key role in animal abuse prevention and intervention, offering a wide range of engaging and effective programmes for children and young people. By working together, professionals can support children and adolescents, their families and the animals in their lives.

Concerning trends in animal abuse: Online risks

Animal abuse has a range of motivations and legal penalties for perpetrators of animal abuse are increasing. However, there is sometimes a drive to engage in new forms of animal abuse or different methods of hiding abuse. The accessibility of the digital world continues to advance and during the Covid-19 pandemic many facets of life moved online including: education (Adedoyin & Soykan, 2020), shopping (Koch and colleagues, 2020) and even legal proceedings (Puddister & Small, 2020). Many people relied on social media and video conferencing tools as means of socialisation (e.g., Duncan and colleagues, 2021) and to share views on animal abuse (Whyke & López-Múgica, 2020). Animal abuse footage is being shared online, including by animal welfare activists to shine a light on abuse (e.g., Buddle and colleagues, 2018), and social media is implicated in organised animal abuse, such as dog fighting (Montrose and colleagues, 2021) and badger baiting. Furthermore, people use social media and online platforms to buy and sell pets and to post information about their pets. Thus, social media and digital platforms are sources of information, images and communities associated with animal abuse.

Exposure to and normalisation of violence is a risk for childhood animal harm (Wauthier, Scottish SPCA & Williams 2022) and can be fuelled not just by what happens in a home and community but also by what young people see online. The RSPCA carried out a survey that found that nearly a quarter of UK schoolchildren aged between 10 and 18 years old had witnessed animal abuse or neglect on social media (RSPCA, 2022). Ofcom (2022) looked at media use and attitudes of children and parents, and found that in 2021 nearly all children and young people (aged 3–17) in the UK went online (99%) and 95% chose to use video-sharing platforms (VSPs) such as YouTube or TikTok. They also found that among all types of online platforms, YouTube was the most widely used platform by children (89%) but TikTok was more popular for posting content (Ofcom, 2022). Given the high percentage of young people who have access to online content and the link between witnessing animal abuse and violence towards others (See Chapters 2 and 3) new UK legislation, such as the Online Safety Bill currently progressing through Westminster, might be an opportunity to reduce animal abuse content online. We know that animal abuse content online is underreported and more work needs to be done to raise awareness of how to report such content. Case example 1 below, provided by the charity SWGfl (South West Grid for Learning Trust, 2022), highlights that the issue of exposure to animal abuse footage online is real and greater awareness is needed on how to report such footage.

Case example 1

A young person aged 15 got in touch in 2020 after the Netflix series 'Don't F*ck with cats' had aired. They reported a number of Instagram accounts that they said were showing live streams of cats being tortured at certain times of the day. Our practitioners examined the accounts concerned and realised that in fact, the accounts were not posting the video content but rather a link to an independent site which would show this at certain times of the day. The independent site was hosted outside of the UK and outside of our scope, however, the Instagram accounts were continuing to enable access to the content. The young person had reported the accounts to Instagram for violence using the in-app reporting feature but to no avail. SWGfl were able to escalate with additional context about the accounts that were facilitating the viewing of the violent animal abuse content, and they were removed that week.

New directions for intervention and treatment of animal abuse

Whilst we have outlined a range of prevention and treatment interventions in Chapter 8 and provided a guide for the development and evaluation of animal welfare education interventions in Chapter 9, there is much work to be done if we are to reduce the incidence of animal abuse in society and promote compassion towards animals.

New prevention interventions for animal abuse

In the UK the majority of animal welfare charities who engage in education programmes focus efforts on animal abuse prevention with primary school-aged children (5-11-year-olds). In a recent study of animal welfare educators (Muldoon & Williams, 2021a; 2021b) it was found, however, that there was a lack of consensus among professionals working in this field about how to define animal cruelty, and a divergence in views about the need to take a universal approach providing a level of education for all, versus a tailored approach to meet the needs of specific children. There was also a concern about evaluation among practitioners, which led to the development of the evaluation toolkit presented in Chapter 9. The activities of animal welfare education teams have led to a plethora of educational materials for primary school aged children, and efforts in the UK to share good practice across charities (e.g., Animal Welfare Education Alliance and Scottish Animal Welfare Educators Network), but a dearth of educational activities in other areas.

Few educational interventions have been developed for pre-school children. Yet we know that unintentional and accidental harm to animals can involve children of this age range, and educational interventions to enhance more animal welfare understanding and behavioural skills required for safe animal handling might prevent animal harm and also reduce harm to children (Meints & De Keuster, 2009). Animal bites are more common among younger children and may be the result of inappropriate handling of animals, misunderstanding of animal behaviour or unsupervised interventions with animals. Thus, there is a need to develop interventions which are evidence-based and age-appropriate for pre-school children and their parents/carers.

While there is some evidence that intentional animal abuse may increase in adolescence, few animal welfare educational interventions are designed for this age range compared to primary school children. A challenge to engaging this age range in animal welfare education is the structure of school classes around subjects, and the lack of clear curriculum-fit for animal welfare/animal abuse prevention interventions. As discussed in Chapter 7 animal abuse is relevant to a range of subjects from personal and social education, psychology, history, to biology. There is a growing call for animal welfare education to be included in the curriculum in the UK with 84% of the population supporting this call (RSPCA & Scottish SPCA, 2022). Animal welfare education interventions for adolescents would need to be adolescent-appropriate, recognising the cognitive, social, wellbeing and behavioural opportunities and challenges of this phase of development. Reaching adolescents outside of school in communities most affected by exposure to violence should also be considered.

While most animal welfare and abuse prevention education programmes focus on teaching children and young people, the extent to which they can put their new skills and knowledge into practice is affected by their parents/carers and families. Children may have learned that their rabbit needs a large hutch and run with daily access to hay and clean water, but they may not have control over whether these needs are met due to parental control of finances and pet care (Muldoon and colleagues, 2015). While there is a growing range of educational materials on pet care and welfare for adults, there are limited educational resources specifically on animal abuse identification and prevention for parents/carers. Parents and carers are key models of behaviour for children (see Chapter 7), so it is important that parents meet the welfare needs of animals in the home to promote this behaviour among their children. This is an area for future development and is likely to involve joint work between welfare charities and commercial partners in the pet and pet food industries. Parents need to know about a dog's needs when considering purchasing a puppy but they also need to have some information about managing positive interactions between children and pets. As research on children's interactions with pets, and pet effects on children's development is relatively new (e.g., Purewal and colleagues, 2017) this is an area of intervention which is ripe for development.

In most cases, participation in intervention programmes for those (child or adult) who have been involved in either intentional or unintentional abuse towards animals is currently on a voluntary basis. It is important that professionals in roles supporting a young person or adult who has been involved in animal abuse have knowledge of services that are available in their area to help safeguard the welfare of both humans and animals. Any programme that is developed must be properly evaluated to ensure that it does make a difference, changes abusive patterns of behaviour and prevents repeat abuse.

New psychological therapies and non-custodial approaches for animal abuse

Animal abuse in children and adults is sometimes associated with psychological risk factors (e.g., conduct disorder), behavioural profiles (e.g., aggression and violence) and developmental contexts (e.g., Adverse Childhood Experiences) that require a deeper approach to understanding the precipitating factors for animal abuse in order to prevent recurrence. A psychological therapy approach rather than an educational intervention is required. At the moment the only therapeutic approach specifically designed for treating animal abuse is the Ani-Care programme for adults (Shapiro & Henderson, 2016; Levitt and colleagues, 2017) and Ani-Care Child programme for children and young people (Shapiro and colleagues, 2013). These USA interventions (see Chapter 8) have not been formally evaluated and have, to date, not been used in the UK. In a study of psychological risk factors for animal abuse among children the theoretical basis of Ani-Care Child was supported (Wauthier, Farnfield, Scottish SPCA & Williams, 2022), but there has been no adoption of this intervention in mainstream psychological services for children and young people in the UK. Until there is evidence of it's efficacy there is not likely to be an uptake of this therapy. For the sub-set of people who engage in animal cruelty intentionally, with associated psychological risk factors (such as low empathy, behaviour and emotional dysregulation, and psychopathic traits), therapeutic intervention is essential. Efforts are therefore required to develop and evaluate new psychological therapies for children and adults who engage in intentional, repeated and severe animal abuse.

In the UK, and in particular in Scotland, there is a need to develop non-custodial sentences for animal abuse, in cases where serious psychological risk factors are not indicated. These might include restorative justice approaches and adapting of 'empathy-based' approaches (which have been developed for children) to make them age-appropriate for adolescents and adults. There are a number of barriers to implementing restorative justice approaches, including who would speak for the animal and who would be involved in the approach (Scottish Government, 2022). A key issue will be matching the interventions to the nature of the offence. For example, where profit has been a motive (e.g. illegal puppy dealing) then high financial penalty would be appropriate, when psychological issues underpin animal abuse psychological therapy should be required as part of the penalty; where someone had little appreciation of the harm they had caused through their behaviour, restorative justice to increase their understanding of the consequences of their actions might be appropriate.

New directions for research

While the scale of animal abuse is difficult to discern there is growing recognition of it's importance. Surprisingly there has been very limited research on animal abuse, especially in contrast to research on human-directed aggression and violence (e.g., Wauthier & Williams, 2022). While there has been an exponential growth in research on human-animal interactions over recent years (e.g., Herzog, 2011) the focus has been mainly on the positive effects of animals on human health and the potential benefits of animal-assisted interventions. The darker side of human-animal interactions, animal abuse, has received scant research, so there is a range of unresolved issues and gaps in evidence.

Much of the research on childhood and adolescent animal abuse has focused on psychological and social risk factors (e.g., Hawkins and colleagues, 2017; Wauthier & Williams, 2022). Early research was strongly guided by work on the Macdonald Triad (Macdonald, 1963) and Dark Triad (Kavanagh and colleagues, 2013) linking psychopathic traits and callous-unemotional traits with animal abuse. This has tended to 'pathologise' animal abuse and focus research on the more extreme end of the spectrum (Wauthier & Williams, 2022). It is notable that despite this focus on clearly psychologically driven pathological abuse in research, therapeutic interventions for animal abuse are in their relative infancy. Wauthier and colleagues (Wauthier, Farnfield, Scottish SPCA & Williams, 2022) in an exploratory study of children who have harmed animals found that these children were more likely than matched children who were low risk for animal harm to have attachment issues, executive functioning issues and externalising behaviours. Thus, further research is required to investigate psychological risk factors that are amenable to intervention, such as behavioural regulation and attachment issues. Once research identifies risk factors, this evidence could be used to refine interventions to reduce these risks.

The lack of research on animal abuse is partly due to a lack of measures. So a key focus of research should be to develop reliable measures of both animal harm and psychological risk factors. For example, we have developed a measure of children's attachment to pets (Marsa-Sambola and colleagues, 2016), children's belief in animal minds (Hawkins & Williams, 2016) and children's attitudes to animal cruelty (Hawkins and colleagues, 2020). We are currently developing a measure of children's empathy to animals, which focuses on how children interpret emotional cues in images of people and animals interacting (Wauthier, Scottish SPCA & Williams, in preparation). Developing new research measures is vital for assessing risk factors for animal abuse, animal abuse behaviour and also for evaluating the impact of interventions.

There is extensive evidence on The Link between animal abuse and human abuse, but there remain gaps in evidence. For example, current qualitative research with care experienced young people carried out by the authors and colleagues has shown that while exposure to family trauma can be associated with a higher risk of childhood animal abuse, it can lead to animal protection in some cases. The following quotes are examples of how young people who have experienced family trauma sometimes step in to protect an animal in the home (names changed for anonymity):

He [pet cat] had rotting teeth [...] he could not eat and [...] before my parents got divorced, I talked about helping them pay for surgery or whatever [...] and they were kind of like, "Oh yeah, sure", you know, and then brushed me off. Well, then they got divorced and I was like, "You know what, forget it, I'm gonna do it myself. [...] So I went to the house, I picked up [cat] and I took him to the vet and I got his surgery done

(Sarah)

I think there was some moments where I think there could have been a little bit of neglect? But that's on her [biological mother] part, not mine, 'cos as soon as I noticed, I would do something about it, because I don't like it? Like, I'm not 100% an animal person, but if I see something that I don't believe is right, I will go in there and I will correct that. [...] And I've always been like that, ever since I was little.

(Patricia)

As much of the research on childhood animal cruelty is based on reports of parents or professionals rather than children, there is a need for further research with children themselves. As there is evidence that psychological risks change with age, research is required to plot risk factors over age. Ideally, longitudinal methods tracking development of children who are at high and low risk of cruelty throughout childhood and adolescence should be employed. We also need to conduct research with vulnerable children who may have psychological risk factors for animal abuse but who might also form very strong attachments to their pets and develop strong motivations to protect animals.

We have learned a lot about risk factors for unintentional animal cruelty, including: low knowledge about animal welfare and how this can be improved (Hawkins, Williams & Scottish SPCA 2017a), low attachment to pets (Hawkins, Scottish SPCA & Williams, 2017b), low belief that animals are sentient and have minds (Hawkins & Williams, 2016) and that attitudes that cruelty is acceptable are predictive of animal abuse (Hawkins and colleagues, 2020). There are still large gaps in knowledge, especially around how these factors predict behaviour and how behaviour change can be promoted. Many animal welfare education interventions do not assess actual animal abuse behaviour or track behaviour change over time, so a key task for future research is to develop accurate and reliable behaviour measures that can be used in research and to assess the effectiveness of interventions for reducing animal abuse behaviour.

Most of the research on animal abuse has been carried out in Western contexts, and even that work has tended to overlook within culture differences such as socioeconomic, ethnicity and religious differences that impact our views of and our behaviour towards animals. As animal abuse is a global issue and is influenced by cultural norms there is a need to engage a wider range of researchers from different cultural contexts in research on risk factors for animal abuse, and interventions to reduce it.

From research to impact

Much of the research on animal abuse is highly applied rather than theoretical, and a key motivation for research is to have a positive impact on the lives of animals and people. Research identifying risk factors or animal abuse has formed the evidence-base for interventions to prevent animal abuse and intervene in cases of animal harm (see Chapters 2 and 3). Similarly, evaluation research on animal abuse prevention interventions is designed to provide evidence of what works, how and for whom, so that interventions can be refined to become more effective (see Chapters 8 and 9). Research on legal contexts informs future legislation to ensure there are penalties for animal abuse that can be enforced (see Chapters 4 and 5). Research on vets' experiences of treating animal abuse and their perspectives on the issue has led to guidelines to support their practice (see Chapter 6). This model of academic research leading to impact on professional practice and societal change underpins much of the work we do, and was a key motivator for this book. By taking a 'research aware' approach, professionals across a range of areas can work together to develop 'evidence-based practice' to reduce animal abuse in our society.

Putting what you have learnt into practice

This book has covered a broad spectrum of topics from the legalities involved in dealing with the consequences of animal abuse, the link between animal abuse and other human-perpetrated crimes, through to a variety of intervention techniques that support those who have committed animal abuse or witnessed animal abuse. It has also been evident that people can learn how to engage in positive interactions with animals through formal and informal education. Finally, we have identified the wide array of professionals who may become involved when an animal abuse incident has occurred where both humans and animals are at risk of harm or have already been harmed.

As a reader you have been introduced to a variety of case studies, and learned about different approaches to identifying your involvement in a case and what actions you can take. For example, the **ANIMAL** approach is just one technique you can use for taking action. Hopefully you have identified how recognising animal abuse and it's link with human welfare relates to you within your profession, as a parent/carer, and as a member of society. Here is one final case example, which is a hypothetical one, but has similarities to real incidents that have been reported. Read the case, review the **ANIMAL** approach (Figure 10.1) and then use the knowledge that you have learned throughout this book to answer the questions.

ASSESS

What is the situation?
Is the person
vulnerable? Are they
in immediate danger?
Where is the animal
concerned?

LISTEN

Listen and learn. What
is the impact of your
decision? What have
you learnt from the
experience? What
would you do
differently next time?

NEED

What does the person
need? What does the
animal need?

Take the ANIMAL approach

ACTION

Put the safeguarding
four R's into action–
Recognise, Respond,
Refer, Record.
(NSPCC, 2021)

INSIGHT

What information do
you have that will help
you make a decision?
Is the person minor?
Do you know if other
agencies are involved?

MAKE A DECISION

What are you going to
do? Do you take
action? Do you wait
and monitor? Do you
seek advice? If so
from who?

The ANIMAL approach a decision making process when faced with an animal abuse incident

Figure 10.1 Scottish SPCA's ANIMAL approach to an abuse incident.

In your current role (e.g., vet, teacher, social worker, police officer or parent/carer) answer the following questions:

- Who is at risk?
- If you have been told this information/witnessed this event, who do you need to speak to for support?
- What immediate action will you take?
- Who can help you take that action?
- What information will you record?
- Is your decision process and proposed action plan different now from what you would have done prior to reading this book?

Case 1

Reports have come in regarding concerns relating to a family with multiple animals and three children (aged, 9, 6 and 2). Within the house there are two dogs (a Jack Russell and a Labrador), one cat and three kittens, a guinea pig and a bearded dragon. The children have been witnessed being very rough with the animals in the garden, in particular, with the Jack Russell, one of the kittens and the guinea pig. One of the kittens has been reported as having a 'wonky' tail. The two-year-old child has noticeable scratch and bite marks on their face, down their arms and on their legs. The children are often seen out playing with the animals during school hours. The adults have been heard arguing a lot at night time and sometimes one or more of the children are heard crying during this time. The adults have also been heard shouting at the children. It has been reported that the dogs are barking a lot within the house and that often they are then shut out in the garden whilst arguments between the adults continue. Sometimes the dogs are left out all night.

Case 1 involves both humans and animals at risk of harm.
   Noticeable concerns are:

- There is a young child with scratch and bite marks;
- The children have been observed playing outside with the animals during school hours;
- There are animals that appear to be getting rough handled;
- One of the animals may be injured (the kitten with the 'wonky' tail);
- Other animals are being shut outside for long periods (i.e., the dogs being shut outside at night);
- There are arguments between adults and shouting at children on a regular basis, which could be an indicator of other concerns within the household (e.g., domestic abuse).

Which professionals should be involved? Think back to Chapter 1 and the other Chapters that focused on each of the key professions. In particular, re-visit Figure 10.2 (first included in Chapter 1) illustrating various professionals' roles when involved in an animal abuse incident. Are you one of these professionals? Are you the person who would contact one of these professionals?
   In relation to this case, a range of professionals would need to be involved in: the action plan, what happens next and the ongoing support that could be put in place.

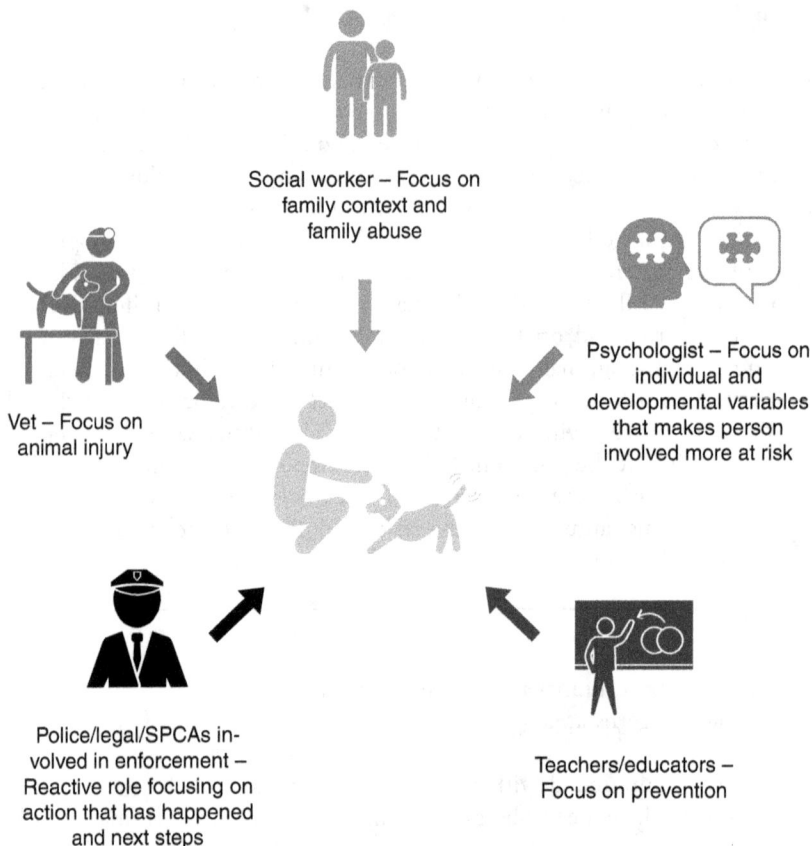

Social worker – Focus on family context and family abuse

Psychologist – Focus on individual and developmental variables that makes person involved more at risk

Vet – Focus on animal injury

Police/legal/SPCAs involved in enforcement – Reactive role focusing on action that has happened and next steps

Teachers/educators – Focus on prevention

Types of professionals that are linked with animal abuse cases

Figure 10.2 Professionals engagement with animal abuse cases.

- The veterinary profession would be required to support the ongoing health of all animals involved.
- The enforcement professionals, such as the local SPCA or police, may remain in contact for a considerable time after the report ensuring animal welfare is being maintained and the family has all the knowledge and access to what they need to care for their animals properly.
- Social workers will support the family dynamics and provide additional support/make referrals to other teams such as mental health support teams if required or even domestic abuse support if deemed necessary.
- Psychologists and mental health professionals may be involved to develop the adult's and children's health and wellbeing support plan.

- Teachers/Educators will be involved in ensuring the children of school age are actually attending school and there may be additional support provided by educators such as from animal welfare organisations with regards to promoting positive human-animal interactions.

Final questions to consider

Think about the other professions that have been mentioned throughout this book and how they have been involved in animal abuse cases. Reflecting on Case 1 consider the following questions:

1   What do you think their perspectives would be?
2   Would it differ from the approach you would take?
3   Would you know how to contact other professionals who could support you?
4   Who would be on the list of your key contacts?
5   How important do you think applying a multi-agency approach to animal abuse is?

Conclusions

This chapter has focused on new trends in animal abuse, new areas of intervention and new directions for research. We have also used a case study to illustrate the roles different people can play in identifying and intervening in animal abuse. At the start of this book we outlined the strength of the human-animal bond and discussed how it can influence the treatment of animals and the impact that animals can have on a person's life. Each chapter has endeavoured to provide a synthesis of key research findings and evidence based guides to support those working with animals and people. This book provides an evidence-based guide to preventing animal abuse, and intervening effectively in animal abuse cases. By working together, we can prevent abuse and suffering, save lives and offer much-needed support to the animals and people whose lives are affected by animal abuse.

Final Key Messages

- Animal abuse is a social issue.
- We have demonstrated that interventions for animal abuse can be effective, but more work is required to develop new intervention strategies.

- Research has told us a lot but we still have a lot to learn about the risk factors and contexts of animal abuse and how these change over age and cultural context.
- Inter-agency collaboration is needed and a range of professionals have a role in preventing and intervening in animal abuse.
- All professionals who work with animals and people have an important role to play:

  - **Partnerships are key** – identify who your local support team would be if you came across a case that involved both animal and human abuse. Do you know who your local SPCA inspector is? Do you know who your local police officer or social worker is? Have you attended a case conference meeting where you think an agency is missing?
  - **Speak up** – Even if you are not sure whether what you have observed or heard needs looked into always speak up, speak to someone you trust and seek that advice. Sometimes an ongoing investigation just needs that extra bit of information in order to take action and protect the welfare of an animal or human or both.

References

Adedoyin, O. B., & Soykan, E. (2020). Covid-19 pandemic and online learning: The challenges and opportunities. *Interactive Learning Environments*, 1–13. 10.1080/10494820. 2020.1813180.

Buddle, E. A., Bray, H. J., & Ankeny, R. A. (2018). Why would we believe them? Meat consumers' reactions to online farm animal welfare activism in Australia. *Communication Research and Practice*, 4(3), 246–260.

Currie, C. L. (2006). Animal cruelty by children exposed to domestic violence. *Child Abuse & Neglect*, 30(4), 425–435.

Duncan, T., Dwyer, R., Savic, M., Pennay, A., & MacLean, S. (2021). 'Super googs on a Zoom, are you kidding me?': The pleasures and constraints of digitally-mediated alcohol and other drug consumption. *Drug and Alcohol Review*, 41(6), 1293–1303.

Herzog, H. (2011). The impact of pets on human health and psychological well-being: Fact, fiction, or hypothesis? *Current Directions in Psychological Science*, 20(4), 236–239.

Hawkins, R. D., & Williams, J. M. (2016). Children's beliefs about animal minds (Child-BAM): Associations with positive and negative child–animal interactions. *Anthrozoös*, 29(3), 503–519.

Hawkins, R. D., Hawkins, E. L., & Williams, J. M. (2017). Psychological risk factors for childhood nonhuman animal cruelty: A systematic review. *Society & Animals*, 25(3), 280–312.

Hawkins, R. D., Williams, J. M., & Scottish SPCA. (2017a). Assessing effectiveness of a nonhuman animal welfare education program for primary school children. *Journal of Applied Animal Welfare Science*, 20(3), 240–256.

Hawkins, R. D., Williams, J. M., & Scottish SPCA. (2017b). Childhood attachment to pets: Associations between pet attachment, attitudes to animals, compassion, and humane behaviour. *International Journal of Environmental Research and Public Health*, *14*(5), 490.

Hawkins, R. D., Scottish SPCA, & Williams, J. M. (2020). Children's attitudes towards animal cruelty: Exploration of predictors and socio-demographic variations. *Psychology, Crime & Law*, *26*(3), 226–247.

Kavanagh, P. S., Signal, T. D., & Taylor, N. (2013). The Dark Triad and animal cruelty: Dark personalities, dark attitudes, and dark behaviors. *Personality and Individual Differences*, *55*(6), 666–670.

Koch, J., Frommeyer, B., & Schewe, G. (2020). Online shopping motives during the COVID-19 pandemic—Lessons from the crisis. *Sustainability*, *12*(24), 10247.

Levitt, L. (2017). The identification, assessment, and treatment of adults who abuse animals: the AniCare approach and the assessment and treatment of children who abuse animals: The AniCare Child Approach. *Anthrozoös*, *30*(1), 167–169. DOI: 10.1080/08927936. 2016.1215536

Macdonald, J. M. (1963). The threat to kill. *American Journal of Psychiatry*, *120*(2), 125–130.

McDonald, S. E., Collins, E. A., Nicotera, N., Hageman, T. O., Ascione, F. R., Williams, J. H., & Graham-Bermann, S. A. (2015). Children's experiences of companion animal maltreatment in households characterized by intimate partner violence. *Child Abuse & Neglect*, *50*, 116–127.

Marsa-Sambola, F., Muldoon, J., Williams, J., Lawrence, A., Connor, M., & Currie, C. (2016). The short attachment to pets scale (SAPS) for children and young people: Development, psychometric qualities and demographic and health associations. *Child Indicators Research*, *9*(1), 111–131.

Meints, K., & De Keuster, T. (2009). Brief report: Don't kiss a sleeping dog: the first assessment of "the blue dog" bite prevention program. *Journal of Pediatric Psychology*, *34*(10), 1084–1090.

Montrose, V. T., Kogan, L. R., & Oxley, J. A. (2021). The role of social media in promoting organised dog fighting. *The Veterinary Nurse*, *12*(8), 386–391.

Muldoon, J. C., Williams, J. M., & Lawrence, A. (2015). 'Mum cleaned it and I just played with it': Childrens perceptions of their roles and responsibilities in the care of family pets. Childhood, 22, 201–216.

Muldoon, J. C., & Williams, J. M. (2021a). Establishing consensus on the best ways to educate children about animal welfare and prevent harm: An online Delphi study. *Animal Welfare*, *30*(2), 179–195.

Muldoon, J. C., & Williams, J. M. (2021b). The challenges and future development of animal welfare education in the UK. *Animal Welfare*, *30*(2), 197–209.

Ofcom (2022, August 22). *Children and parents: media use and attitudes report 2022*. https://www.ofcom.org.uk/research-and-data/media-literacy-research/childrens/children-and-parents-media-use-and-attitudes-report-2022

Puddister, K., & Small, T. A. (2020). Trial by Zoom? The response to COVID-19 by Canada's Courts. *Canadian Journal of Political Science/Revue canadienne de science politique*, *53*(2), 373–377.

Purewal, R., Christley, R., Kordas, K., Joinson, C., Meints, K., Gee, N., & Westgarth, C. (2017). Companion animals and child/adolescent development: A systematic review of the evidence. *International Journal of Environmental Research and Public Health*, *14*(3), 234.

RSPCA (2022, August 2) RSPCA News October 2018. *23 percent of kids have seen animal abuse online.* https://www.rspca.org.uk/-/16_10_18_genkind

RSPCA Kindness Index Report (2022, August 22nd). *RSPCA Kindness Index Report.* https://www.rspca.org.uk/whatwedo/latest/kindnessindex/report

Scottish Government. (2022) Restorative justice and empathy-based interventions for animal welfare and wildlife crimes. https://www.gov.scot/publications/restorative-justice-empathy-based-interventions-animal-welfare-wildlife-crimes/documents/.

SWFGL (South West Grid for Learning Trust). (2022). https://swgfl.org.uk/

Shapiro, K., & Henderson, A. J. Z. (2016). *The identification, assessment, and treatment of adults who abuse animals: The AniCare approach.* Switzerland: Springer International Publishing. ISBN: 978-3-319-27360-0.

Shapiro, K., Randour, M. L., Krinsk, S., & Wolf, J. L. (2013). *The assessment and treatment of children who abuse animals: The AniCare child approach.* Springer Science & Business Media.

Wauthier, L. M., & Williams, J. M. (2022). Understanding and conceptualizing childhood animal harm: A meta-narrative systematic review. *Anthrozoös, 35*(2), 165–202.

Wauthier, L., Scottish SPCA, & Williams, J. M. (2022). A qualitative study of children's accounts of cruelty to animals: Uncovering the roles of trauma, exposure to violence, and attachment. *Journal of Interpersonal Violence, 37*(9-10), NP6405–NP6438.

Wauthier, L. M., Farnfield, S., Scottish SPCA, & Williams, J. M. (2022). A preliminary exploration of the psychological risk factors for childhood animal cruelty: The roles of attachment, self-regulation, and empathy. *Anthrozoös,* 1–23.

Wauthier, Scottish SPCA & Williams (in preparation). A measure of animal and human-directed empathy.

Whyke, T. W., & López-Múgica, J. (2020). Content and discourse analysis of cruelty towards stray dogs as presented in Chinese social media. *Society & Animals, 1*(aop), 1–20.

Index

Note: **Bold** page numbers refer to tables, *italic* page numbers refer to figures, and page numbers followed by "n" indicate notes.

For Product Safety Concerns and Information please contact our EU
representative GPSR@taylorandfrancis.com
Taylor & Francis Verlag GmbH, Kaufingerstraße 24, 80331 München, Germany

www.ingramcontent.com/pod-product-compliance
Lightning Source LLC
Chambersburg PA
CBHW052007270326
41929CB00015B/2817

9 7 8 0 3 6 7 7 6 1 1 3 4